THE

TRUMP INDICTMENTS

THE TRUMP INDICTMENTS

The 91 Criminal Counts Against
the Former President of the United States

Edited and Introduced by
ALI VELSHI

MARINER BOOKS
New York Boston

THE TRUMP INDICTMENTS. Introduction copyright © 2023 by Ali Velshi. All rights reserved. Printed in the United States of America. No part of this book may be used or reproduced in any manner whatsoever without written permission except in the case of brief quotations embodied in critical articles and reviews. For information, address HarperCollins Publishers, 195 Broadway, New York, NY 10007.

HarperCollins books may be purchased for educational, business, or sales promotional use. For information, please email the Special Markets Department at SPsales@harpercollins.com.

FIRST EDITION

Designed by Renata DiBiase

Library of Congress Cataloging-in-Publication Data has been applied for.

ISBN 978-0-06-338258-9

23 24 25 26 27 LBC 5 4 3 2 1

CONTENTS

INTRODUCTION

JUSTICE ON TRIAL

Ali Velshi

> The Defendant, Donald J. Trump, did knowingly combine, conspire, confederate and agree with co-conspirators, known and unknown to the Grand Jury, to injure, oppress, threaten and intimidate one or more persons in free exercise and enjoyment of a right and privilege secured to them by the Constitution and laws of the United States—that is, the right to vote, and to have one's vote counted.
>
> (In violation of Title 18, United States Code, Section 241)
>
> Jack Smith
> Special Counsel
> United States Department of Justice
> August 1, 2023.

So ends the initial filing of *United States of America v. Donald J. Trump, Defendant*, the federal election interference indictment of the 45th president of the United States—his THIRD indictment of four, and the second by Special Counsel Jack Smith.

Of the four charges in this indictment, it is count four, which accuses Donald Trump of "conspiracy against rights" that gets the fewest words, and no explanation in the text. For good reason. In the effort to preserve our American democracy, this final, simple charge is perhaps the most relevant, and the most salient, to the lay reader. For any American citizen who lives and breathes democracy, now maybe more than any time in recent memory, it is the charge least in need of explanation.

As you will read in the following pages, numerous federal and state laws are alleged to have been broken; as of this writing, ninety-one by the former president himself, often with the aid of a tightly knit cabal of co-conspirators. Then there's a whole list of separate allegations made against a variety of other characters, some of them indicted, some simply named, and still others who remain anonymous and, as yet, uncharged. The pages contain so many charges, and those charges are so detailed, that we risk becoming numb to their monumental importance, particularly those of us who lack formal legal training.

Hence, this book.

Typically, the layperson is happy to leave legal briefs to the lawyers and scientific studies to the scientists. But there are some matters of such import that we must read and form our own opinions about them. These multiple indictments of, and charges against, a former president of the United States, a man who is alleged to have attempted to undermine the infrastructure that protects our democracy, fall into that category. We must read these words, and not merely read them but sit with them, digest them, and comprehend them. We cannot allow their meaning, nor the legal doctrines which underpin them, to get past us. In order to argue—and defend—the belief that "no one is above the law," we cannot simply leave these charges to the interpretation of others.

These indictments, along with the decisions that will ultimately be rendered by the respective juries of your fellow citizens, will become some of the most significant political and legal documents in our nation's history. Buried in the details are matters that are not just relevant to the defendants, but are of critical importance to you and to those around the world who still hold America's democracy as the gold standard to which they aspire.

This book contains the indictments in four cases, in four separate jurisdictions, brought by three prosecutors.

CASE 1: FEDERAL ELECTION INTERFERENCE

United States of America v. Donald J. Trump

On August 1, 2023, Donald Trump was charged with four counts by Special Counsel Jack Smith, who was appointed by Attorney General Merrick Garland. This federal case is about Trump and his confederates' alleged sweeping efforts to retain power after the 2020 election, specifically pertaining to the January 6, 2021, attack on the Capitol. The four charges outlined in the forty-five-page indictment are one count of conspiracy to violate rights, one count of conspiracy to defraud the government, and one count each of obstructing an official proceeding and conspiring to do so.

The central thesis of Smith's indictment of Donald Trump is that, regardless of whether or not Trump had a "sincere belief" that he had won the election, his advisors, lawyers, his own Department of Justice, election recount audits, and several court cases proved otherwise. Despite all the evidence, Trump and six "unindicted co-conspirators" persisted in their efforts to prevent the certification of Joe Biden as president of the United States on January 6, 2021, and the peaceful transition of power.

The trial is currently scheduled to begin on March 4, 2024. If convicted, Donald Trump could face fifty-five years in prison.

CASE 2: MAR-A-LAGO CLASSIFIED DOCUMENTS

United States of America v. Donald J. Trump, et al.

On June 9, 2023, Special Counsel Jack Smith charged Donald Trump with thirty-seven counts. This case involves Trump's handling of sensitive government documents that were the property of the U.S. government, and that he improperly took with him upon leaving office to his residence in Mar-a-Lago, in Palm Beach, Florida. The forty-nine-page indictment alleges that Trump was involved with unauthorized retention of national security secrets and obstruction of efforts by the government to retrieve the files. His aide, Waltine Nauta, is also named in the indictment.

On July 27, 2023, Jack Smith filed what's called a "superseding indictment" in addition to the existing charges related to the classified documents. That indictment, also included herein, charges Donald Trump with three additional counts, alleging that he obstructed the investigation by attempting to delete Mar-a-Lago security footage sought by the grand jury. It also brings charges against Carlos De Oliveira, a property manager at Trump's Mar-a-Lago residence, for his alleged involvement, and involves Nauta again.

In total, Trump is charged with forty counts within these two indictments: thirty-two counts related to unauthorized retention of national security secrets, seven counts related to obstructing the investigation, and three counts related to false statements between Trump, Nauta, and De Oliveira.

The trial is currently scheduled to begin on May 20, 2024. If convicted, Donald Trump could face 460 years in prison.

CASE 3: GEORGIA

The State of Georgia v. Donald John Trump, et al.

On August 14, 2023, Donald Trump and eighteen co-conspirators were charged with forty-one counts by Fulton County district attorney Fani T. Willis. Trump is facing thirteen of those counts. The case is unique in that it relies on Georgia's RICO—Racketeering Influenced and Corrupt Organizations—statute, alleging a vast conspiracy to reverse Trump's 2020 election loss in Georgia and other states. It is alleged that Trump and his co-conspirators attempted to overturn the state's election results and subvert the will of Georgia voters. In the ninety-eight-page indictment, nineteen defendants are charged with twenty-two counts related to forgery or false documents and statements, eight counts related to soliciting or impersonating public officers, three counts related to influencing witnesses, three counts related to election fraud or defrauding the state, three counts related to computer tampering, one count related to racketeering, and one count related to perjury. If convicted, Donald Trump could face seventy-six and a half years in prison.

CASE 4: MANHATTAN
People of the State of New York v. Trump

On March 30, 2023, Donald Trump was charged with thirty-four counts by Manhattan County, New York's elected district attorney Alvin L. Bragg. The case revolves around hush-money payments related to Donald Trump's first presidential campaign in 2016. It alleges that in 2017, Trump falsified Trump Organization business records related to reimbursing his then lawyer, Michael D. Cohen, for payments made to the adult film actress known as Stormy Daniels. The twenty-nine-page indictment outlines eleven counts related to invoices from Cohen, eleven counts related to checks, and twelve counts related to ledger entries. The trial is scheduled to begin on March 25, 2024, in New York state court in Manhattan. If convicted, Donald Trump could face 136 years in prison, though experts think this is unlikely.

The indictments that you'll find in these pages will serve as roadmaps to these trials, the outcomes of which will have a direct impact upon the right of American citizens to participate in free and fair elections—the "right to vote, and to have one's vote counted," as Jack Smith put it. They will have a direct impact on that right, as well as the method and the means by which we are able to contest the outcome of elections, via recounts, audits, and judicial appeals. The historic trials will underscore

Booking photograph, Fulton County Jail,
Atlanta, Georgia, August 24, 2023

our protections, but also our obligations as citizens when those rights are subverted. And they will put a spotlight on not just those accused of doing the wrong thing, but also on those who stood fast and did the right thing, perhaps saving our democracy in the process, thus giving us this opportunity to examine and understand its weaknesses, and buttress it against future attacks.

And yet, beyond all these existential rationales, there is another—maybe a better—reason to keep this book of indictments near. With this in your hand, you will have access to the same criminal charges the juries in these cases will have. Those charges have been variously described as a "slam dunk" or a "layup," while simultaneously being called "politicized." The indictments have also been billed as part of a coordinated "witch hunt" and, without irony, "election interference." Reading them, you will be able to evaluate those claims against the evidence laid out. But even that will not be simple. Some say these indictments are an easy read, but they are filled with concepts that may feel unfamiliar, terms that don't roll off the tongue. It will be on the jurors to understand these concepts, and it will be on the prosecutors to make them accessible and easy to follow—and, ultimately, to prove that laws were broken in the pursuit of a criminal, antidemocratic enterprise. By having this book, when the verdicts come down you will understand why the juries came to the conclusions they did.

Finally, there is the issue of "free speech" and protections afforded to Defendant Trump under the First Amendment of the Constitution. This issue will be endlessly raised in the months ahead, and Special Counsel Jack Smith perhaps puts it best when he states on page 2, paragraph 3 of his election interference indictment:

> The Defendant had a right, like every American, to speak publicly about the election and even to claim, falsely, that there had been outcome-determinative fraud during the election and that he had won. He was also entitled to formally challenge the results of the election through lawful and appropriate means, such as by seeking recounts or audits of the popular vote in states or filing lawsuits challenging ballots or procedures. Indeed, in many cases, the Defendant did pursue these methods of contesting the election results. His efforts to change the outcome in any state through recounts, audits or legal challenges were uniformly unsuccessful.

This explicit recognition of Trump's First Amendment rights—including the right to deny the outcome of the election, and to lie about it—is critical. Despite protestations to the contrary, that's not what he is being prosecuted for, not in federal court, nor in Georgia. These prosecutions are for alleged criminal acts. Donald Trump cannot—and will not—be convicted for publicly denying the validity and outcome of the 2020 election. That, as damaging as it may be, is a political matter, not a legal one. What he tried to do as a result of it is what is at issue.

There is also a constitutional question that is not addressed in these indictments but which will be hovering over and around the trials. It relates to whether or not Donald Trump already has been, or will be, found responsible for what many believe to have been an insurrection. Section 3 of the Fourteenth Amendment of the Constitution states:

> No person shall be a Senator or Representative in Congress, or elector of President and Vice-President, or hold any office, civil or military, under the United States, or under any State, who, having previously taken an oath, as a member of Congress, or as an officer of the United States, or as a member of any State legislature, or as an executive or judicial officer of any State, to support the Constitution of the United States, shall have engaged in insurrection or rebellion against the same, or given aid or comfort to the enemies thereof. But Congress may by a vote of two-thirds of each House, remove such disability.

Does this amendment disqualify Trump from assuming office, should he run for president again, and win? Some of the country's greatest legal minds say it does. Two scholars affiliated with the conservative Federalist Society, William Baude of the University of Chicago and Michael Stokes Paulsen of the University of St. Thomas, as well as Conservative former federal court judge J. Michael Luttig and liberal Harvard constitutional expert Laurence Tribe, share the view that Trump cannot again hold office. But they all seem to recognize that there is no obvious existing mechanism to enforce this. Presidential elections are not federal; there are fifty separate state elections for president, so it may fall to the secretaries of state of the individual states, or governors, or state legislatures, to determine Donald Trump's eligibility to appear on the ballot, and to be certified and assume office if he wins. Some argue that his culpability has been established by his impeachment and the work of the House Select Committee to Investigate the January 6th Attack on the United States Capitol. Others say those were both political procedures. Should Donald Trump prevail in the Republican presidential nomination, would a conviction in the federal or Georgia cases be the support state officials need to keep him off the ballot? That is but one of the monumental unknowns we face as a nation.

Long after the adjudication of these indictments, we will still be debating whether these charges and the resulting trials were the upholding of democracy, or the politicized subjugation of it. Because of that, the prosecutors and judges in these cases, conscious of the valid scrutiny they will face, will have to redouble their efforts to make sure they aren't viewed as political or zealous or simply unfair. These four cases, and the ninety-one charges therein against a former president of the United States, will form the backbone of whether, and how, we choose to strengthen our democracy against future direct assaults on it. The trials will refer heavily to the acts and charges contained in these pages, so much so that you will want to keep this volume close to where you most frequently consume your news; a constant reference so that we, as citizens and voters, can consult the actual allegations as we hear the cases being made, and the counterarguments being presented, ready with pen or pencil or Post-it to note our first thoughts, the words or ideas that come to us, in our mutual quest for justice and a more perfect Union.

THE TRUMP INDICTMENTS

I.

UNITED STATES OF AMERICA v. DONALD J. TRUMP

IN THE UNITED STATES DISTRICT COURT
FOR THE DISTRICT OF COLUMBIA

United States of America	*	Violations:
	*	
v.	*	Count 1: 18 U.S.C. § 371
	*	(Conspiracy to Defraud the
Donald J. Trump,	*	United States)
	*	
Defendant.	*	Count 2: 18 U.S.C. § 1512(k)
	*	(Conspiracy to Obstruct an
	*	Official Proceeding)
	*	
	*	Count 3: 18 U.S.C. §§ 1512(c)(2), 2
	*	(Obstruction of and Attempt to
	*	Obstruct an Official Proceeding)
	*	
	*	Count 4: 18 U.S.C. § 241
	*	(Conspiracy Against Rights)

INDICTMENT

The Grand Jury charges that, at all times material to this Indictment, on or about the dates and at the approximate times stated below:

INTRODUCTION

1. The Defendant, **DONALD J. TRUMP,** was the forty-fifth President of the United States and a candidate for re-election in 2020. The Defendant lost the 2020 presidential election.

2. Despite having lost, the Defendant was determined to remain in power. So for more than two months following election day on November 3, 2020, the Defendant spread lies that there had been outcome-determinative fraud in the election and that he had actually won. These claims were false, and the Defendant knew that they were false. But the Defendant repeated and widely disseminated them anyway—to make his knowingly false claims appear legitimate, create an intense national atmosphere of mistrust and anger, and erode public faith in the administration of the election.

3. The Defendant had a right, like every American, to speak publicly about the election and even to claim, falsely, that there had been outcome-determinative fraud during the election and that he had won. He was also entitled to formally challenge the results of the election through lawful and appropriate means, such as by seeking recounts or audits of the popular vote in states or filing lawsuits challenging ballots and procedures. Indeed, in many cases, the Defendant did pursue these methods of contesting the election results. His efforts to change the outcome in any state through recounts, audits, or legal challenges were uniformly unsuccessful.

4. Shortly after election day, the Defendant also pursued unlawful means of discounting legitimate votes and subverting the election results. In so doing, the Defendant perpetrated three criminal conspiracies:

a. A conspiracy to defraud the United States by using dishonesty, fraud, and deceit to impair, obstruct, and defeat the lawful federal government function by which the results of the presidential election are collected, counted, and certified by the federal government, in violation of 18 U.S.C. § 371;

b. A conspiracy to corruptly obstruct and impede the January 6 congressional proceeding at which the collected results of the presidential election are counted and certified ("the certification proceeding"), in violation of 18 U.S.C. § 1512(k); and

c. A conspiracy against the right to vote and to have one's vote counted, in violation of 18 U.S.C. § 241.

Each of these conspiracies—which built on the widespread mistrust the Defendant was creating through pervasive and destabilizing lies about election fraud—targeted a bedrock function of the United States federal government: the nation's process of collecting, counting, and certifying the results of the presidential election ("the federal government function").

COUNT ONE

(Conspiracy to Defraud the United States—18 U.S.C. § 371)

5. The allegations contained in paragraphs 1 through 4 of this Indictment are realleged and fully incorporated here by reference.

The Conspiracy

6. From on or about November 14, 2020, through on or about January 20, 2021, in the District of Columbia and elsewhere, the Defendant,

DONALD J. TRUMP,

did knowingly combine, conspire, confederate, and agree with co-conspirators, known and unknown to the Grand Jury, to defraud the United States by using dishonesty, fraud, and deceit to impair, obstruct, and defeat the lawful federal government function by which the results of the presidential election are collected, counted, and certified by the federal government.

Purpose of the Conspiracy

7. The purpose of the conspiracy was to overturn the legitimate results of the 2020 presidential election by using knowingly false claims of election fraud to obstruct the federal government function by which those results are collected, counted, and certified.

The Defendant's Co-Conspirators

8. The Defendant enlisted co-conspirators to assist him in his criminal efforts to overturn the legitimate results of the 2020 presidential election and retain power. Among these were:

a. Co-Conspirator 1, an attorney who was willing to spread knowingly false claims and pursue strategies that the Defendant's 2020 re-election campaign attorneys would not.

b. Co-Conspirator 2, an attorney who devised and attempted to implement a strategy to leverage the Vice President's ceremonial role overseeing the certification proceeding to obstruct the certification of the presidential election.

c. Co-Conspirator 3, an attorney whose unfounded claims of election fraud the Defendant privately acknowledged to others sounded "crazy." Nonetheless, the Defendant embraced and publicly amplified Co-Conspirator 3's disinformation.

d. Co-Conspirator 4, a Justice Department official who worked on civil matters and who, with the Defendant, attempted to use the Justice Department to open sham election crime investigations and influence state legislatures with knowingly false claims of election fraud.

e. Co-Conspirator 5, an attorney who assisted in devising and attempting to implement a plan to submit fraudulent slates of presidential electors to obstruct the certification proceeding.

f. Co-Conspirator 6, a political consultant who helped implement a plan to submit fraudulent slates of presidential electors to obstruct the certification proceeding.

The Federal Government Function

9. The federal government function by which the results of the election for President of the United States are collected, counted, and certified was established through the Constitution and the Electoral Count Act (ECA), a federal law enacted in 1887. The Constitution provided that individuals called electors select the president, and that each state determine for itself how to appoint the electors apportioned to it. Through state laws, each of the fifty states and the District of Columbia chose to select their electors based on the popular vote in the state. After election day, the ECA required each state to formally determine—or "ascertain"—the electors who would represent the state's voters by casting electoral votes on behalf of the candidate who had won the popular vote, and required the executive of each state to certify to the federal govern-

ment the identities of those electors. Then, on a date set by the ECA, each state's ascertained electors were required to meet and collect the results of the presidential election—that is, to cast electoral votes based on their state's popular vote, and to send their electoral votes, along with the state executive's certification that they were the state's legitimate electors, to the United States Congress to be counted and certified in an official proceeding. Finally, the Constitution and ECA required that on the sixth of January following election day, the Congress meet in a Joint Session for a certification proceeding, presided over by the Vice President as President of the Senate, to count the electoral votes, resolve any objections, and announce the result—thus certifying the winner of the presidential election as president-elect. This federal government function—from the point of ascertainment to the certification—is foundational to the United States' democratic process, and until 2021, had operated in a peaceful and orderly manner for more than 130 years.

Manner and Means

10. The Defendant's conspiracy to impair, obstruct, and defeat the federal government function through dishonesty, fraud, and deceit included the following manner and means:

a. The Defendant and co-conspirators used knowingly false claims of election fraud to get state legislators and election officials to subvert the legitimate election results and change electoral votes for the Defendant's opponent, Joseph R. Biden, Jr., to electoral votes for the Defendant. That is, on the pretext of baseless fraud claims, the Defendant pushed officials in certain states to ignore the popular vote; disenfranchise millions of voters; dismiss legitimate electors; and ultimately, cause the ascertainment of and voting by illegitimate electors in favor of the Defendant.

b. The Defendant and co-conspirators organized fraudulent slates of electors in seven targeted states (Arizona, Georgia, Michigan, Nevada, New Mexico, Pennsylvania, and Wisconsin), attempting to mimic the procedures that the legitimate electors were supposed to follow under the Constitution and other federal and state laws. This included causing the fraudulent electors to meet on the day appointed by federal law on which legitimate electors were to gather and cast their votes; cast fraudulent votes for the Defendant; and sign certificates falsely representing that they were legitimate electors. Some fraudulent electors were tricked into participating based on the understanding that their votes would be used only if the Defendant succeeded in outcome-determinative lawsuits within their state, which the Defendant never did. The Defendant and co-conspirators then caused these fraudulent electors to transmit their false certificates to the Vice President and other government officials to be counted at the certification proceeding on January 6.

c. The Defendant and co-conspirators attempted to use the power and authority of the Justice Department to conduct sham election crime investigations and to send a letter to the targeted states that falsely claimed that the Justice Department had identified significant concerns that may have impacted the election outcome; that sought to advance the Defendant's fraudulent elector plan by using the Justice Department's authority to falsely present the fraudulent electors as a valid alternative to the legitimate electors; and that urged, on behalf of the Justice

Department, the targeted states' legislatures to convene to create the opportunity to choose the fraudulent electors over the legitimate electors.

d. The Defendant and co-conspirators attempted to enlist the Vice President to use his ceremonial role at the January 6 certification proceeding to fraudulently alter the election results. First, using knowingly false claims of election fraud, the Defendant and co-conspirators attempted to convince the Vice President to use the Defendant's fraudulent electors, reject legitimate electoral votes, or send legitimate electoral votes to state legislatures for review rather than counting them. When that failed, on the morning of January 6, the Defendant and co-conspirators repeated knowingly false claims of election fraud to gathered supporters, falsely told them that the Vice President had the authority to and might alter the election results, and directed them to the Capitol to obstruct the certification proceeding and exert pressure on the Vice President to take the fraudulent actions he had previously refused.

e. After it became public on the afternoon of January 6 that the Vice President would not fraudulently alter the election results, a large and angry crowd—including many individuals whom the Defendant had deceived into believing the Vice President could and might change the election results—violently attacked the Capitol and halted the proceeding. As violence ensued, the Defendant and co-conspirators exploited the disruption by redoubling efforts to levy false claims of election fraud and convince Members of Congress to further delay the certification based on those claims.

The Defendant's Knowledge of the Falsity of His Election Fraud Claims

11. The Defendant, his co-conspirators, and their agents made knowingly false claims that there had been outcome-determinative fraud in the 2020 presidential election. These prolific lies about election fraud included dozens of specific claims that there had been substantial fraud in certain states, such as that large numbers of dead, non-resident, non-citizen, or otherwise ineligible voters had cast ballots, or that voting machines had changed votes for the Defendant to votes for Biden. These claims were false, and the Defendant knew that they were false. In fact, the Defendant was notified repeatedly that his claims were untrue—often by the people on whom he relied for candid advice on important matters, and who were best positioned to know the facts—and he deliberately disregarded the truth. For instance:

a. The Defendant's Vice President—who personally stood to gain by remaining in office as part of the Defendant's ticket and whom the Defendant asked to study fraud allegations—told the Defendant that he had seen no evidence of outcome-determinative fraud.

b. The senior leaders of the Justice Department—appointed by the Defendant and responsible for investigating credible allegations of election crimes—told the Defendant on multiple occasions that various allegations of fraud were unsupported.

c. The Director of National Intelligence—the Defendant's principal advisor on intelligence matters related to national security—disabused the Defendant of the notion that the Intelligence Community's findings regarding foreign interference would change the outcome of the election.

d. The Department of Homeland Security's Cybersecurity and Infrastructure Security Agency ("CISA")—whose existence the Defendant signed into law to protect the nation's cybersecurity infrastructure from attack—joined an official multi-agency statement that there was no evidence any voting system had been compromised and that declared the 2020 election "the most secure in American history." Days later, after the CISA Director—whom the Defendant had appointed—announced publicly that election security experts were in agreement that claims of computer-based election fraud were unsubstantiated, the Defendant fired him.

e. Senior White House attorneys—selected by the Defendant to provide him candid advice—informed the Defendant that there was no evidence of outcome-determinative election fraud, and told him that his presidency would end on Inauguration Day in 2021.

f. Senior staffers on the Defendant's 2020 re-election campaign ("Defendant's Campaign" or "Campaign")—whose sole mission was the Defendant's re-election—told the Defendant on November 7, 2020, that he had only a five to ten percent chance of prevailing in the election, and that success was contingent on the Defendant winning ongoing vote counts or litigation in Arizona, Georgia, and Wisconsin. Within a week of that assessment, the Defendant lost in Arizona—meaning he had lost the election.

g. State legislators and officials—many of whom were the Defendant's political allies, had voted for him, and wanted him to be re-elected—repeatedly informed the Defendant that his claims of fraud in their states were unsubstantiated or false and resisted his pressure to act based upon them.

h. State and federal courts—the neutral arbiters responsible for ensuring the fair and even-handed administration of election laws—rejected every outcome-determinative post-election lawsuit filed by the Defendant, his co-conspirators, and allies, providing the Defendant real-time notice that his allegations were meritless.

12. The Defendant widely disseminated his false claims of election fraud for months, despite the fact that he knew, and in many cases had been informed directly, that they were not true. The Defendant's knowingly false statements were integral to his criminal plans to defeat the federal government function, obstruct the certification, and interfere with others' right to vote and have their votes counted. He made these knowingly false claims throughout the post-election time period, including those below that he made immediately before the attack on the Capitol on January 6:

a. The Defendant insinuated that more than ten thousand dead voters had voted in Georgia. Just four days earlier, Georgia's Secretary of State had explained to the Defendant that this was false.

b. The Defendant asserted that there had been 205,000 more votes than voters in Pennsylvania. The Defendant's Acting Attorney General and Acting Deputy Attorney General had explained to him that this was false.

c. The Defendant said that there had been a suspicious vote dump in Detroit, Michigan. The Defendant's Attorney General had explained to the Defendant that this was false, and the Defendant's allies in the Michigan state legislature—the Speaker of the House of Representatives and Majority Leader of the Senate—had publicly announced that there was no evidence of substantial fraud in the state.

d. The Defendant claimed that there had been tens of thousands of double votes and other fraud in Nevada. The Nevada Secretary of State had previously rebutted the Defendant's fraud claims by publicly posting a "Facts vs. Myths" document explaining that Nevada judges had reviewed and rejected them, and the Nevada Supreme Court had rendered a decision denying such claims.

e. The Defendant said that more than 30,000 non-citizens had voted in Arizona. The Defendant's own Campaign Manager had explained to him that such claims were false, and the Speaker of the Arizona House of Representatives, who had supported the Defendant in the election, had issued a public statement that there was no evidence of substantial fraud in Arizona.

f. The Defendant asserted that voting machines in various contested states had switched votes from the Defendant to Biden. The Defendant's Attorney General, Acting Attorney General, and Acting Deputy Attorney General all had explained to him that this was false, and numerous recounts and audits had confirmed the accuracy of voting machines.

THE CRIMINAL AGREEMENT AND ACTS TO EFFECT THE OBJECT OF THE CONSPIRACY

The Defendant's Use of Deceit to Get State Officials to Subvert the Legitimate Election Results and Change Electoral Votes

13. Shortly after election day—which fell on November 3, 2020—the Defendant launched his criminal scheme. On November 13, the Defendant's Campaign attorneys conceded in court that he had lost the vote count in the state of Arizona—meaning, based on the assessment the Defendant's Campaign advisors had given him just a week earlier, the Defendant had lost the election. So the next day, the Defendant turned to Co-Conspirator 1, whom he announced would spearhead his efforts going forward to challenge the election results. From that point on, the Defendant and his co-conspirators executed a strategy to use knowing deceit in the targeted states to impair, obstruct, and defeat the federal government function, including as described below.

Arizona

14. On November 13, 2020, the Defendant had a conversation with his Campaign Manager, who informed him that a claim that had been circulating, that a substantial number of non-citizens had voted in Arizona, was false.

15. On November 22, eight days before Arizona's Governor certified the ascertainment of the state's legitimate electors based on the popular vote, the Defendant and Co-Conspirator 1 called the Speaker of the Arizona House of Representatives and made knowingly false claims of election fraud aimed at interfering with the ascertainment of and voting by Arizona's electors, as follows:

a. The Defendant and Co-Conspirator 1 falsely asserted, among other things, that a substantial number of non-citizens, non-residents, and dead people had voted fraudulently in Arizona.

The Arizona House Speaker asked Co-Conspirator 1 for evidence of the claims, which Co-Conspirator 1 did not have, but claimed he would provide. Co-Conspirator 1 never did so.

b. The Defendant and Co-Conspirator 1 asked the Arizona House Speaker to call the legislature into session to hold a hearing based on their claims of election fraud. The Arizona House Speaker refused, stating that doing so would require a two-thirds vote of its members, and he would not allow it without actual evidence of fraud.

c. The Defendant and Co-Conspirator 1 asked the Arizona House Speaker to use the legislature to circumvent the process by which legitimate electors would be ascertained for Biden based on the popular vote, and replace those electors with a new slate for the Defendant. The Arizona House Speaker refused, responding that the suggestion was beyond anything he had ever heard or thought of as something within his authority.

16. On December 1, Co-Conspirator 1 met with the Arizona House Speaker. When the Arizona House Speaker again asked Co-Conspirator 1 for evidence of the outcome-determinative election fraud he and the Defendant had been claiming, Co-Conspirator 1 responded with words to the effect of, "We don't have the evidence, but we have lots of theories."

17. On December 4, the Arizona House Speaker issued a public statement that said, in part:

> No election is perfect, and if there were evidence of illegal votes or an improper count, then Arizona law provides a process to contest the

> election: a lawsuit under state law. But the law does not authorize the Legislature to reverse the results of an election.
>
> As a conservative Republican, I don't like the results of the presidential election. I voted for President Trump and worked hard to reelect him. But I cannot and will not entertain a suggestion that we violate current law to change the outcome of a certified election.
>
> I and my fellow legislators swore an oath to support the U.S. Constitution and the constitution and laws of the state of Arizona. It would violate that oath, the basic principles of republican government, and the rule of law if we attempted to nullify the people's vote based on unsupported theories of fraud. Under the laws that we wrote and voted upon, Arizona voters choose who wins, and our system requires that their choice be respected.

18. On the morning of January 4, 2021, Co-Conspirator 2 called the Arizona House Speaker to urge him to use a majority of the legislature to decertify the state's legitimate electors. Arizona's validly ascertained electors had voted three weeks earlier and sent their votes to Congress, which was scheduled to count those votes in Biden's favor in just two days' time at the January 6 certification proceeding. When the Arizona House Speaker explained that state investigations had uncovered no evidence of substantial fraud in the state, Co-Conspirator 2 conceded that he "[didn't] know enough about facts on the ground" in Arizona, but nonetheless told the Arizona House Speaker to decertify and "let the courts sort it out." The Arizona House Speaker refused, stating that he would not "play with the oath" he had taken to uphold the United States Constitution and Arizona law.

19. On January 6, the Defendant publicly repeated the knowingly false claim that 36,000 non-citizens had voted in Arizona.

Georgia

20. On November 16, 2020, on the Defendant's behalf, his executive assistant sent Co-Conspirator 3 and others a document containing bullet points critical of a certain voting machine company, writing, "See attached—Please include as is, or almost as is, in lawsuit." Co-Conspirator 3 responded nine minutes later, writing, "IT MUST GO IN ALL SUITS IN GA AND PA IMMEDIATELY WITH A FRAUD CLAIM THAT REQUIRES THE ENTIRE ELECTION TO BE SET ASIDE in those states and machines impounded for non-partisan professional inspection." On November 25, Co-Conspirator 3 filed a lawsuit against the Governor of Georgia falsely alleging "massive election fraud" accomplished through the voting machine company's election software and hardware. Before the lawsuit was even filed, the Defendant retweeted a post promoting it. The Defendant did this despite the fact that when he had discussed Co-Conspirator 3's far-fetched public claims regarding the voting machine company in private with advisors, the Defendant had conceded that they were unsupported and that Co-Conspirator 3 sounded "crazy." Co-Conspirator 3's Georgia lawsuit was dismissed on December 7.

21. On December 3, Co-Conspirator 1 orchestrated a presentation to a Judiciary Subcommittee of the Georgia State Senate, with the intention of misleading state senators into blocking the ascertainment of legitimate electors. During the presentation:

a. An agent of the Defendant and Co-Conspirator 1 falsely claimed that more than 10,000 dead people voted in Georgia. That afternoon, a Senior Advisor to the Defendant told the Defendant's Chief of Staff through text messages, "Just an FYI. [A Campaign lawyer] and his team verified that the 10k+ supposed dead people voting in GA is not accurate. . . . It was alleged in [Co-Conspirator 1's] hearing today." The Senior Advisor clarified that he believed that the actual number was 12.

b. Another agent of the Defendant and Co-Conspirator 1 played a misleading excerpt of a video recording of ballot-counting at State Farm Arena in Atlanta and insinuated that it showed election workers counting "suitcases" of illegal ballots.

c. Co-Conspirator 2 encouraged the legislators to decertify the state's legitimate electors based on false allegations of election fraud.

22. Also on December 3, the Defendant issued a Tweet amplifying the knowingly false claims made in Co-Conspirator 1's presentation in Georgia: "Wow! Blockbuster testimony taking place right now in Georgia. Ballot stuffing by Dems when Republicans were forced to leave the large counting room. Plenty more coming, but this alone leads to an easy win of the State!"

23. On December 4, the Georgia Secretary of State's Chief Operating Officer debunked the claims made at Co-Conspirator 1's presentation the previous day, issuing a Tweet stating, "The 90 second video of election workers at State Farm arena, purporting to show fraud was watched in its entirety (hours) by @GaSecofState investigators. Shows normal ballot processing. Here is the fact check on it." On December 7, he reiterated during a press conference that the claim that there had been misconduct at State Farm Arena was false.

24. On December 8, the Defendant called the Georgia Attorney General to pressure him to support an election lawsuit filed in the Supreme Court by another state's attorney general. The Georgia Attorney General told the Defendant that officials had investigated various claims of election fraud in the state and were not seeing evidence to support them.

25. Also on December 8, a Senior Campaign Advisor—who spoke with the Defendant on a daily basis and had informed him on multiple occasions that various fraud claims were untrue—expressed frustration that many of Co-Conspirator 1 and his legal team's claims could not be substantiated. As early as mid-November, for instance, the Senior Campaign Advisor had informed the Defendant that his claims of a large number of dead voters in Georgia were untrue. With respect to the persistent false claim regarding State Farm Arena, on December 8, the Senior Campaign Advisor wrote in an email, "When our research and campaign legal team can't back up any of the claims made by our Elite Strike Force Legal Team, you can see why we're 0-32 on our cases. I'll obviously hustle to help on all fronts, but it's tough to own any of this when it's all just conspiracy shit beamed down from the mothership."

26. On December 10, four days before Biden's validly ascertained electors were scheduled to cast votes and send them to Congress, Co-Conspirator 1 appeared at a hearing before the Georgia House of Representatives' Government Affairs Committee. Co-Conspirator 1 played the State Farm Arena video again, and falsely claimed that it showed "voter fraud right in front of people's eyes" and was "the tip of the iceberg." Then, he cited two election workers by name, baselessly accused them of "quite obviously surreptitiously passing around USB ports as if they are vials of heroin or cocaine," and suggested that they were criminals whose "places of work, their homes, should have been searched for evidence of ballots, for evidence of USB ports, for evidence of voter fraud." Thereafter, the two election workers received numerous death threats.

27. On December 15, the Defendant summoned the incoming Acting Attorney General, the incoming Acting Deputy Attorney General, and others to the Oval Office to discuss allegations of election fraud. During the meeting, the Justice Department officials specifically refuted the Defendant's claims about State Farm Arena, explaining to him that the activity shown on the tape Co-Conspirator 1 had used was "benign."

28. On December 23, a day after the Defendant's Chief of Staff personally observed the signature verification process at the Cobb County Civic Center and notified the Defendant that state election officials were "conducting themselves in an exemplary fashion" and would find fraud if it existed, the Defendant tweeted that the Georgia officials administering the signature verification process were trying to hide evidence of election fraud and were "[t]errible people!"

29. In a phone call on December 27, the Defendant spoke with the Acting Attorney General and Acting Deputy Attorney General. During the call, the Defendant again pressed the unfounded claims regarding State Farm Arena, and the two top Justice Department officials again rebutted the allegations, telling him that the Justice Department had reviewed videotape and interviewed witnesses, and had not identified any suspicious conduct.

30. On December 31, the Defendant signed a verification affirming false election fraud allegations made on his behalf in a lawsuit filed in his name against the Georgia Governor. In advance of the filing, Co-Conspirator 2—who was advising the Defendant on the lawsuit—acknowledged in an email that he and the Defendant had, since signing a previous verification, "been made aware that some of the allegations (and evidence proffered by the experts) has been inaccurate" and that signing a new affirmation "with that knowledge (and incorporation by reference) would not be accurate." The Defendant and Co-Conspirator 2 caused the Defendant's signed verification to be filed nonetheless.

31. On January 2, four days before Congress's certification proceeding, the Defendant and others called Georgia's Secretary of State. During the call, the Defendant lied to the Georgia Secretary of State to induce him to alter Georgia's popular vote count and call into question the validity of the Biden electors' votes, which had been transmitted to Congress weeks before, including as follows:

a. The Defendant raised allegations regarding the State Farm Arena video and repeatedly disparaged one of the same election workers that Co-Conspirator 1 had maligned on December 10, using her name almost twenty times and falsely referring to her as "a professional vote scammer and hustler." In response, the Georgia Secretary of State refuted this: "You're talking about the State Farm video. And I think it's extremely unfortunate that [Co-Conspirator 1] or his people, they sliced and diced that video and took it out of context." When the Georgia Secretary of State then offered a link to a video that would disprove Co-Conspirator 1's claims, the Defendant responded, "I don't care about a link, I don't need it. I have a much, [Georgia Secretary of State], I have a much better link."

b. The Defendant asked about rumors that paper ballots cast in the election were being destroyed, and the Georgia Secretary of State's Counsel explained to him that the claim had been investigated and was not true.

c. The Defendant claimed that 5,000 dead people voted in Georgia, causing the Georgia Secretary of State to respond, "Well, Mr. President, the challenge that you have is the data you have is wrong. . . . The actual number were two. Two. Two people that were dead that voted. And so [your information]'s wrong, that was two."

d. The Defendant claimed that thousands of out-of-state voters had cast ballots in Georgia's election, which the Georgia Secretary of State's Counsel refuted, explaining, "We've been going through each of those as well, and those numbers that we got, that [Defendant's counsel] was just saying, they're not accurate. Every one we've been through are people that lived in Georgia, moved to a different state, but then moved back to Georgia legitimately . . . they moved back in years ago. This was not like something just before the election."

e. In response to multiple other of the Defendant's allegations, the Georgia Secretary of State's Counsel told the Defendant that the Georgia Bureau of Investigation was examining all such claims and finding no merit to them.

f. The Defendant said that he needed to "find" 11,780 votes, and insinuated that the Georgia Secretary of State and his Counsel could be subject to criminal prosecution if they failed to find election fraud as he demanded, stating, "And you are going to find that they are—which is totally illegal—it's, it's, it's more illegal for you than it is for them because you know what they did and you're not reporting it. That's a criminal, you know, that's a criminal offense. And you know, you can't let that happen. That's a big risk to you and to [the Georgia Secretary of State's Counsel], your lawyer."

32. The next day, on January 3, the Defendant falsely claimed that the Georgia Secretary of State had not addressed the Defendant's allegations, publicly stating that the Georgia Secretary of State "was unwilling, or unable, to answer questions such as the 'ballots under table' scam, ballot destruction, out of state 'voters', dead voters, and more. He has no clue!"

33. On January 6, the Defendant publicly repeated the knowingly false insinuation that more than 10,300 dead people had voted in Georgia.

Michigan

34. On November 5, 2020, the Defendant claimed that there had been a suspicious dump of votes—purportedly illegitimate ballots—stating, "In Detroit, there were hours of unexplained delay in delivering many of the votes for counting. The final batch did not arrive until four in the morning and—even though the polls closed at eight o'clock. So they brought it in, and the batches came in, and nobody knew where they came from."

35. On November 20, three days before Michigan's Governor signed a certificate of ascertainment notifying the federal government that, based on the popular vote, Biden's electors were to represent Michigan's voters, the Defendant held a meeting in the Oval Office with the Speaker of the Michigan House of Representatives and the Majority Leader of the Michigan Senate. In the meeting, the Defendant raised his false claim, among others, of an illegitimate vote dump in Detroit. In response, the Michigan Senate Majority Leader told the Defendant that he had lost Michigan not because of fraud, but because the Defendant had underperformed with certain voter populations in the state. Upon leaving their meeting, the Michigan House Speaker and Michigan Senate Majority Leader issued a statement reiterating this:

> The Senate and House Oversight Committees are actively engaged in a thorough review of Michigan's elections process and we have faith in the committee process to provide greater transparency and accountability to our citizens. We have not yet been made aware of any information that would change the outcome of the election in Michigan and as legislative leaders, we will follow the law and follow the normal process regarding Michigan's electors, just as we have said throughout this election.

36. On December 1, the Defendant raised his Michigan vote dump claim with the Attorney General, who responded that what had occurred in Michigan had been the normal vote-counting process and that there was no indication of fraud in Detroit.

37. Despite this, the next day, the Defendant made a knowingly false statement that in Michigan, "[a]t 6:31 in the morning, a vote dump of 149,772 votes came in unexpectedly. We were winning by a lot. That batch was received in horror. Nobody knows anything about it. . . . It's corrupt. Detroit is corrupt. I have a lot of friends in Detroit. They know it. But Detroit is totally corrupt."

38. On December 4, Co-Conspirator 1 sent a text message to the Michigan House Speaker reiterating his unsupported claim of election fraud and attempting to get the Michigan House Speaker to assist in reversing the ascertainment of the legitimate Biden electors, stating, "Looks like Georgia may well hold some factual hearings and change the certification under Art II sec 1 cl 2 of the Constitution. As [Co-Conspirator 2] explained they don't just have the right to do it but the obligation. . . . Help me get this done in Michigan."

39. Similarly, on December 7, despite still having established no fraud in Michigan, Co-Conspirator 1 sent a text intended for the Michigan Senate Majority Leader: "So I need you to pass a joint resolution from the Michigan legislature that states that, * the election is in dispute, * there's an ongoing investigation by the Legislature, and * the Electors sent by Governor Whitmer are not the official Electors of the State of Michigan and do not fall within the Safe Harbor deadline of Dec 8 under Michigan law."

40. On December 14—the day that electors in states across the country were required to vote and submit their votes to Congress—the Michigan House Speaker and Michigan Senate Majority Leader announced that, contrary to the Defendant's requests, they would not decertify the legitimate election results or electors in Michigan. The Michigan

Senate Majority Leader's public statement included, "[W]e have not received evidence of fraud on a scale that would change the outcome of the election in Michigan." The Michigan House Speaker's public statement read, in part:

> We've diligently examined these reports of fraud to the best of our ability. . . .
>
> . . . I fought hard for President Trump. Nobody wanted him to win more than me. I think he's done an incredible job. But I love our republic, too. I can't fathom risking our norms, traditions and institutions to pass a resolution retroactively changing the electors for Trump, simply because some think there may have been enough widespread fraud to give him the win. That's unprecedented for good reason. And that's why there is not enough support in the House to cast a new slate of electors. I fear we'd lose our country forever. This truly would bring mutually assured destruction for every future election in regards to the Electoral College. And I can't stand for that. I won't.

41. On January 6, 2021, the Defendant publicly repeated his knowingly false claim regarding an illicit dump of more than a hundred thousand ballots in Detroit.

Pennsylvania

42. On November 11, 2020, the Defendant publicly maligned a Philadelphia City Commissioner for stating on the news that there was no evidence of widespread fraud in Philadelphia. As a result, the Philadelphia City Commissioner and his family received death threats.

43. On November 25, the day after Pennsylvania's Governor signed a certificate of ascertainment and thus certified to the federal govern-

ment that Biden's electors were the legitimate electors for the state, Co-Conspirator 1 orchestrated an event at a hotel in Gettysburg attended by state legislators. Co-Conspirator 1 falsely claimed that Pennsylvania had issued 1.8 million absentee ballots and received 2.5 million in return. In the days thereafter, a Campaign staffer wrote internally that Co-Conspirator 1's allegation was "just wrong" and "[t]here's no way to defend it." The Deputy Campaign Manager responded, "We have been saying this for a while. It's very frustrating."

44. On December 4, after four Republican leaders of the Pennsylvania legislature issued a public statement that the General Assembly lacked the authority to overturn the popular vote and appoint its own slate of electors, and that doing so would violate the state Election Code and Constitution, the Defendant re-tweeted a post labeling the legislators cowards.

45. On December 31 and January 3, the Defendant repeatedly raised with the Acting Attorney General and Acting Deputy Attorney General the allegation that in Pennsylvania, there had been 205,000 more votes than voters. Each time, the Justice Department officials informed the Defendant that his claim was false.

46. On January 6, 2021, the Defendant publicly repeated his knowingly false claim that there had been 205,000 more votes than voters in Pennsylvania.

Wisconsin

47. On November 29, 2020, a recount in Wisconsin that the Defendant's Campaign had petitioned and paid for did not change the election result, and in fact increased the Defendant's margin of defeat.

48. On December 14, the Wisconsin Supreme Court rejected an election challenge by the Campaign. One Justice wrote, "[N]othing in this case casts any legitimate doubt that the people of Wisconsin lawfully

chose Vice President Biden and Senator Harris to be the next leaders of our great country."

49. On December 21, as a result of the state Supreme Court's decision, the Wisconsin Governor—who had signed a certificate of ascertainment on November 30 identifying Biden's electors as the state's legitimate electors—signed a certificate of final determination in which he recognized that the state Supreme Court had resolved a controversy regarding the appointment of Biden's electors, and confirmed that Biden had received the highest number of votes in the state and that his electors were the state's legitimate electors.

50. That same day, in response to the court decision that had prompted the Wisconsin Governor to sign a certificate of final determination, the Defendant issued a Tweet repeating his knowingly false claim of election fraud and demanding that the Wisconsin legislature overturn the election results that had led to the ascertainment of Biden's electors as the legitimate electors.

51. On December 27, the Defendant raised with the Acting Attorney General and Acting Deputy Attorney General a specific fraud claim—that there had been more votes than voters in Wisconsin. The Acting Deputy Attorney General informed the Defendant that the claim was false.

52. On January 6, 2021, the Defendant publicly repeated knowingly false claims that there had been tens of thousands of unlawful votes in Wisconsin.

The Defendant's Use of Dishonesty, Fraud, and Deceit to Organize Fraudulent Slates of Electors and Cause Them to Transmit False Certificates to Congress

53. As the Defendant's attempts to obstruct the electoral vote through deceit of state officials met with repeated failure, beginning in early December 2020, he and co-conspirators developed a new plan: to

marshal individuals who would have served as the Defendant's electors, had he won the popular vote, in seven targeted states—Arizona, Georgia, Michigan, Nevada, New Mexico, Pennsylvania, and Wisconsin—and cause those individuals to make and send to the Vice President and Congress false certifications that they were legitimate electors. Under the plan, the submission of these fraudulent slates would create a fake controversy at the certification proceeding and position the Vice President—presiding on January 6 as President of the Senate—to supplant legitimate electors with the Defendant's fake electors and certify the Defendant as president.

54. The plan capitalized on ideas presented in memoranda drafted by Co-Conspirator 5, an attorney who was assisting the Defendant's Campaign with legal efforts related to a recount in Wisconsin. The memoranda evolved over time from a legal strategy to preserve the Defendant's rights to a corrupt plan to subvert the federal government function by stopping Biden electors' votes from being counted and certified, as follows:

a. November 18 Memorandum ("Wisconsin Memo") advocated that, because of the ongoing recount in Wisconsin, the Defendant's electors there should meet and cast votes on December 14—the date the ECA required appointed electors to vote—to preserve the alternative of the Defendant's Wisconsin elector slate in the event the Defendant ultimately prevailed in the state.

b. The December 6 Memorandum ("Fraudulent Elector Memo") marked a sharp departure from Co-Conspirator 5's Wisconsin Memo, advocating that the alternate electors originally conceived of to preserve rights in Wisconsin instead be used in a number of states as fraudulent electors to prevent Biden from receiving the 270 electoral votes necessary to secure the presidency on January 6. The Fraudulent Elector Memo suggested that the Defendant's electors in six purportedly "contested" states (Arizona, Georgia, Michigan, Nevada, Pennsylvania, and Wisconsin) should meet and mimic as best as possible the actions of the legitimate Biden electors, and that on January 6, the Vice President should open and count the fraudulent votes, setting up a fake controversy that would derail the proper certification of Biden as president-elect.

c. The December 9 Memorandum ("Fraudulent Elector Instructions") consisted of Co-Conspirator 5's instructions on how fraudulent electors could mimic legitimate electors in Arizona, Georgia, Michigan, Nevada, Pennsylvania, and Wisconsin. Co-Conspirator 5 noted that in some states, it would be virtually impossible for the fraudulent electors to successfully take the same steps as the legitimate electors because state law required formal participation in the process by state officials, or access to official resources.

55. The plan began in early December, and ultimately, the conspirators and the Defendant's Campaign took the Wisconsin Memo and expanded it to any state that the Defendant claimed was "contested"—even New Mexico, which the Defendant had lost by more than ten percent of the popular vote. This expansion was forecast by emails the Defendant's Chief of Staff sent on December 6, forwarding the Wisconsin Memo to Campaign staff and writing, "We just need to have someone coordinating the electors for states."

56. On December 6, the Defendant and Co-Conspirator 2 called the Chairwoman of the Republican National Committee to ensure that the plan was in motion. During the call, Co-Conspirator 2 told the

Chairwoman that it was important for the RNC to help the Defendant's Campaign gather electors in targeted states, and falsely represented to her that such electors' votes would be used only if ongoing litigation in one of the states changed the results in the Defendant's favor. After the RNC Chairwoman consulted the Campaign and heard that work on gathering electors was underway, she called and reported this information to the Defendant, who responded approvingly.

57. On December 7, Co-Conspirator 1 received the Wisconsin Memo and the Fraudulent Elector Memo. Co-Conspirator 1 spoke with Co-Conspirator 6 regarding attorneys who could assist in the fraudulent elector effort in the targeted states, and he received from Co-Conspirator 6 an email identifying attorneys in Arizona, Georgia, Michigan, Nevada, New Mexico, Pennsylvania, and Wisconsin.

58. The next day, on December 8, Co-Conspirator 5 called the Arizona attorney on Co-Conspirator 6's list. In an email after the call, the Arizona attorney recounted his conversation with Co-Conspirator 5 as follows:

> I just talked to the gentleman who did that memo, [Co-Conspirator 5]. His idea is basically that all of us (GA, WI, AZ, PA, etc.) have our electors send in their votes (even though the votes aren't legal under federal law—because they're not signed by the Governor); so that members of Congress can fight about whether they should be counted on January 6th. (They could potentially argue that they're not bound by federal law because they're Congress and make the law, etc.) Kind of wild/creative—I'm happy to discuss. My comment to him was that I guess there's no harm in it, (legally at least)—i.e. we would just be sending in "fake" electoral votes to Pence so that "someone" in Congress can make an objection when they start counting votes, and start arguing that the "fake" votes should be counted.

59. At Co-Conspirator 1's direction, on December 10, Co-Conspirator 5 sent to points of contact in all targeted states except Wisconsin (which had already received his memos) and New Mexico a streamlined version of the Wisconsin Memo—which did not reveal the intended fraudulent use of the Defendant's electors—and the Fraudulent Elector Instructions, along with fraudulent elector certificates that he had drafted.

60. The next day, on December 11, through Co-Conspirator 5, Co-Conspirator 1 suggested that the Arizona lawyer file a petition for certiorari in the Supreme Court as a pretext to claim that litigation was pending in the state, to provide cover for the convening and voting of the Defendant's fraudulent electors there. Co-Conspirator 5 explained that Co-Conspirator 1 had heard from a state official and state provisional elector that "it could appear **treasonous** for the AZ electors to vote on Monday if there is no pending court proceeding. . . ."

61. To manage the plan in Pennsylvania, on December 12, Co-Conspirator 1, Co-Conspirator 5, and Co-Conspirator 6 participated in a conference call organized by the Defendant's Campaign with the Defendant's electors in that state. When the Defendant's electors expressed concern about signing certificates representing themselves as legitimate electors, Co-Conspirator 1 falsely assured them that their certificates would be used only if the Defendant succeeded in litigation. Subsequently, Co-Conspirator 6 circulated proposed conditional language to that effect for potential inclusion in the fraudulent elector certificates. A Campaign official cautioned not to offer the conditional language to other states because "[t]he other States are signing what he prepared—if it gets out we changed the language for PA it could snowball." In some cases, the Defendant's electors refused to participate in the plan.

62. On December 13, Co-Conspirator 5 sent Co-Conspirator 1 an email memorandum that further confirmed that the conspirators'

plan was not to use the fraudulent electors only in the circumstance that the Defendant's litigation was successful in one of the targeted states—instead, the plan was to falsely present the fraudulent slates as an alternative to the legitimate slates at Congress's certification proceeding.

63. On December 13, the Defendant asked the Senior Campaign Advisor for an update on "what was going on" with the elector plan and directed him to "put out [a] statement on electors." As a result, Co-Conspirator 1 directed the Senior Campaign Advisor to join a conference call with him, Co-Conspirator 6, and others. When the Senior Campaign Advisor related these developments in text messages to the Deputy Campaign Manager, a Senior Advisor to the Defendant, and a Campaign staffer, the Deputy Campaign Manager responded, "Here's the thing the way this has morphed it's a crazy play so I don't know who wants to put their name on it." The Senior Advisor wrote, "Certifying illegal votes." In turn, the participants in the group text message refused to have a statement regarding electors attributed to their names because none of them could "stand by it."

64. Also on December 13, at a Campaign staffer's request, Co-Conspirator 5 drafted and sent fraudulent elector certificates for the Defendant's electors in New Mexico, which had not previously been among the targeted states, and where there was no pending litigation on the Defendant's behalf. The next day, the Defendant's Campaign filed an election challenge suit in New Mexico at 11:54 a.m., six minutes before the noon deadline for the electors' votes, as a pretext so that there was pending litigation there at the time the fraudulent electors voted.

65. On December 14, the legitimate electors of all 50 states and the District of Columbia met in their respective jurisdictions to formally cast their votes for president, resulting in a total of 232 electoral votes for the Defendant and 306 for Biden. The legitimate electoral votes that Biden won in the states that the Defendant targeted, and the Defendant's margin of defeat, were as follows: Arizona (11 elec-

toral votes; 10,457 votes), Georgia (16 electoral votes; 11,779 votes), Michigan (16 electoral votes; 154,188 votes), Nevada (6 electoral votes; 33,596 votes), New Mexico (5 electoral votes; 99,720 votes), Pennsylvania (20 electoral votes; 80,555 votes), and Wisconsin (10 electoral votes; 20,682 votes).

66. On the same day, at the direction of the Defendant and Co-Conspirator 1, fraudulent electors convened sham proceedings in the seven targeted states to cast fraudulent electoral ballots in favor of the Defendant. In some states, in order to satisfy legal requirements set forth for legitimate electors under state law, state officials were enlisted to provide the fraudulent electors access to state capitol buildings so that they could gather and vote there. In many cases, however, as Co-Conspirator 5 had predicted in the Fraudulent Elector Instructions, the fraudulent electors were unable to satisfy the legal requirements.

67. Nonetheless, as directed in the Fraudulent Elector Instructions, shortly after the fraudulent electors met on December 14, the targeted states' fraudulent elector certificates were mailed to the President of the Senate, the Archivist of the United States, and others. The Defendant and co-conspirators ultimately used the certificates of these fraudulent electors to deceitfully target the government function, and did so contrary to how fraudulent electors were told they would be used.

68. Unlike those of the fraudulent electors, consistent with the ECA, the legitimate electors' signed certificates were annexed to the state executives' certificates of ascertainment before being sent to the President of the Senate and others.

69. That evening, at 6:26 p.m., the RNC Chairwoman forwarded to the Defendant, through his executive assistant, an email titled, "Electors Recap—Final," which represented that in "Six Contested States"—Arizona, Georgia, Michigan, Nevada, Pennsylvania, and Wisconsin—the Defendant's electors had voted in parallel to Biden's electors. The Defendant's executive assistant responded, "It's in front of him!"

The Defendant's Attempt to Leverage the Justice Department to Use Deceit to Get State Officials to Replace Legitimate Electors and Electoral Votes with the Defendant's

70. In late December 2020, the Defendant attempted to use the Justice Department to make knowingly false claims of election fraud to officials in the targeted states through a formal letter under the Acting Attorney General's signature, thus giving the Defendant's lies the backing of the federal government and attempting to improperly influence the targeted states to replace legitimate Biden electors with the Defendant's.

71. On December 22, the Defendant met with Co-Conspirator 4 at the White House. Co-Conspirator 4 had not informed his leadership at the Justice Department of the meeting, which was a violation of the Justice Department's written policy restricting contacts with the White House to guard against improper political influence.

72. On December 26, Co-Conspirator 4 spoke on the phone with the Acting Attorney General and lied about the circumstances of his meeting with the Defendant at the White House, falsely claiming that the meeting had been unplanned. The Acting Attorney General directed Co-Conspirator 4 not to have unauthorized contacts with the White House again, and Co-Conspirator 4 said he would not.

73. The next morning, on December 27, contrary to the Acting Attorney General's direction, Co-Conspirator 4 spoke with the Defendant on the Defendant's cell phone for nearly three minutes.

74. That afternoon, the Defendant called the Acting Attorney General and Acting Deputy Attorney General and said, among other things, "People tell me [Co-Conspirator 4] is great. I should put him in." The Defendant also raised multiple false claims of election fraud, which the Acting Attorney General and Acting Deputy Attorney General refuted. When the Acting Attorney General told the Defendant that the Justice Department could not and would not change the outcome of the

election, the Defendant responded, "Just say that the election was corrupt and leave the rest to me and the Republican congressmen."

75. On December 28, Co-Conspirator 4 sent a draft letter to the Acting Attorney General and Acting Deputy Attorney General, which he proposed they all sign. The draft was addressed to state officials in Georgia, and Co-Conspirator 4 proposed sending versions of the letter to elected officials in other targeted states. The proposed letter contained numerous knowingly false claims about the election and the Justice Department, including that:

a. The Justice Department had "identified significant concerns that may have impacted the outcome of the election in multiple States[.]"

b. The Justice Department believed that in Georgia and other states, two valid slates of electors had gathered at the proper location on December 14, and that both sets of ballots had been transmitted to Congress. That is, Co-Conspirator 4's letter sought to advance the Defendant's fraudulent elector plan by using the authority of the Justice Department to falsely present the fraudulent electors as a valid alternative to the legitimate electors.

c. The Justice Department urged that the state legislature convene a special legislative session to create the opportunity to, among other things, choose the fraudulent electors over the legitimate electors.

76. The Acting Deputy Attorney General promptly responded to Co-Conspirator 4 by email and told him that his proposed letter was false, writing, "Despite dramatic claims to the contrary, we have not seen the

type of fraud that calls into question the reported (and certified) results of the election." In a meeting shortly thereafter, the Acting Attorney General and Acting Deputy Attorney General again directed Co-Conspirator 4 not to have unauthorized contact with the White House.

77. On December 31, the Defendant summoned to the Oval Office the Acting Attorney General, Acting Deputy Attorney General, and other advisors. In the meeting, the Defendant again raised claims about election fraud that Justice Department officials already had told him were not true—and that the senior Justice Department officials reiterated were false—and suggested he might change the leadership in the Justice Department.

78. On January 2, 2021, just four days before Congress's certification proceeding, Co-Conspirator 4 tried to coerce the Acting Attorney General and Acting Deputy Attorney General to sign and send Co-Conspirator 4's draft letter, which contained false statements, to state officials. He told them that the Defendant was considering making Co-Conspirator 4 the new Acting Attorney General, but that Co-Conspirator 4 would decline the Defendant's offer if the Acting Attorney General and Acting Deputy Attorney General would agree to send the proposed letter to the targeted states. The Justice Department officials refused.

79. The next morning, on January 3, despite having uncovered no additional evidence of election fraud, Co-Conspirator 4 sent to a Justice Department colleague an edited version of his draft letter to the states, which included a change from its previous claim that the Justice Department had "concerns" to a stronger false claim that "[a]s of today, there is evidence of significant irregularities that may have impacted the outcome of the election in multiple States. . . ."

80. Also on the morning of January 3, Co-Conspirator 4 met with the Defendant at the White House—again without having informed senior Justice Department officials—and accepted the Defendant's offer that he become Acting Attorney General.

81. On the afternoon of January 3, Co-Conspirator 4 spoke with a Deputy White House Counsel. The previous month, the Deputy White House Counsel had informed the Defendant that "there is no world, there is no option in which you do not leave the White House [o]n January 20th." Now, the same Deputy White House Counsel tried to dissuade Co-Conspirator 4 from assuming the role of Acting Attorney General. The Deputy White House Counsel reiterated to Co-Conspirator 4 that there had not been outcome-determinative fraud in the election and that if the Defendant remained in office nonetheless, there would be "riots in every major city in the United States." Co-Conspirator 4 responded, "Well, [Deputy White House Counsel], that's why there's an Insurrection Act."

82. Also that afternoon, Co-Conspirator 4 met with the Acting Attorney General and told him that the Defendant had decided to put Co-Conspirator 4 in charge of the Justice Department. The Acting Attorney General responded that he would not accept being fired by a subordinate and immediately scheduled a meeting with the Defendant for that evening.

83. On the evening of January 3, the Defendant met for a briefing on an overseas national security issue with the Chairman of the Joint Chiefs of Staff and other senior national security advisors. The Chairman briefed the Defendant on the issue—which had previously arisen in December—as well as possible ways the Defendant could handle it. When the Chairman and another advisor recommended that the Defendant take no action because Inauguration Day was only seventeen days away and any course of action could trigger something unhelpful, the Defendant calmly agreed, stating, "Yeah, you're right, it's too late for us. We're going to give that to the next guy."

84. The Defendant moved immediately from this national security briefing to the meeting that the Acting Attorney General had requested earlier that day, which included Co-Conspirator 4, the Acting Attorney

General, the Acting Deputy Attorney General, the Justice Department's Assistant Attorney General for the Office of Legal Counsel, the White House Counsel, a Deputy White House Counsel, and a Senior Advisor. At the meeting, the Defendant expressed frustration with the Acting Attorney General for failing to do anything to overturn the election results, and the group discussed Co-Conspirator 4's plans to investigate purported election fraud and to send his proposed letter to state officials—a copy of which was provided to the Defendant during the meeting. The Defendant relented in his plan to replace the Acting Attorney General with Co-Conspirator 4 only when he was told that it would result in mass resignations at the Justice Department and of his own White House Counsel.

85. At the meeting in the Oval Office on the night of January 3, Co-Conspirator 4 suggested that the Justice Department should opine that the Vice President could exceed his lawful authority during the certification proceeding and change the election outcome. When the Assistant Attorney General for the Office of Legal Counsel began to explain why the Justice Department should not do so, the Defendant said, "No one here should be talking to the Vice President. I'm talking to the Vice President," and ended the discussion.

The Defendant's Attempts to Enlist the Vice President to Fraudulently Alter the Election Results at the January 6 Certification Proceeding

86. As the January 6 congressional certification proceeding approached and other efforts to impair, obstruct, and defeat the federal government function failed, the Defendant sought to enlist the Vice President to use his ceremonial role at the certification to fraudulently alter the election results. The Defendant did this first by using knowingly false claims of election fraud to convince the Vice President to accept the Defendant's fraudulent electors, reject legitimate electoral votes, or send

legitimate electoral votes to state legislatures for review rather than count them. When that failed, the Defendant attempted to use a crowd of supporters that he had gathered in Washington, D.C., to pressure the Vice President to fraudulently alter the election results.

87. On December 19, 2020, after cultivating widespread anger and resentment for weeks with his knowingly false claims of election fraud, the Defendant urged his supporters to travel to Washington on the day of the certification proceeding, tweeting, "Big protest in D.C. on January 6th. Be there, will be wild!" Throughout late December, he repeatedly urged his supporters to come to Washington for January 6.

88. On December 23, the Defendant re-tweeted a memo titled "Operation 'PENCE' CARD," which falsely asserted that the Vice President could, among other things, unilaterally disqualify legitimate electors from six targeted states.

89. On the same day, Co-Conspirator 2 circulated a two-page memorandum outlining a plan for the Vice President to unlawfully declare the Defendant the certified winner of the presidential election. In the memorandum, Co-Conspirator 2 claimed that seven states had transmitted two slates of electors and proposed that the Vice President announce that "because of the ongoing disputes in the 7 States, there are no electors that can be deemed validly appointed in those States." Next, Co-Conspirator 2 proposed steps that he acknowledged violated the ECA, advocating that, in the end, "Pence then gavels President Trump as re-elected." Just two months earlier, on October 11, Co-Conspirator 2 had taken the opposite position, writing that neither the Constitution nor the ECA provided the Vice President discretion in the counting of electoral votes, or permitted him to "make the determination on his own."

90. On several private phone calls in late December and early January, the Defendant repeated knowingly false claims of election fraud and directly pressured the Vice President to use his ceremonial role at the cer-

tification proceeding on January 6 to fraudulently overturn the results of the election, and the Vice President resisted, including:

a. On December 25, when the Vice President called the Defendant to wish him a Merry Christmas, the Defendant quickly turned the conversation to January 6 and his request that the Vice President reject electoral votes that day. The Vice President pushed back, telling the Defendant, as the Vice President already had in previous conversations, "You know I don't think I have the authority to change the outcome."

b. On December 29, as reflected in the Vice President's contemporaneous notes, the Defendant falsely told the Vice President that the "Justice Dept [was] finding major infractions."

c. On January 1, the Defendant called the Vice President and berated him because he had learned that the Vice President had opposed a lawsuit seeking a judicial decision that, at the certification, the Vice President had the authority to reject or return votes to the states under the Constitution. The Vice President responded that he thought there was no constitutional basis for such authority and that it was improper. In response, the Defendant told the Vice President, "You're too honest." Within hours of the conversation, the Defendant reminded his supporters to meet in Washington before the certification proceeding, tweeting, "The BIG Protest Rally in Washington, D.C., will take place at 11:00 A.M. on January 6th. Locational details to follow. StopTheSteal!"

d. On January 3, the Defendant again told the Vice President that at the certification proceeding, the Vice President had the absolute right to reject electoral votes and the ability to overturn the election. The Vice President responded that he had no such authority, and that a federal appeals court had rejected the lawsuit making that claim the previous day.

91. On January 3, Co-Conspirator 2 circulated a second memorandum that included a new plan under which, contrary to the ECA, the Vice President would send the elector slates to the state legislatures to determine which slate to count.

92. On January 4, the Defendant held a meeting with Co-Conspirator 2, the Vice President, the Vice President's Chief of Staff, and the Vice President's Counsel for the purpose of convincing the Vice President, based on the Defendant's knowingly false claims of election fraud, that the Vice President should reject or send to the states Biden's legitimate electoral votes, rather than count them. The Defendant deliberately excluded his White House Counsel from the meeting because the White House Counsel previously had pushed back on the Defendant's false claims of election fraud.

93. During the meeting, as reflected in the Vice President's contemporaneous notes, the Defendant made knowingly false claims of election fraud, including, "Bottom line—won every state by 100,000s of votes" and "We won every state," and asked—regarding a claim his senior Justice Department officials previously had told him was false, including as recently as the night before—"What about 205,000 votes more in PA than voters?" The Defendant and Co-Conspirator 2 then asked the Vice President to either unilaterally reject the legitimate electors from the seven targeted states, or send the question of which slate was legitimate to the targeted states' legislatures. When the Vice President challenged Co-Conspirator 2 on whether the proposal to return the question to the states was defensible, Co-Conspirator 2 responded, "Well, nobody's tested it before." The Vice President then told the Defendant, "Did you

hear that? Even your own counsel is not saying I have that authority." The Defendant responded, "That's okay, I prefer the other suggestion" of the Vice President rejecting the electors unilaterally.

94. Also on January 4, when Co-Conspirator 2 acknowledged to the Defendant's Senior Advisor that no court would support his proposal, the Senior Advisor told Co-Conspirator 2, "[Y]ou're going to cause riots in the streets." Co-Conspirator 2 responded that there had previously been points in the nation's history where violence was necessary to protect the republic. After that conversation, the Senior Advisor notified the Defendant that Co-Conspirator 2 had conceded that his plan was "not going to work."

95. On the morning of January 5, at the Defendant's direction, the Vice President's Chief of Staff and the Vice President's Counsel met again with Co-Conspirator 2. Co-Conspirator 2 now advocated that the Vice President do what the Defendant had said he preferred the day before: unilaterally reject electors from the targeted states. During this meeting, Co-Conspirator 2 privately acknowledged to the Vice President's Counsel that he hoped to prevent judicial review of his proposal because he understood that it would be unanimously rejected by the Supreme Court. The Vice President's Counsel expressed to Co-Conspirator 2 that following through with the proposal would result in a "disastrous situation" where the election might "have to be decided in the streets."

96. That same day, the Defendant encouraged supporters to travel to Washington on January 6, and he set the false expectation that the Vice President had the authority to and might use his ceremonial role at the certification proceeding to reverse the election outcome in the Defendant's favor, including issuing the following Tweets:

a. At 11:06 a.m., "The Vice President has the power to reject fraudulently chosen electors." This was within 40 minutes of the Defendant's earlier reminder, "See you in D.C."

b. At 5:05 p.m., "Washington is being inundated with people who don't want to see an election victory stolen . . . Our Country has had enough, they won't take it anymore! We hear you (and love you) from the Oval Office."

c. At 5:43 p.m., "I will be speaking at the SAVE AMERICA RALLY tomorrow on the Ellipse at 11AM Eastern. Arrive early—doors open at 7AM Eastern. BIG CROWDS!"

97. Also on January 5, the Defendant met alone with the Vice President. When the Vice President refused to agree to the Defendant's request that he obstruct the certification, the Defendant grew frustrated and told the Vice President that the Defendant would have to publicly criticize him. Upon learning of this, the Vice President's Chief of Staff was concerned for the Vice President's safety and alerted the head of the Vice President's Secret Service detail.

98. As crowds began to gather in Washington and were audible from the Oval Office, the Defendant remarked to advisors that the crowd the following day on January 6 was going to be "angry."

99. That night, the Defendant approved and caused the Defendant's Campaign to issue a public statement that the Defendant knew, from his meeting with the Vice President only hours earlier, was false: "The Vice President and I are in total agreement that the Vice President has the power to act."

100. On January 6, starting in the early morning hours, the Defendant again turned to knowingly false statements aimed at pressuring the Vice President to fraudulently alter the election outcome, and raised publicly the false expectation that the Vice President might do so:

a. At 1:00 a.m., the Defendant issued a Tweet that falsely claimed, "If Vice President @Mike_Pence comes through for us, we will win the Presidency. Many States want to decertify the mistake they made in certifying incorrect & even fraudulent numbers in a process NOT approved by their State Legislatures (which it must be). Mike can send it back!"

b. At 8:17 a.m., the Defendant issued a Tweet that falsely stated, "States want to correct their votes, which they now know were based on irregularities and fraud, plus corrupt process never received legislative approval. All Mike Pence has to do is send them back to the States, AND WE WIN. Do it Mike, this is a time for extreme courage!"

101. On the morning of January 6, an agent of the Defendant contacted a United States Senator to ask him to hand-deliver documents to the Vice President. The agent then facilitated the receipt by the Senator's staff of the fraudulent certificates signed by the Defendant's fraudulent electors in Michigan and Wisconsin, which were believed not to have been delivered to the Vice President or Archivist by mail. When one of the Senator's staffers contacted a staffer for the Vice President by text message to arrange for delivery of what the Senator's staffer had been told were "[a]lternate slate[s] of electors for MI and WI because archivist didn't receive them," the Vice President's staffer rejected them.

102. At 11:15 a.m., the Defendant called the Vice President and again pressured him to fraudulently reject or return Biden's legitimate electoral votes. The Vice President again refused. Immediately after the call, the Defendant decided to single out the Vice President in public remarks he would make within the hour, reinserting language that he had personally drafted earlier that morning—falsely claiming that the Vice President had authority to send electoral votes to the states—but that advisors had previously successfully advocated be removed.

103. Earlier that morning, the Defendant had selected Co-Conspirator 2 to join Co-Conspirator 1 in giving public remarks before his own. When they did so, based on knowingly false election fraud claims, Co-Conspirator 1 and Co-Conspirator 2 intensified pressure on the Vice President to fraudulently obstruct the certification proceeding:

a. Co-Conspirator 1 told the crowd that the Vice President could "cast [the ECA] aside" and unilaterally "decide on the validity of these crooked ballots[.]" He also lied when he claimed to "have letters from five legislatures begging us" to send elector slates to the legislatures for review, and called for "trial by combat."

b. Co-Conspirator 2 told the crowd, "[A]ll we are demanding of Vice President Pence is this afternoon at one o'clock he let the legislatures of the state look into this so we get to the bottom of it and the American people know whether we have control of the direction of our government or not. We no longer live in a self-governing republic if we can't get the answer to this question."

104. Next, beginning at 11:56 a.m., the Defendant made multiple knowingly false statements integral to his criminal plans to defeat the federal government function, obstruct the certification, and interfere with others' right to vote and have their votes counted. The Defendant repeated false claims of election fraud, gave false hope that the Vice President might change the election outcome, and directed the crowd in front of him to go to the Capitol as a means to obstruct the certification and pressure the Vice President to fraudulently obstruct the certification. The Defendant's knowingly false statements for these purposes included:

da. The Defendant falsely claimed that, based on fraud, the Vice President could alter the outcome of the election results, stating:

> I hope Mike is going to do the right thing. I hope so. I hope so.
>
> Because if Mike Pence does the right thing, we win the election. All he has to do—all, this is, this is from the number one, or certainly one of the top, Constitutional lawyers in our country—he has the absolute right to do it. We're supposed to protect our country, support our country, support our Constitution, and protect our Constitution.
>
> States want to revote. The states got defrauded. They were given false information. They voted on it. Now they want to recertify. They want it back. All Vice President Pence has to do is send it back to the states to recertify and we become president and you are the happiest people.

b. After the Defendant falsely stated that the Pennsylvania legislature wanted "to recertify their votes. They want to recertify. But the only way that can happen is if Mike Pence agrees to send it back," the crowd began to chant, "Send it back."

c. The Defendant also said that regular rules no longer applied, stating, "And fraud breaks up everything, doesn't it? When you catch somebody in a fraud, you're allowed to go by very different rules."

d. Finally, after exhorting that "we fight. We fight like hell. And if you don't fight like hell, you're not going to have a country anymore," the Defendant directed the people in front of him to head to the Capitol, suggested he was going with them, and told them to give Members of Congress "the kind of pride and boldness that they need to take back our country."

105. During and after the Defendant's remarks, thousands of people marched toward the Capitol.

The Defendant's Exploitation of the Violence and Chaos at the Capitol

106. Shortly before 1:00 p.m., the Vice President issued a public statement explaining that his role as President of the Senate at the certification proceeding that was about to begin did not include "unilateral authority to determine which electoral votes should be counted and which should not."

107. Before the Defendant had finished speaking, a crowd began to gather at the Capitol. Thereafter, a mass of people—including individuals who had traveled to Washington and to the Capitol at the Defendant's direction—broke through barriers cordoning off the Capitol grounds and advanced on the building, including by violently attacking law enforcement officers trying to secure it.

108. The Defendant, who had returned to the White House after concluding his remarks, watched events at the Capitol unfold on the television in the dining room next to the Oval Office.

109. At 2:13 p.m., after more than an hour of steady, violent advancement, the crowd at the Capitol broke into the building.

110. Upon receiving news that individuals had breached the Capitol, the Defendant's advisors told him that there was a riot there and that rioters had breached the building. When advisors urged the Defendant to issue a calming message aimed at the rioters, the Defendant refused,

instead repeatedly remarking that the people at the Capitol were angry because the election had been stolen.

111. At 2:24 p.m., after advisors had left the Defendant alone in his dining room, the Defendant issued a Tweet intended to further delay and obstruct the certification: "Mike Pence didn't have the courage to do what should have been done to protect our Country and our Constitution, giving States a chance to certify a corrected set of facts, not the fraudulent or inaccurate ones which they were asked to previously certify. USA demands the truth!"

112. One minute later, at 2:25 p.m., the United States Secret Service was forced to evacuate the Vice President to a secure location.

113. At the Capitol, throughout the afternoon, members of the crowd chanted, "Hang Mike Pence!"; "Where is Pence? Bring him out!"; and "Traitor Pence!"

114. The Defendant repeatedly refused to approve a message directing rioters to leave the Capitol, as urged by his most senior advisors—including the White House Counsel, a Deputy White House Counsel, the Chief of Staff, a Deputy Chief of Staff, and a Senior Advisor. Instead, the Defendant issued two Tweets that did not ask rioters to leave the Capitol but instead falsely suggested that the crowd at the Capitol was being peaceful, including:

a. At 2:38 p.m., "Please support our Capitol Police and Law Enforcement. They are truly on the side of our Country. Stay peaceful!"

b. At 3:13 p.m., "I am asking for everyone at the U.S. Capitol to remain peaceful. No violence! Remember, WE are the Party of Law & Order—respect the Law and our great men and women in Blue. Thank you!"

115. At 3:00 p.m., the Defendant had a phone call with the Minority Leader of the United States House of Representatives. The Defendant told the Minority Leader that the crowd at the Capitol was more upset about the election than the Minority Leader was.

116. At 4:17 p.m., the Defendant released a video message on Twitter that he had just taped in the White House Rose Garden. In it, the Defendant repeated the knowingly false claim that "[w]e had an election that was stolen from us," and finally asked individuals to leave the Capitol, while telling them that they were "very special" and that "we love you."

117. After the 4:17 p.m. Tweet, as the Defendant joined others in the outer Oval Office to watch the attack on the Capitol on television, the Defendant said, "See, this is what happens when they try to steal an election. These people are angry. These people are really angry about it. This is what happens."

118. At 6:01 p.m., the Defendant tweeted, "These are the things and events that happen when a sacred landslide election victory is so unceremoniously & viciously stripped away from great patriots who have been badly & unfairly treated for so long. Go home with love & in peace. Remember this day forever!"

119. On the evening of January 6, the Defendant and Co-Conspirator 1 attempted to exploit the violence and chaos at the Capitol by calling lawmakers to convince them, based on knowingly false claims of election fraud, to delay the certification, including:

a. The Defendant, through White House aides, attempted to reach two United States Senators at 6:00 p.m.

b. From 6:59 p.m. until 7:18 p.m., Co-Conspirator 1 placed calls to five United States Senators and one United States Representative.

c. Co-Conspirator 6 attempted to confirm phone numbers for six United States Senators whom the Defendant had directed Co-Conspirator 1 to call and attempt to enlist in further delaying the certification.

d. In one of the calls, Co-Conspirator 1 left a voicemail intended for a United States Senator that said, "We need you, our Republican friends, to try to just slow it down so we can get these legislatures to get more information to you. And I know they're reconvening at eight tonight but the only strategy we can follow is to object to numerous states and raise issues so that we get ourselves into tomorrow—ideally until the end of tomorrow."

e. In another message intended for another United States Senator, Co-Conspirator 1 repeated knowingly false allegations of election fraud, including that the vote counts certified by the states to Congress were incorrect and that the governors who had certified knew they were incorrect; that "illegal immigrants" had voted in substantial numbers in Arizona; and that "Georgia gave you a number in which 65,000 people who were underage voted." Co-Conspirator 1 also claimed that the Vice President's actions had been surprising and asked the Senator to "object to every state and kind of spread this out a little bit like a filibuster[.]"

120. At 7:01 p.m., while Co-Conspirator 1 was calling United States Senators on behalf of the Defendant, the White House Counsel called the Defendant to ask him to withdraw any objections and allow the certification. The Defendant refused.

121. The attack on the Capitol obstructed and delayed the certification for approximately six hours, until the Senate and House of Repre-

sentatives came back into session separately at 8:06 p.m. and 9:02 p.m., respectively, and came together in a Joint Session at 11:35 p.m.

122. At 11:44 p.m., Co-Conspirator 2 emailed the Vice President's Counsel advocating that the Vice President violate the law and seek further delay of the certification. Co-Conspirator 2 wrote, "I implore you to consider one more relatively minor violation [of the ECA] and adjourn for 10 days to allow the legislatures to finish their investigations, as well as to allow a full forensic audit of the massive amount of illegal activity that has occurred here."

123. At 3:41 a.m. on January 7, as President of the Senate, the Vice President announced the certified results of the 2020 presidential election in favor of Biden.

124. The Defendant and his co-conspirators committed one or more of the acts to effect the object of the conspiracy alleged above in Paragraphs 13, 15–16, 18–22, 24, 26, 28, 30–33, 35, 37–39, 41, 43–44, 46, 50, 52, 54, 56, 57–64, 67, 71–75, 78–82, 84, 85, 87–97, 99–100, 102–104, 111, 114, 116, 118–119, and 122.

(In violation of Title 18, United States Code, Section 371)

<u>COUNT TWO</u>

(Conspiracy to Obstruct an Official Proceeding—18 U.S.C. § 1512(k))

125. The allegations contained in paragraphs 1 through 4 and 8 through 123 of this Indictment are re-alleged and fully incorporated here by reference.

126. From on or about November 14, 2020, through on or about January 7, 2021, in the District of Columbia and elsewhere, the Defendant,

DONALD J. TRUMP,

did knowingly combine, conspire, confederate, and agree with co-conspirators, known and unknown to the Grand Jury, to corruptly obstruct and impede an official proceeding, that is, the certification of the electoral vote, inviolation of Title 18, United States Code, Section 1512(c)(2).

(In violation of Title 18, United States Code, Section 1512(k))

COUNT THREE

(Obstruction of, and Attempt to Obstruct, an Official Proceeding—18 U.S.C. §§ 1512(c)(2), 2)

127. The allegations contained in paragraphs 1 through 4 and 8 through 123 of this Indictment are re-alleged and fully incorporated here by reference.

128. From on or about November 14, 2020, through on or about January 7, 2021, in the District of Columbia and elsewhere, the Defendant,

DONALD J. TRUMP,

attempted to, and did, corruptly obstruct and impede an official proceeding, that is, the certification of the electoral vote.

(In violation of Title 18, United States Code, Sections 1512(c)(2), 2)

COUNT FOUR

(Conspiracy Against Rights—18 U.S.C. § 241)

129. The allegations contained in paragraphs 1 through 4 and 8 through 123 of this Indictment are re-alleged and fully incorporated here by reference.

130. From on or about November 14, 2020, through on or about January 20, 2021, in the District of Columbia and elsewhere, the Defendant,

DONALD J. TRUMP,

did knowingly combine, conspire, confederate, and agree with co-conspirators, known and unknown to the Grand Jury, to injure, oppress, threaten, and intimidate one or more persons in the free exercise and enjoyment of a right and privilege secured to them by the Constitution and laws of the United States that is, the right to vote, and to have one's vote counted.

(In violation of Title 18, United States Code, Section 241)

JACK SMITH
SPECIAL COUNSEL
UNITED STATES
DEPARTMENT OF JUSTICE

2.

UNITED STATES OF AMERICA v. DONALD J. TRUMP, WALTINE NAUTA, AND CARLOS DE OLIVEIRA

UNITED STATES DISTRICT COURT
SOUTHERN DISTRICT OF FLORIDA
Case No. 23-CR-80101-CANNON(s)
18 U.S.C. § 793(e)
18 U.S.C. § 1512(k)
18 U.S.C. § 1512(b)(2)(A)
18 U.S.C. § 1512(b)(2)(B)
18 U.S.C. § 1512(c)(1)
18 U.S.C. § 1519
18 U.S.C. § 1001(a)(1)
18 U.S.C. § 1001(a)(2)
18 U.S.C. § 2

UNITED STATES OF AMERICA

v.

DONALD J. TRUMP,

WALTINE NAUTA, and

CARLOS DE OLIVEIRA,

Defendants.

SUPERSEDING INDICTMENT

The Grand Jury charges that:

GENERAL ALLEGATIONS

At times material to this Superseding Indictment, on or about the dates and approximate times stated below:

Introduction

1. Defendant **DONALD J. TRUMP** was the forty-fifth President of the United States of America. He held office from January 20, 2017, until January 20, 2021. As president, **TRUMP** had lawful access to the most sensitive classified documents and national defense information gathered and owned by the United States government, including information from the agencies that comprise the United States Intelligence Community and the United States Department of Defense.

2. Over the course of his presidency, **TRUMP** gathered newspapers, press clippings, letters, notes, cards, photographs, official documents, and other materials in cardboard boxes that he kept in the White House. Among the materials **TRUMP** stored in his boxes were hundreds of classified documents.

3. The classified documents **TRUMP** stored in his boxes included information regarding defense and weapons capabilities of both the United States and foreign countries; United States nuclear programs; potential vulnerabilities of the United States and its allies to military attack; and plans for possible retaliation in response to a foreign attack. The unauthorized disclosure of these classified documents could put at risk the

national security of the United States, foreign relations, the safety of the United States military, and human sources and the continued viability of sensitive intelligence collection methods.

4. At 12:00 p.m. on January 20, 2021, **TRUMP** ceased to be president. As he departed the White House, **TRUMP** caused scores of boxes, many of which contained classified documents, to be transported to The Mar-a-Lago Club in Palm Beach, Florida, where he maintained his residence. **TRUMP** was not authorized to possess or retain those classified documents.

5. The Mar-a-Lago Club was an active social club, which, between January 2021 and August 2022, hosted events for tens of thousands of members and guests. After **TRUMP**'s presidency, The Mar-a-Lago Club was not an authorized location for the storage, possession, review, display, or discussion of classified documents. Nevertheless, **TRUMP** stored his boxes containing classified documents in various locations at The Mar-a-Lago Club—including in a ballroom, a bathroom and shower, an office space, his bedroom, and a storage room.

6. On two occasions in 2021, **TRUMP** showed classified documents to others, as follows:

a. In July 2021, at Trump National Golf Club in Bedminster, New Jersey ("The Bedminster Club"), during an audio-recorded meeting with a writer, a publisher, and two members of his staff, none of whom possessed a security clearance, **TRUMP** showed and described a "plan of attack" that **TRUMP** said was prepared for him by the Department of Defense and a senior military official. **TRUMP** told the individuals that the plan was "highly confidential" and "secret." **TRUMP** also said, "as president I could have declassified it," and, "Now I can't, you know, but this is still a secret."

b. In August or September 2021, at The Bedminster Club, **TRUMP** showed a representative of his political action committee who did not possess a security clearance a classified map related to a military operation and told the representative that he should not be showing it to the representative and that the representative should not get too close.

7. On March 30, 2022, the Federal Bureau of Investigation ("FBI") opened a criminal investigation into the unlawful retention of classified documents at The Mar-a-Lago Club. A federal grand jury investigation began the next month. The grand jury issued a subpoena requiring **TRUMP** to turn over all documents with classification markings. **TRUMP** endeavored to obstruct the FBI and grand jury investigations and conceal his continued retention of classified documents by, among other things:

a. suggesting that his attorney falsely represent to the FBI and grand jury that **TRUMP** did not have documents called for by the grand jury subpoena;

b. directing defendant **WALTINE NAUTA** to move boxes of documents to conceal them from **TRUMP**'s attorney, the FBI, and the grand jury;

c. suggesting that his attorney hide or destroy documents called for by the grand jury subpoena;

d. providing to the FBI and grand jury just some of the documents called for by the grand jury subpoena, while claiming that he was cooperating fully;

e. causing a certification to be submitted to the FBI and grand jury falsely representing that all documents called for by the grand jury subpoena had been produced—while knowing that, in fact, not all such documents had been produced; and

f. attempting to delete security camera footage at The Mar-a-Lago Club to conceal information from the FBI and grand jury.

8. As a result of **TRUMP**'s retention of classified documents after his presidency and refusal to return them, hundreds of classified documents were not recovered by the United States government until 2022, as follows:

a. On January 17, nearly one year after **TRUMP** left office, and after months of demands by the National Archives and Records Administration for **TRUMP** to provide all missing presidential records, **TRUMP** provided only 15 boxes, which contained 197 documents with classification markings.

b. On June 3, in response to a grand jury subpoena demanding the production of all documents with classification markings, **TRUMP**'s attorney provided to the FBI 38 more documents with classification markings.

c. On August 8, pursuant to a court-authorized search warrant, the FBI recovered from **TRUMP**'s office and a storage room at The Mar-a-Lago Club 102 more documents with classification markings.

TRUMP's Co-Conspirators

9. Defendant **NAUTA** was a member of the United States Navy stationed as a valet in the White House during **TRUMP**'s presidency. Beginning in August 2021, **NAUTA** became an executive assistant in The Office of Donald J. Trump and served as **TRUMP**'s personal aide or "body man." **NAUTA** reported to **TRUMP,** worked closely with **TRUMP,** and traveled with **TRUMP.**

10. Beginning in January 2022, Defendant **CARLOS DE OLIVEIRA** was employed as the property manager at The Mar-a-Lago Club. Prior to holding the position of property manager, **DE OLIVEIRA** was employed as a valet at The Mar-a-Lago Club.

The Mar-a-Lago Club

11. The Mar-a-Lago Club was located on South Ocean Boulevard in Palm Beach, Florida, and included **TRUMP**'s residence, more than 25 guest rooms, two ballrooms, a spa, a gift store, exercise facilities, office space, and an outdoor pool and patio. As of January 2021, The Mar-a-Lago Club had hundreds of members and was staffed by more than 150 full-time, part-time, and temporary employees.

12. Between January 2021 and August 2022, The Mar-a-Lago Club hosted more than 150 social events, including weddings, movie premieres, and fundraisers that together drew tens of thousands of guests.

13. The United States Secret Service (the "Secret Service") provided protection services to **TRUMP** and his family after he left office, including at The Mar-a-Lago Club, but it was not responsible for the protection of **TRUMP**'s boxes or their contents. **TRUMP** did not inform the Secret Service that he was storing boxes containing classified documents at The Mar-a-Lago Club.

Classified Information

14. National security information was information owned by, produced by, produced for, and under the control of the United States government. Pursuant to Executive Order 12958, signed on April 17, 1995, as amended by Executive Order 13292 on March 25, 2003, and Executive Order 13526 on December 29, 2009, national security information was classified as "TOP SECRET," "SECRET," or "CONFIDENTIAL," as follows:

a. Information was classified as TOP SECRET if the unauthorized disclosure of that information reasonably could be expected to cause exceptionally grave damage to the national security that the original classification authority was able to identify or describe.

b. Information was classified as SECRET if the unauthorized disclosure of that information reasonably could be expected to cause serious damage to the national security that the original classification authority was able to identify or describe.

c. Information was classified as CONFIDENTIAL if the unauthorized disclosure of that information reasonably could be expected to cause damage to the national security that the original classification authority was able to identify or describe.

15. The classification marking "NOFORN" stood for "Not Releasable to Foreign Nationals" and denoted that dissemination of that information was limited to United States persons.

16. Classified information related to intelligence sources, methods, and analytical processes was designated as Sensitive Compartmented Information ("SCI"). SCI was to be processed, stored, used, or discussed in an accredited Sensitive Compartmented Information Facility ("SCIF"), and only individuals with the appropriate security clearance and additional SCI permissions were authorized to have access to such national security information.

17. When the vulnerability of, or threat to, specific classified information was exceptional, and the normal criteria for determining eligibility for access to classified information were insufficient to protect the information from unauthorized disclosure, the United States could establish Special Access Programs ("SAPs") to further protect the classified information. The number of these programs was to be kept to an absolute minimum and limited to programs in which the number of persons who ordinarily would have access would be reasonably small and commensurate with the objective of providing enhanced protection for the information involved. Only individuals with the appropriate security clearance and additional SAP permissions were authorized to have access to such national security information, which was subject to enhanced handling and storage requirements.

18. Pursuant to Executive Order 13526, information classified at any level could be lawfully accessed only by persons determined by an appropriate United States government official to be eligible for access to classified information and who had signed an approved non-disclosure agreement, who received a security clearance, and who had a "need-to-know" the classified information. After his presidency, **TRUMP** was not authorized to possess or retain classified documents.

19. Executive Order 13526 provided that a former president could obtain a waiver of the "need-to-know" requirement, if the agency head or senior agency official of the agency that originated the classified information: (1) determined in writing that access was consistent with the inter-

est of national security and (2) took appropriate steps to protect classified information from unauthorized disclosure or compromise and ensured that the information was safeguarded in a manner consistent with the order. **TRUMP** did not obtain any such waiver after his presidency.

The Executive Branch Departments and Agencies Whose Classified Documents TRUMP Retained After His Presidency

20. As part of his official duties as president, **TRUMP** received intelligence briefings from high-level United States government officials, including briefings from the Director of the Central Intelligence Agency, the Chairman of the Joint Chiefs of Staff, senior White House officials, and a designated briefer. He regularly received a collection of classified intelligence from the United States Intelligence Community ("USIC") known as the "President's Daily Brief."

21. The USIC's mission was to collect, analyze, and deliver foreign intelligence and counterintelligence information to America's leaders, including the president, policymakers, law enforcement, and the military, so they could make sound decisions to protect the United States. The USIC consisted of United States executive branch departments and agencies responsible for the conduct of foreign relations and the protection of national security.

22. After his presidency, **TRUMP** retained classified documents originated by, or implicating the equities of, multiple USIC members and other executive branch departments and agencies, including the following:

a. **The Central Intelligence Agency ("CIA").** CIA was responsible for providing intelligence on foreign countries and global issues to the president and other policymakers to help them make national security decisions.

b. **The Department of Defense ("DoD").** DoD was responsible for providing the military forces needed to deter war and ensure national security. Some of the executive branch agencies comprising the USIC were within DoD.

c. **The National Security Agency.** The National Security Agency was a combat support agency within DoD and a member of the USIC responsible for foreign signals intelligence and cybersecurity. This included collecting, processing, and disseminating to United States policymakers and military leaders foreign intelligence derived from communications and information systems; protecting national security systems; and enabling computer network operations.

d. **The National Geospatial Intelligence Agency.** The National Geospatial Intelligence Agency was a combat support agency within DoD responsible for the exploitation and analysis of imagery, imagery intelligence, and geospatial information in support of the national security objectives of the United States and the geospatial intelligence requirements of DoD, the Department of State, and other federal agencies.

e. **The National Reconnaissance Office.** The National Reconnaissance Office was an agency within DoD responsible for developing, acquiring, launching, and operating space-based surveillance and reconnaissance systems that collected and delivered intelligence to enhance national security.

f. **The Department of Energy.** The Department of Energy was responsible for maintaining a safe, secure, and effective nuclear deterrent to protect national security, including ensuring the effectiveness of the United States nuclear weapons stockpile without nuclear explosive testing.

g. **The Department of State and Bureau of Intelligence and Research.** The Department of State was responsible for protecting and promoting United States security, prosperity, and democratic values. Within the Department of State, the Bureau of Intelligence and Research was a member of the USIC and responsible for providing intelligence to inform diplomacy and support United States diplomats.

TRUMP's Public Statements on Classified Information

23. As a candidate for President of the United States, **TRUMP** made the following public statements, among others, about classified information:

a. On August 18, 2016, **TRUMP** stated, "In my administration I'm going to enforce all laws concerning the protection of classified information. No one will be above the law."

b. On September 6, 2016, **TRUMP** stated, "We also need to fight this battle by collecting intelligence and then protecting, protecting our classified secrets. . . . We can't have someone in the Oval Office who doesn't understand the meaning of the word confidential or classified."

c. On September 7, 2016, **TRUMP** stated, "[O]ne of the first things we must do is to enforce all classification rules and to enforce all laws relating to the handling of classified information."

d. On September 19, 2016, **TRUMP** stated, "We also need the best protection of classified information."

e. On November 3, 2016, **TRUMP** stated, "Service members here in North Carolina have risked their lives to acquire classified intelligence to protect our country."

24. As President of the United States, on July 26, 2018, **TRUMP** issued the following statement about classified information:

> As the head of the executive branch and Commander in Chief, I have a unique, Constitutional responsibility to protect the Nation's classified information, including by controlling access to it. . . . More broadly, the issue of [a former executive branch official's] security clearance raises larger questions about the practice of former officials maintaining access to our Nation's most sensitive secrets long after their time in Government has ended. Such access is particularly inappropriate when former officials have transitioned into highly partisan positions and seek to use real or perceived access to sensitive information to validate their political attacks. Any access granted to our Nation's secrets should be in furtherance of national, not personal, interests.

TRUMP's Retention of Classified Documents After His Presidency

25. In January 2021, as he was preparing to leave the White House, **TRUMP** and his White House staff, including **NAUTA,** packed items, including some of **TRUMP**'s boxes. **TRUMP** was personally involved in this process. **TRUMP** caused his boxes, containing hundreds of classified documents, to be transported from the White House to The Mar-a-Lago Club.

26. From January through March 15, 2021, some of **TRUMP**'s boxes were stored in The Mar-a-Lago Club's White and Gold Ballroom,

in which events and gatherings took place. **TRUMP**'s boxes were for a time stacked on the ballroom's stage, as depicted in the photograph below (redacted to obscure an individual's identity).

27. In March 2021, **NAUTA** and others moved some of **TRUMP**'s boxes from the White and Gold Ballroom to the business center at The Mar-a-Lago Club.

28. On April 5, 2021, an employee of The Office of Donald J. Trump ("Trump Employee 1") texted another employee of that office ("Trump Employee 2") to ask whether **TRUMP**'s boxes could be moved out of the business center to make room for staff to use it as an office. Trump Employee 2 replied, "Woah!! Ok so potus specifically asked Walt for those boxes to be in the business center because they are his 'papers.'" Later that day, Trump Employee 1 and Trump Employee 2 exchanged the following text messages:

Trump Employee 2:

> We can definitely make it work if we move his papers into the lake room?

Trump Employee 1:

> There is still a little room in the shower where his other stuff is. Is it only his papers he cares about? Theres some other stuff in there that are not papers. Could that go to storage? Or does he want everything in there on property

Trump Employee 2:

> Yes—anything that's not the beautiful mind paper boxes can definitely go to storage. Want to take a look at the space and start moving tomorrow AM?

29. After the text exchange between Trump Employee 1 and Trump Employee 2, in April 2021, some of **TRUMP**'s boxes were moved from the business center to a bathroom and shower in The Mar-a-Lago Club's Lake Room, as depicted in the photograph below.

30. In May 2021, **TRUMP** directed that a storage room on the ground floor of The Mar-a-Lago Club (the "Storage Room") be cleaned out so that it could be used to store his boxes. The hallway

leading to the Storage Room could be reached from multiple outside entrances, including one accessible from The Mar-a-Lago Club pool patio through a doorway that was often kept open. The Storage Room was near the liquor supply closet, linen room, lock shop, and various other rooms.

31. On June 24, 2021, **TRUMP**'s boxes that were in the Lake Room were moved to the Storage Room. After the move, there were more than 80 boxes in the Storage Room, as depicted in the photographs below.

32. On December 7, 2021, **NAUTA** found several of **TRUMP**'s boxes fallen and their contents spilled onto the floor of the Storage Room, including a document marked "SECRET//REL TO USA, FVEY," which denoted that the information in the document was releasable only to the Five Eyes intelligence alliance consisting of Australia, Canada, New Zealand, the United Kingdom, and the United States. **NAUTA** texted Trump Employee 2, "I opened the door and found this . . ." **NAUTA** also attached two photographs he took of the spill. Trump Employee 2 replied, "Oh no oh no," and "I'm sorry potus had my phone." One of the photographs **NAUTA** texted to Trump Employee 2 is depicted below with the visible classified information redacted. **TRUMP**'s unlawful retention of this document is charged in Count 8 of this Superseding Indictment.

TRUMP's Disclosures of Classified Information in Private Meetings

33. In May 2021, **TRUMP** caused some of his boxes to be brought to his summer residence at The Bedminster Club. Like The Mar-a-Lago Club, after **TRUMP**'s presidency, The Bedminster Club was not an authorized location for the storage, possession, review, display, or discussion of classified documents.

34. On July 21, 2021, when he was no longer president, **TRUMP** gave an interview in his office at The Bedminster Club to a writer and a publisher in connection with a then-forthcoming book. Two members of **TRUMP**'s staff also attended the interview, which was recorded with **TRUMP**'s knowledge and consent. Before the interview, the media had published reports that, at the end of **TRUMP**'s term as president, a senior military official (the "Senior Military Official") purportedly feared that **TRUMP** might order an attack on Country A and that the Senior Military Official advised **TRUMP** against doing so.

35. Upon greeting the writer, publisher, and his two staff members, **TRUMP** stated, "Look what I found, this was [the Senior Military Official's] plan of attack, read it and just show . . . it's interesting." Later in the interview, **TRUMP** engaged in the following exchange:

TRUMP: Well, with [the Senior Military Official]—uh, let me see that, I'll show you an example. He said that I wanted to attack [Country A]. Isn't it amazing? I have a big pile of papers, this thing just came up. Look. This was him. They presented me this—this is off the record, but—they presented me this. This was him. This was the Defense Department and him.

WRITER: Wow.

TRUMP: We looked at some. This was him. This wasn't done by me, this was him. All sorts of stuff—pages long, look.

STAFFER: Mm.

TRUMP: Wait a minute, let's see here.

STAFFER: *[Laughter]* Yeah.

TRUMP: I just found, isn't that amazing? This totally wins my case, you know.

STAFFER: Mm-hm.

TRUMP: Except it is like, highly confidential.

STAFFER: Yeah. *[Laughter]*

TRUMP: Secret. This is secret information. Look, look at this. You attack, and—

* * *

TRUMP: By the way. Isn't that incredible?

STAFFER: Yeah.

TRUMP: I was just thinking, because we were talking about it. And you know, he said, "he wanted to attack [Country A], and what . . ."

STAFFER: You did.

TRUMP: This was done by the military and given to me. Uh, I think we can probably, right?

STAFFER: I don't know, we'll, we'll have to see. Yeah, we'll have to try to—

TRUMP: Declassify it.

STAFFER: —figure out a—yeah.

TRUMP: See as president I could have declassified it.

STAFFER: Yeah. *[Laughter]*

TRUMP: Now I can't, you know, but this is still a secret.

STAFFER: Yeah. *[Laughter]* Now we have a problem.

TRUMP: Isn't that interesting?

At the time of this exchange, the writer, the publisher, and **TRUMP**'s two staff members did not have security clearances or any need-to-know any classified information about a plan of attack on Country A. The document that **TRUMP** possessed and showed on July 21, 2021, is charged as Count 32 in this Superseding Indictment.

36. In August or September 2021, when he was no longer president, **TRUMP** met in his office at The Bedminster Club with a representative of his political action committee (the "PAC Representative"). During the meeting, **TRUMP** commented that an ongoing military operation in Country B was not going well. **TRUMP** showed the PAC Representative a classified map of Country B and told the PAC Representative that he should not be showing the map to the PAC Representative and to not get too close. The PAC Representative did not have a security clearance or any need-to-know classified information about the military operation.

37. On February 16, 2017, four years before **TRUMP**'s disclosures of classified information set forth above, **TRUMP** said at a press conference:

> The first thing I thought of when I heard about it is, how does the press get this information that's classified? How do they do it? You know why? Because it's an illegal process, and the press should be ashamed of themselves. But more importantly, the people that gave out the information to the press should be ashamed of themselves. Really ashamed.

TRUMP's Production of 15 Cardboard Boxes to the National Archives and Records Administration

38. Beginning in May 2021, the National Archives and Records Administration ("NARA"), which was responsible for archiving presidential records, repeatedly demanded that **TRUMP** turn over presidential records that he had kept after his presidency. On multiple occasions, beginning in June, NARA warned **TRUMP** through his representatives that if he did not comply, it would refer the matter of the missing records to the Department of Justice.

39. Between November 2021 and January 2022, **NAUTA** and Trump Employee 2—at **TRUMP**'s direction—brought boxes from the Storage Room to **TRUMP**'s residence for **TRUMP** to review.

40. On November 12, 2021, Trump Employee 2 provided **TRUMP** a photograph of his boxes in the Storage Room by taping it to one of the boxes that Trump Employee 2 had placed in **TRUMP**'s residence. Trump Employee 2 provided **TRUMP** the photograph so that **TRUMP** could see how many of his boxes were stored in the Storage Room. The photograph, shown below, depicted a wall of the Storage Room against which dozens of **TRUMP**'s boxes were stacked.

41. On November 17, 2021, **NAUTA** texted Trump Employee 2 about the photograph Trump Employee 2 had provided to **TRUMP,** stating, "He mentioned about a picture of the 'boxes' he wants me to see it?" Trump Employee 2 replied, "Calling you shortly."

42. On November 25, 2021, Trump Employee 2 texted **NAUTA** about **TRUMP**'s review of the contents of his boxes, asking, "Has he mentioned boxes to you? I delivered some, but I think he may need more. Could you ask if he'd like more in pine hall?" Pine Hall was an entry room in **TRUMP**'s residence. **NAUTA** replied in three successive text messages:

> Nothing about boxes yet
>
> He has one he's working on in pine hall
>
> Knocked out 2 boxes yesterday

43. On November 29, 2021, Trump Employee 2 texted **NAUTA,** asking, "Next you are on property (no rush) could you help me bring 4 more boxes up?" **NAUTA** replied, "Yes!! Of course."

44. On December 29, 2021, Trump Employee 2 texted a **TRUMP** representative who was in contact with NARA ("Trump Representative 1"), "box answer will be wrenched out of him today, promise!" The next day, Trump Representative 1 replied in two successive text messages:

> Hey—Just checking on Boxes . . .
>
> would love to have a number to them today

Trump Employee 2 spoke to **TRUMP** and then responded a few hours later in two successive text messages:

> 12
>
> Is his number

45. On January 13, 2022, **NAUTA** texted Trump Employee 2 about **TRUMP**'s "tracking" of boxes, stating, "He's tracking the boxes, more to follow today on whether he wants to go through more today or tomorrow." Trump Employee 2 replied, "Thank you!"

46. On January 15, 2022, **NAUTA** sent Trump Employee 2 four successive text messages:

> One thing he asked
>
> Was for new covers for the boxes, for Monday m.
>
> Morning
>
> *can we get new box covers before giving these to them on Monday? They have too much writing on them..I marked too much

Trump Employee 2 replied, "Yes, I will get that!"

47. On January 17, 2022, Trump Employee 2 and **NAUTA** gathered 15 boxes from **TRUMP**'s residence, loaded the boxes in **NAUTA**'s car, and took them to a commercial truck for delivery to NARA.

48. When interviewed by the FBI in May 2022 regarding the location and movement of boxes before the production to NARA, **NAUTA** made false and misleading statements as set forth in Count 38 of this Superseding Indictment, including:

a. falsely stating that he was not aware of **TRUMP**'s boxes being brought to **TRUMP**'s residence for his review before **TRUMP** provided 15 boxes to NARA in January 2022;

b. falsely stating that he did not know how the boxes that he and Trump Employee 2 brought from **TRUMP**'s residence to the commercial truck for delivery to NARA on January 17, 2022, had gotten to the residence; and

c. when asked whether he knew where **TRUMP**'s boxes had been stored before they were in **TRUMP**'s residence and whether they had been in a secure or locked location, **NAUTA** falsely responded, "I wish, I wish I could tell you. I don't know. I don't—I honestly just don't know."

49. When the 15 boxes that **TRUMP** had provided reached NARA in January 2022, NARA reviewed the contents and determined that 14 of the boxes contained documents with classification markings. Specifically, as the FBI later determined, the boxes contained 197 documents with classification markings, of which 98 were marked "SECRET," 30 were marked "TOP SECRET," and the remainder were marked "CONFIDENTIAL." Some of those documents also contained SCI and SAP markings.

50. On February 9, 2022, NARA referred the discovery of classified documents in **TRUMP**'s boxes to the Department of Justice for investigation.

The FBI and Grand Jury Investigations

51. On March 30, 2022, the FBI opened a criminal investigation.
52. On April 26, 2022, a federal grand jury opened an investigation.

The Defendants' Concealment of Boxes

53. On May 11, 2022, the grand jury issued a subpoena (the "May 11 Subpoena") to The Office of Donald J. Trump requiring the production of all documents with classification markings in the possession, custody, or control of **TRUMP** or The Office of Donald J. Trump. Two attorneys representing **TRUMP** ("Trump Attorney 1" and "Trump Attorney 2") informed **TRUMP** of the May 11 Subpoena, and he authorized Trump Attorney 1 to accept service.
54. On May 22, 2022, **NAUTA** entered the Storage Room at 3:47 p.m. and left approximately 34 minutes later, carrying one of **TRUMP**'s boxes.
55. On May 23, 2022, **TRUMP** met with Trump Attorney 1 and Trump Attorney 2 at The Mar-a-Lago Club to discuss the response to the May 11 Subpoena. Trump Attorney 1 and Trump Attorney 2 told **TRUMP** that they needed to search for documents that would be responsive to the subpoena and provide a certification that there had been compliance with the subpoena. **TRUMP**, in sum and substance, made the following statements, among others, as memorialized by Trump Attorney 1:

a. I don't want anybody looking, I don't want anybody looking through my boxes, I really don't, I don't want you looking through my boxes.

b. Well what if we, what happens if we just don't respond at all or don't play ball with them?

c. Wouldn't it be better if we just told them we don't have anything here?

d. Well look isn't it better if there are no documents?

56. While meeting with Trump Attorney 1 and Trump Attorney 2 on May 23, **TRUMP**, in sum and substance, told the following story, as memorialized by Trump Attorney 1:

> [Attorney], he was great, he did a great job. You know what? He said, he said that it—that it was him. That he was the one who deleted all of her emails, the 30,000 emails, because they basically dealt with her scheduling and her going to the gym and her having beauty appointments. And he was great. And he, so she didn't get in any trouble because he said that he was the one who deleted them.

TRUMP related the story more than once that day.

57. On May 23, **TRUMP** also confirmed his understanding with Trump Attorney 1 that Trump Attorney 1 would return to The Mar-a-Lago Club on June 2 to search for any documents with classification markings to produce in response to the May 11 Subpoena. Trump Attorney 1 made it clear to **TRUMP** that Trump Attorney 1 would conduct the search for responsive documents by looking through **TRUMP**'s boxes that had been transported from the White House and remained in storage at The Mar-a-Lago Club. **TRUMP** indicated that he wanted to be at The Mar-a-Lago Club when Trump Attorney 1 returned to review his boxes on June 2, and that **TRUMP** would change his summer travel plans

to do so. **TRUMP** told Trump Attorney 2 that Trump Attorney 2 did not need to be present for the review of boxes.

58. After meeting with Trump Attorney 1 and Trump Attorney 2 on May 23, **TRUMP** delayed his departure from The Mar-a-Lago Club to The Bedminster Club for the summer so that he would be present at The Mar-a-Lago Club on June 2, when Trump Attorney 1 returned to review the boxes.

59. Between **TRUMP**'s May 23 meeting with Trump Attorney 1 and Trump Attorney 2 to discuss the May 11 Subpoena, and June 2, when Trump Attorney 1 returned to The Mar-a-Lago Club to review the boxes in the Storage Room, **NAUTA** removed—at **TRUMP**'s direction—a total of approximately 64 boxes from the Storage Room and brought them to **TRUMP**'s residence, as set forth below:

a. On May 24, 2022, between 5:30 p.m. and 5:38 p.m., **NAUTA** removed three boxes from the Storage Room.

b. On May 30, 2022, at 9:08 a.m., **TRUMP** and **NAUTA** spoke by phone for approximately 30 seconds. Between 10:02 a.m. and 11:51 a.m., **NAUTA** removed a total of approximately 50 boxes from the Storage Room.

c. On May 30, 2022, at 12:33 p.m., a Trump family member texted **NAUTA**:

> Good afternoon Walt,
>
> Happy Memorial Day!
>
> I saw you put boxes to Potus room. Just FYI and I will tell him as well:

> Not sure how many he wants to take on Friday on the plane. We will NOT have a room for them. Plane will be full with luggage.
>
> Thank you!

NAUTA replied:

> Good Afternoon Ma'am [Smiley Face Emoji]
>
> Thank you so much.
>
> I think he wanted to pick from them. I don't imagine him wanting to take the boxes.
>
> He told me to put them in the room and that he was going to talk to you about them.

d. On June 1, 2022, beginning at 12:52 p.m., **NAUTA** removed approximately 11 boxes from the Storage Room.

60. On June 1, 2022, **TRUMP** spoke with Trump Attorney 1 by phone and asked whether Trump Attorney 1 was coming to The Mar-a-Lago Club the next day and for exactly what purpose. Trump Attorney 1 reminded **TRUMP** that Trump Attorney 1 was going to review the boxes that had been transported from the White House and remained in storage at The Mar-a-Lago Club so that Trump Attorney 1 could have a custodian of records certify that the May 11 subpoena had been complied with fully.

61. On June 2, 2022, the day that Trump Attorney 1 was scheduled to review **TRUMP**'s boxes in the Storage Room, **TRUMP** spoke with **NAUTA** on the phone at 9:29 a.m. for approximately 24 seconds.

62. Later that day, between 12:33 p.m. and 12:52 p.m., **NAUTA** and **DE OLIVEIRA** moved approximately 30 boxes from **TRUMP**'s residence to the Storage Room.

63. In sum, between May 23, 2022, and June 2, 2022, before Trump Attorney 1's review of **TRUMP**'s boxes in the Storage Room, **NAUTA**—at **TRUMP**'s direction—moved approximately 64 boxes from the Storage Room to **TRUMP**'s residence, and **NAUTA** and **DE OLIVEIRA** brought to the Storage Room only approximately 30 boxes. Neither **TRUMP** nor **NAUTA** informed Trump Attorney 1 of this information.

The False Certification to the FBI and the Grand Jury

64. On the afternoon of June 2, 2022, as **TRUMP** had been informed, Trump Attorney 1 arrived at The Mar-a-Lago Club to review **TRUMP**'s boxes to look for documents with classification markings in response to the May 11 Subpoena. **TRUMP** met with Trump Attorney 1 before Trump Attorney 1 conducted the review. **NAUTA** escorted Trump Attorney 1 to the Storage Room.

65. Between 3:53 p.m. and 6:23 p.m., Trump Attorney 1 reviewed the contents of **TRUMP**'s boxes in the Storage Room. Trump Attorney 1 located 38 documents with classification markings inside the boxes, which Trump Attorney 1 removed and placed in a Redweld folder. Trump Attorney 1 contacted **NAUTA** and asked him to bring clear duct tape to the Storage Room, which **NAUTA** did. Trump Attorney 1 used the clear duct tape to seal the Redweld folder with the documents with classification markings inside.

66. After Trump Attorney 1 finished sealing the Redweld folder containing the documents with classification markings that he had found inside **TRUMP**'s boxes, **NAUTA** took Trump Attorney 1 to a dining room in The Mar-a-Lago Club to meet with **TRUMP**. After Trump Attorney 1 confirmed that he was finished with his search of the Storage Room, **TRUMP** asked, "Did you find anything? . . . Is it bad? Good?"

67. **TRUMP** and Trump Attorney 1 then discussed what to do with the Redweld folder containing documents with classification mark-

ings and whether Trump Attorney 1 should bring them to his hotel room and put them in a safe there. During that conversation, **TRUMP** made a plucking motion, as memorialized by Trump Attorney 1:

> He made a funny motion as though—well okay why don't you take them with you to your hotel room and if there's anything really bad in there, like, you know, pluck it out. And that was the motion that he made. He didn't say that.

68. That evening, Trump Attorney 1 contacted the Department of Justice and requested that an FBI agent meet him at The Mar-a-Lago Club the next day, June 3, so that he could turn over the documents responsive to the May 11 Subpoena.

69. Also that evening, Trump Attorney 1 contacted another **TRUMP** attorney ("Trump Attorney 3") and asked her if she would come to The Mar-a-Lago Club the next morning to act as a custodian of records and sign a certification regarding the search for documents with classification markings in response to the May 11 Subpoena. Trump Attorney 3, who had no role in the review of **TRUMP**'s boxes in the Storage Room, agreed.

70. The next day, on June 3, 2022, at Trump Attorney 1's request, Trump Attorney 3 signed a certification as the custodian of records for The Office of Donald J. Trump and took it to The Mar-a-Lago Club to provide it to the Department of Justice and FBI. In the certification, Trump Attorney 3—who performed no search of **TRUMP**'s boxes, had not reviewed the May 11 Subpoena, and had not reviewed the contents of the Redweld folder—stated, among other things, that "[b]ased upon the information that [had] been provided to" her:

a. "A diligent search was conducted of the boxes that were moved from the White House to Florida";

b. "This search was conducted after receipt of the subpoena, in order to locate any and all documents that are responsive to the subpoena"; and

c. "Any and all responsive documents accompany this certification."

71. These statements were false because, among other reasons, **TRUMP** had directed **NAUTA** to move boxes before Trump Attorney 1's June 2 review, so that many boxes were not searched and many documents responsive to the May 11 Subpoena could not be found—and in fact were not found—by Trump Attorney 1.

72. Shortly after Trump Attorney 3 executed the false certification, on June 3, 2022, Trump Attorney 1 and Trump Attorney 3 met at The Mar-a-Lago Club with personnel from the Department of Justice and FBI. Trump Attorney 1 and Trump Attorney 3 turned over the Redweld folder containing documents with classification markings, as well as the false certification signed by Trump Attorney 3 as custodian of records. **TRUMP,** who had delayed his departure from The Mar-a-Lago Club, joined Trump Attorney 1 and Trump Attorney 3 for some of the meeting. **TRUMP** claimed to the Department of Justice and FBI that he was "an open book."

73. Earlier that same day, **NAUTA, DE OLIVEIRA,** and others loaded several of **TRUMP**'s boxes along with other items on aircraft that flew **TRUMP** and his family north for the summer.

The Attempt to Delete Security Camera Footage

74. On June 3, 2022, when FBI agents were at The Mar-a-Lago Club to collect the documents with classification markings from Trump Attorney 1 and Trump Attorney 3, the agents observed that there were surveillance cameras located near the Storage Room.

75. On June 22, 2022, the Department of Justice emailed an attorney for **TRUMP**'s business organization a draft grand jury subpoena requiring the production of certain security camera footage from The Mar-a-Lago Club, including footage from cameras "on ground floor (basement)," where the Storage Room was located.

76. On June 23, 2022, at 8:46 p.m., **TRUMP** called **DE OLIVEIRA** and they spoke for approximately 24 minutes.

77. On Friday, June 24, 2022, the Department of Justice emailed the attorney for **TRUMP**'s business organization the final grand jury subpoena, which required the production of "[a]ny and all surveillance records, videos, images, photographs and/or CCTV from internal cameras" at certain locations at The Mar-a-Lago Club, including "on ground floor (basement)," from January 10, 2022, to June 24, 2022.

78. That same day, June 24, 2022, at 1:25 p.m., Trump Attorney 1 spoke with **TRUMP** by phone regarding the subpoena for security camera footage. At 3:44 p.m., **NAUTA** received a text message from a co-worker, Trump Employee 3, indicating that **TRUMP** wanted to see **NAUTA.** Less than two hours later, **NAUTA**—who was scheduled to travel with **TRUMP** to Illinois the next day—changed his travel schedule and began to make arrangements to go to Palm Beach, Florida, instead.

79. **NAUTA** provided inconsistent explanations to colleagues for his sudden travel to Florida. At 7:14 p.m. on June 24, he texted one person that he would not be traveling with **TRUMP** the next day because he had a family emergency and used "shushing" emojis; at 9:48 p.m. that night, he texted a Secret Service agent that he had to check on a family member in Florida; and after he arrived in Florida on June 25, he texted the same Secret Service agent that he was in Florida working.

80. Around the same time on June 24 that **NAUTA** was making his travel plans to go to Florida, **NAUTA** and **DE OLIVEIRA** contacted Trump Employee 4, who was the Director of Information Technology ("IT") at The Mar-a-Lago Club, as follows:

a. At 5:02 p.m., NAUTA sent text messages to Trump Employee 4 asking, "Hey bro You around this weekend."

b. At 5:05 p.m., NAUTA texted DE OLIVEIRA, asking, "Hey brother You working today?" DE OLIVEIRA responded, "Yes I just left." NAUTA then called DE OLIVEIRA and they spoke for approximately two minutes.

c. At 5:09 p.m., Trump Employee 4 texted a response to NAUTA, "I am local. Entertaining some family that came to visit. What's up?" NAUTA responded to Trump Employee 4, "Ok, cool. No biggie just wanted to see if you where around. Enjoy bro!"

d. At 6:56 p.m., DE OLIVEIRA texted Trump Employee 4, "Hey buddy how are you . . . Walter call me early said it was trying to get in touch with you I guess he's coming down tomorrow I guess needs you for something." Trump Employee 4 responded, "He reached out but he didn't say what he wanted. I told him I was local but entertaining some family that came from NYC this weekend. He told me to no worries."

e. At 6:58 p.m., Trump Employee 4 texted NAUTA, "Bro, if you need me I can get away for a few. Just let me know." NAUTA responded, "Sounds good!! Thank you."

81. On Saturday, June 25, 2022, **NAUTA** traveled from Bedminster, New Jersey, to Palm Beach, Florida. Prior to **NAUTA**'s trip, **DE OLIVEIRA** told a valet at The Mar-a-Lago Club ("Trump Employee 5") that **NAUTA** was coming down. **DE OLIVEIRA** asked Trump Employee 5 not to tell anyone that **NAUTA** was coming down because **NAUTA** wanted the trip to remain secret. **DE OLIVEIRA** also told Trump Em-

ployee 5 that **NAUTA** wanted **DE OLIVEIRA** to talk to Trump Employee 4 to see how long camera footage was stored.

82. Shortly after arriving in Palm Beach on the evening of June 25, **NAUTA** went to The Mar-a-Lago Club and met with **DE OLIVEIRA** at 5:46 p.m. At The Mar-a-Lago Club, **NAUTA** and **DE OLIVEIRA** went to the security guard booth where surveillance video is displayed on monitors, walked with a flashlight through the tunnel where the Storage Room was located, and observed and pointed out surveillance cameras.

83. On Monday, June 27, 2022, at 9:48 a.m., **DE OLIVEIRA** walked to the IT office where Trump Employee 4 was working with another employee in the IT department. **DE OLIVEIRA** requested that Trump Employee 4 step away from the office so that **DE OLIVEIRA** and Trump Employee 4 could talk.

84. At 9:49 a.m., Trump Employee 4 and **DE OLIVEIRA** left the area of the IT office together and walked through a basement tunnel. **DE OLIVEIRA** took Trump Employee 4 to a small room known as an "audio closet" near the White and Gold Ballroom. Once inside the audio closet, **DE OLIVEIRA** and Trump Employee 4 had the following exchange:

a. **DE OLIVEIRA** told Trump Employee 4 that their conversation should remain between the two of them.

b. **DE OLIVEIRA** asked Trump Employee 4 how many days the server retained footage. Trump Employee 4 responded that he believed it was approximately 45 days.

c. **DE OLIVEIRA** told Trump Employee 4 that "the boss" wanted the server deleted. Trump Employee 4 responded that he would not know how to do that, and that he did not believe that he would have the rights to do that. Trump Employee 4 told **DE OLIVEIRA** that **DE OLIVEIRA** would have to reach out to another employee who was a supervisor of security for **TRUMP**'s business organization. **DE OLIVEIRA** then insisted to **TRUMP** Employee 4 that "the boss" wanted the server deleted and asked, "what are we going to do?"

85. At 10:14 a.m., **DE OLIVEIRA** texted **NAUTA**, who was still in Florida, "Hey buddy are you working today?" **DE OLIVEIRA** then called **NAUTA** at 10:15 a.m., and they spoke for approximately one minute.

86. Later that day, at 1:06 p.m., **NAUTA** texted **DE OLIVEIRA**, who was at The Mar-a-Lago Club, "On my way to you." Between 1:31 p.m. and 1:50 p.m., **DE OLIVEIRA** walked through the bushes on the northern edge of The Mar-a-Lago Club property to meet with **NAUTA** on the adjacent property; then walked back to the IT office that he had visited that morning; and then walked again through the bushes on the northern edge of The Mar-a-Lago Club property to meet with **NAUTA** on the adjacent property.

87. At 3:55 p.m., **TRUMP** called **DE OLIVEIRA** and they spoke for approximately three and a half minutes.

The Court-Authorized Search of The Mar-a-Lago Club

88. In July 2022, the FBI and grand jury obtained and reviewed surveillance video from The Mar-a-Lago Club showing the movement of boxes set forth above.

89. On August 8, 2022, the FBI executed a court-authorized search warrant at The Mar-a-Lago Club. The search warrant authorized the FBI to search for and seize, among other things, all documents with classification markings.

90. During the execution of the warrant at The Mar-a-Lago Club, the FBI seized 102 documents with classification markings in **TRUMP**'s office and the Storage Room, as follows:

Location	Number of Documents	Classification Markings
TRUMP's Office	27	Top Secret (6) Secret (18) Confidential (3)
Storage Room	75	Top Secret (11) Secret (36) Confidential (28)

91. Just over two weeks after the FBI discovered classified documents in the Storage Room and **TRUMP**'s office, on August 26, 2022, **NAUTA** called Trump Employee 5 and said words to the effect of, "someone just wants to make sure Carlos is good." In response, Trump Employee 5 told **NAUTA** that **DE OLIVEIRA** was loyal and that **DE OLIVEIRA** would not do anything to affect his relationship with **TRUMP.** That same day, at **NAUTA**'s request, Trump Employee 5 confirmed in a Signal chat group with **NAUTA** and the PAC Representative that **DE OLIVEIRA** was loyal. That same day, **TRUMP** called **DE OLIVEIRA** and told **DE OLIVEIRA** that **TRUMP** would get **DE OLIVEIRA** an attorney.

COUNTS 1–32

Willful Retention of National Defense Information (18 U.S.C. § 793(e))

92. The General Allegations of this Superseding Indictment are re-alleged and fully incorporated here by reference.

93. On or about the dates set forth in the table below, in Palm Beach County, in the Southern District of Florida, and elsewhere, the defendant,

DONALD J. TRUMP,

having unauthorized possession of, access to, and control over documents relating to the national defense, did willfully retain the documents and fail to deliver them to the officer and employee of the United States entitled to receive them; that is—**TRUMP**, without authorization, retained at The Mar-a-Lago Club documents relating to the national defense, including the following:

Count	Date of Offense / Classification Marking / Document Description
1	January 20, 2021 – August 8, 2022
	TOP SECRET//NOFORN//SPECIAL HANDLING
	Document dated May 3, 2018, concerning White House intelligence briefing related to various foreign countries
2	January 20, 2021 – August 8, 2022
	TOP SECRET//SI//NOFORN//SPECIAL HANDLING
	Document dated May 9, 2018, concerning White House intelligence briefing related to various foreign countries
3	January 20, 2021 – August 8, 2022
	TOP SECRET//SI//NOFORN//FISA
	Undated document concerning military capabilities of a foreign country and the United States, with handwritten annotation in black marker
4	January 20, 2021 – August 8, 2022
	TOP SECRET//SPECIAL HANDLING
	Document dated May 6, 2019, concerning White House intelligence briefing related to foreign countries, including military activities and planning of foreign countries
5	January 20, 2021 – August 8, 2022
	TOP SECRET//[redacted]/[redacted]//ORCON/NOFORN
	Document dated June 2020 concerning nuclear capabilities of a foreign country
6	January 20, 2021 – August 8, 2022
	TOP SECRET//SPECIAL HANDLING
	Document dated June 4, 2020, concerning White House intelligence briefing related to various foreign countries

<table>
<tr><td rowspan="3">7</td><td>January 20, 2021 – August 8, 2022</td></tr>
<tr><td>SECRET//NOFORN</td></tr>
<tr><td>Document dated October 21, 2018, concerning communications with a leader of a foreign country</td></tr>
<tr><td rowspan="3">8</td><td>January 20, 2021 – August 8, 2022</td></tr>
<tr><td>SECRET//REL TO USA, FVEY</td></tr>
<tr><td>Document dated October 4, 2019, concerning military capabilities of a foreign country</td></tr>
<tr><td rowspan="3">9</td><td>January 20, 2021 – August 8, 2022</td></tr>
<tr><td>TOP SECRET//[redacted]/[redacted]//ORCON/NOFORN/FISA</td></tr>
<tr><td>Undated document concerning military attacks by a foreign country</td></tr>
<tr><td rowspan="3">10</td><td>January 20, 2021 – August 8, 2022</td></tr>
<tr><td>TOP SECRET//TK//NOFORN</td></tr>
<tr><td>Document dated November 2017 concerning military capabilities of a foreign country</td></tr>
<tr><td rowspan="3">11</td><td>January 20, 2021 – August 8, 2022</td></tr>
<tr><td>No marking</td></tr>
<tr><td>Undated document concerning military contingency planning of the United States</td></tr>
<tr><td rowspan="3">12</td><td>January 20, 2021 – August 8, 2022</td></tr>
<tr><td>SECRET//REL TO USA, FVEY</td></tr>
<tr><td>Pages of undated document concerning projected regional military capabilities of a foreign country and the United States</td></tr>
<tr><td rowspan="3">13</td><td>January 20, 2021 – August 8, 2022</td></tr>
<tr><td>TOP SECRET//SI/TK//NOFORN</td></tr>
<tr><td>Undated document concerning military capabilities of a foreign country and the United States</td></tr>
</table>

<table>
<tr><td rowspan="3">14</td><td>January 20, 2021 – August 8, 2022</td></tr>
<tr><td>SECRET//ORCON/NOFORN</td></tr>
<tr><td>Document dated January 2020 concerning military options of a foreign country and potential effects on United States interests</td></tr>
<tr><td rowspan="3">15</td><td>January 20, 2021 – August 8, 2022</td></tr>
<tr><td>SECRET//ORCON/NOFORN</td></tr>
<tr><td>Document dated February 2020 concerning policies in a foreign country</td></tr>
<tr><td rowspan="3">16</td><td>January 20, 2021 – August 8, 2022</td></tr>
<tr><td>SECRET//ORCON/NOFORN</td></tr>
<tr><td>Document dated December 2019 concerning foreign country support of terrorist acts against United States interests</td></tr>
<tr><td rowspan="3">17</td><td>January 20, 2021 – August 8, 2022</td></tr>
<tr><td>TOP SECRET//[redacted]/TK//ORCON/IMCON/NOFORN</td></tr>
<tr><td>Document dated January 2020 concerning military capabilities of a foreign country</td></tr>
<tr><td rowspan="3">18</td><td>January 20, 2021 – August 8, 2022</td></tr>
<tr><td>SECRET//NOFORN</td></tr>
<tr><td>Document dated March 2020 concerning military operations against United States forces and others</td></tr>
<tr><td rowspan="3">19</td><td>January 20, 2021 – August 8, 2022</td></tr>
<tr><td>SECRET//FORMERLY RESTRICTED DATA</td></tr>
<tr><td>Undated document concerning nuclear weaponry of the United States</td></tr>
<tr><td rowspan="3">20</td><td>January 20, 2021 – August 8, 2022</td></tr>
<tr><td>TOP SECRET//[redacted]//ORCON/NOFORN</td></tr>
<tr><td>Undated document concerning timeline and details of attack in a foreign country</td></tr>
<tr><td rowspan="3">21</td><td>January 20, 2021 – August 8, 2022</td></tr>
<tr><td>SECRET//NOFORN</td></tr>
<tr><td>Undated document concerning military capabilities of foreign countries</td></tr>
</table>

22	January 20, 2021 – June 3, 2022
	TOP SECRET//[redacted]//RSEN/ORCON/NOFORN
	Document dated August 2019 concerning regional military activity of a foreign country
23	January 20, 2021 – June 3, 2022
	TOP SECRET//SPECIAL HANDLING
	Document dated August 30, 2019, concerning White House intelligence briefing related to various foreign countries, with handwritten annotation in black marker
24	January 20, 2021 – June 3, 2022
	TOP SECRET//HCS-P/SI//ORCON-USGOV/NOFORN
	Undated document concerning military activity of a foreign country
25	January 20, 2021 – June 3, 2022
	TOP SECRET//HCS-P/SI//ORCON-USGOV/NOFORN
	Document dated October 24, 2019, concerning military activity of foreign countries and the United States
26	January 20, 2021 – June 3, 2022
	TOP SECRET//[redacted]//ORCON/NOFORN/FISA
	Document dated November 7, 2019, concerning military activity of foreign countries and the United States
27	January 20, 2021 – June 3, 2022
	TOP SECRET//SI/TK//NOFORN
	Document dated November 2019 concerning military activity of foreign countries
28	January 20, 2021 – June 3, 2022
	TOP SECRET//SPECIAL HANDLING
	Document dated October 18, 2019, concerning White House intelligence briefing related to various foreign countries

29	January 20, 2021 – June 3, 2022
	TOP SECRET//[redacted]/SI/TK//ORCON/NOFORN
	Document dated October 18, 2019, concerning military capabilities of a foreign country
30	January 20, 2021 – June 3, 2022
	TOP SECRET//[redacted]//ORCON/NOFORN/FISA
	Document dated October 15, 2019, concerning military activity in a foreign country
31	January 20, 2021 – June 3, 2022
	TOP SECRET//SI/TK//NOFORN
	Document dated February 2017 concerning military activity of a foreign country
32	January 20, 2021 – January 17, 2022
	TOP SECRET//NOFORN
	Presentation concerning military activity in a foreign country

All in violation of Title 18, United States Code, Section 793(e).

COUNT 33

Conspiracy to Obstruct Justice (18 U.S.C. § 1512(k))

94. The General Allegations of this Superseding Indictment are re-alleged and fully incorporated here by reference.

The Conspiracy and Its Objects

95. From on or about May 11, 2022, through in or around August 2022, in Palm Beach County, in the Southern District of Florida, and elsewhere, the defendants,

DONALD J. TRUMP,
WALTINE NAUTA, and
CARLOS DE OLIVEIRA

did knowingly combine, conspire, confederate, and agree with each other and with others known and unknown to the grand jury, to engage in misleading conduct toward another person and corruptly persuade another person to withhold a record, document, and other object from an official proceeding, in violation of 18 U.S.C. § 1512(b)(2)(A); to corruptly persuade another person, with intent to cause and induce any person to alter, destroy, mutilate, and conceal an object with intent to impair the object's integrity and availability for use in an official proceeding, in violation of 18 U.S.C. § 1512(b)(2)(B); and to corruptly alter, destroy, mutilate, and conceal a record, document, and other object from an official proceeding, in violation of 18 U.S.C. § 1512(c)(1).

The Purpose of the Conspiracy

96. The purpose of the conspiracy was for **TRUMP** to keep classified documents he had taken with him from the White House and to hide and conceal them from a federal grand jury.

The Manner and Means of the Conspiracy

97. The manner and means by which the defendants sought to accomplish the objects and purpose of the conspiracy included, among other things, the following:

a. Suggesting that Trump Attorney 1 falsely represent to the FBI and grand jury that **TRUMP** did not have documents called for by the May 11 Subpoena;

b. moving boxes of documents to conceal them from Trump Attorney 1, the FBI, and the grand jury;

c. suggesting that Trump Attorney 1 hide or destroy documents called for by the May 11 Subpoena;

d. providing to the FBI and grand jury just some of the documents called for by the May 11 Subpoena, while **TRUMP** claimed he was cooperating fully;

e. causing a false certification to be submitted to the FBI and grand jury representing that all documents with classification markings had been produced, when in fact they had not; and

f. making false and misleading statements to the FBI; and

g. attempting to delete security camera footage from The Mar-a-Lago Club to conceal the footage from the FBI and grand jury.

All in violation of Title 18, United States Code, Section 1512(k).

COUNT 34

Withholding a Document or Record (18 U.S.C. §§ 1512(b)(2)(A), 2)

98. The General Allegations of this Superseding Indictment are re-alleged and fully incorporated here by reference.

99. From on or about May 11, 2022, through in or around August 2022, in Palm Beach County, in the Southern District of Florida, and elsewhere, the defendants,

DONALD J. TRUMP and
WALTINE NAUTA,

did knowingly engage in misleading conduct toward another person, and knowingly corruptly persuade and attempt to persuade another person, with intent to cause and induce any person to withhold a record, document, and other object from an official proceeding; that is—(1) **TRUMP** attempted to persuade Trump Attorney 1 to hide and conceal documents from a federal grand jury; and (2) **TRUMP** and **NAUTA** misled Trump Attorney 1 by moving boxes that contained documents with classification markings so that Trump Attorney 1 would not find the documents and produce them to a federal grand jury.

All in violation of Title 18, United States Code, Sections 1512(b)(2)(A) and 2.

COUNT 35

Corruptly Concealing a Document or Record
(18 U.S.C. §§ 1512(c)(1), 2)

100. The General Allegations of this Superseding Indictment are re-alleged and fully incorporated here by reference.

101. From on or about May 11, 2022, through in or around August 2022, in Palm Beach County, in the Southern District of Florida, and elsewhere, the defendants,

DONALD J. TRUMP and
WALTINE NAUTA,

did corruptly conceal a record, document, and other object, and attempted to do so, with the intent to impair the object's integrity and availability for use in an official proceeding; that is—**TRUMP** and **NAUTA** hid and concealed boxes that contained documents with classification markings from Trump Attorney 1 so that Trump Attorney 1 would not find the documents and produce them to a federal grand jury.

All in violation of Title 18, United States Code, Sections 1512(c)(1) and 2.

COUNT 36

Concealing a Document in a Federal Investigation (18 U.S.C. §§ 1519, 2)

102. The General Allegations of this Superseding Indictment are re-alleged and fully incorporated here by reference.

103. From on or about May 11, 2022, through in or around August 2022, in Palm Beach County, in the Southern District of Florida, and elsewhere, the defendants,

DONALD J. TRUMP and
WALTINE NAUTA,

did knowingly conceal, cover up, falsify, and make a false entry in any record, document, and tangible object with the intent to impede, obstruct, and influence the investigation and proper administration of any matter within the jurisdiction of a department and agency of the United States, and in relation to and contemplation of any such matter; that is—during a federal criminal investigation being conducted by the FBI, (1) **TRUMP** and **NAUTA** hid, concealed, and covered up from the FBI **TRUMP**'s continued possession of documents with classification markings at The Mar-a-Lago Club; and (2) **TRUMP** caused a false certification to be submitted to the FBI.

All in violation of Title 18, United States Code, Sections 1519 and 2.

COUNT 37

Scheme to Conceal (18 U.S.C. §§ 1001(a)(1), 2)

104. The General Allegations of this Superseding Indictment are re-alleged and fully incorporated here by reference.

105. From on or about May 11, 2022, through in or around August 2022, in Palm Beach County, in the Southern District of Florida, and elsewhere, the defendants,

DONALD J. TRUMP and
WALTINE NAUTA,

in a matter within the jurisdiction of the judicial branch and executive branch of the United States government, did knowingly and willfully falsify, conceal, and cover up by any trick, scheme, and device a material fact; that is—during a federal grand jury investigation and a federal criminal investigation being conducted by the FBI, **TRUMP** and **NAUTA** hid and concealed from the grand jury and the FBI **TRUMP**'s continued possession of documents with classification markings.

All in violation of Title 18, United States Code, Sections 1001(a)(1) and 2.

COUNT 38

False Statements and Representations (18 U.S.C. §§ 1001(a)(2), 2)

106. The General Allegations of this Superseding Indictment are re-alleged and fully incorporated here by reference.

107. On or about June 3, 2022, in Palm Beach County, in the Southern District of Florida, and elsewhere, the defendant,

DONALD J. TRUMP,

in a matter within the jurisdiction of the judicial branch and executive branch of the United States government, did knowingly and willfully make and cause to be made a materially false, fictitious, and fraudulent statement and representation; that is—during a federal grand jury investigation and a federal criminal investigation being conducted by the FBI, **TRUMP** caused the following false statements and representations to be made to the grand jury and the FBI in a sworn certification executed by Trump Attorney 3:

a. "A diligent search was conducted of the boxes that were moved from the White House to Florida";

b. "This search was conducted after receipt of the subpoena, in order to locate any and all documents that are responsive to the subpoena"; and

c. "Any and all responsive documents accompany this certification."

108. The statements and representations set forth above were false, as **TRUMP** knew, because **TRUMP** had directed that boxes be removed from the Storage Room before Trump Attorney 1 conducted the June 2, 2022 search for documents with classification markings, so that Trump Attorney 1's search would not and did not include all of **TRUMP**'s boxes that were removed from the White House; Trump Attorney 1's search would not and did not locate all documents responsive to the May 11 Subpoena; and all responsive documents were not provided to the FBI and the grand jury with the certification. In fact, after June 3, 2022, more than 100 documents with classification markings remained at The Mar-a-Lago Club until the FBI search on August 8, 2022.

All in violation of Title 18, United States Code, Sections 1001(a)(2) and 2.

COUNT 39

False Statements and Representations (18 U.S.C. § 1001(a)(2))

109. The General Allegations of this Superseding Indictment are re-alleged and fully incorporated here by reference.

110. On May 26, 2022, **NAUTA** participated in a voluntary interview with the FBI. During the interview, the FBI explained to **NAUTA** that the FBI was investigating how classified documents had been kept at The Mar-a-Lago Club, and the FBI asked **NAUTA** questions about the location and movement of **TRUMP**'s boxes before **TRUMP** provided 15 boxes to NARA on January 17, 2022. **NAUTA**

was represented by counsel, and the FBI advised **NAUTA** that the interview was voluntary and that he could leave at any time. The FBI also advised **NAUTA** that it was a criminal offense to lie to the FBI. The interview was recorded.

111. On or about May 26, 2022, in Palm Beach County, in the Southern District of Florida, and elsewhere, the defendant,

WALTINE NAUTA,

in a matter within the jurisdiction of the executive branch of the United States government, did knowingly and willfully make a materially false, fictitious, and fraudulent statement and representation; that is—in a voluntary interview during a federal criminal investigation being conducted by the FBI, **NAUTA** was asked the following questions and gave the following false answers:

Question: Does any—are you aware of any boxes being brought to his home—his suite?

Answer: **No.**

Question: All right. So, so to the best of your knowledge, you're saying that those boxes that you brought onto the truck, first time you ever laid eyes on them was just the day of when [Trump Employee 2] needed you to—

Answer: **Correct.**

Question: —to take them. Okay.

Question: In knowing that we're trying to track the life of these boxes and where they could have been kept and stored and all that kind of stuff—

Answer: Mm-hm.

Question: —do you have any information that could—that would—that could help us understand, like, where they were kept, how they were kept, were they secured, were they locked? Something that makes the intelligence community feel better about these things, you know?

Answer: **I wish, I wish I could tell you. I don't know. I don't—I honestly just don't know.**

Question: And what—so, so you only saw the 15 boxes, 15, 17 boxes—

Answer: Mm-hm.

Question: —the day of the move? Even—they just showed up that day?

Answer: They were in Pine Hall. [Trump Employee 2] just asked me, hey, can we move some boxes?

Question: Okay.

Answer: And I was like, okay.

Question: So, you didn't know—had no idea how they got there before?

Answer: **No.**

112. The underscored statements and representations above were false, as **NAUTA** knew, because (1) **NAUTA** did in fact know that the boxes in Pine Hall had come from the Storage Room, as **NAUTA** himself, with the assistance of Trump Employee 2, had moved the boxes

from the Storage Room to Pine Hall; and (2) **NAUTA** had observed the boxes in and moved them to various locations at The Mar-a-Lago Club.

All in violation of Title 18, United States Code, Section 1001(a)(2).

COUNT 40

Altering, Destroying, Mutilating, or Concealing an Object (18 U.S.C. §§ 1512(b)(2)(B), 2)

113. The General Allegations of this Superseding Indictment are re-alleged and fully incorporated here by reference.

114. From on or about June 22, 2022, through in or around August 2022, in Palm Beach County, in the Southern District of Florida, and elsewhere, the defendants,

DONALD J. TRUMP,
WALTINE NAUTA, and
CARLOS DE OLIVEIRA

did knowingly corruptly persuade and attempt to persuade another person, with intent to cause and induce any person to alter, destroy, mutilate, and conceal an object with intent to impair the object's integrity and availability for use in an official proceeding; that is—**TRUMP**, **NAUTA**, and **DE OLIVEIRA** requested that Trump Employee 4 delete security camera footage at The Mar-a-Lago Club to prevent the footage from being provided to a federal grand jury.

All in violation of Title 18, United States Code, Sections 1512(b)(2)(8) and 2.

COUNT 41

Corruptly Altering, Destroying, Mutilating or Concealing a Document, Record, or Other Object (18 U.S.C. §§ 1512(c)(1), 2)

115. The General Allegations of this Superseding Indictment are re-alleged and fully incorporated here by reference.

116. From on or about June 22, 2022, through in or around August 2022, in Palm Beach County, in the Southern District of Florida, and elsewhere, the defendants,

DONALD J. TRUMP,
WALTINE NAUTA, and
CARLOS DE OLIVEIRA

did corruptly alter, destroy, mutilate, and conceal a record, document and other object and attempted to do so, with the intent to impair the object's integrity and availability for use in an official proceeding; that is—**TRUMP**, **NAUTA**, and **DE OLIVEIRA** requested that Trump Employee 4 delete security camera footage at The Mar-a-Lago Club to prevent the footage from being provided to a federal grand jury.

All in violation of Title 18, United States Code, Sections 1512(c)(1) and 2.

COUNT 42

False Statements and Representations (18 U.S.C. § 1001(a)(2))

117. The General Allegations of this Superseding Indictment are re-alleged and fully incorporated here by reference.

118. On January 13, 2023, **DE OLIVEIRA** participated in a voluntary interview with the FBI at **DE OLIVEIRA**'s residence. During the interview, the FBI explained to **DE OLIVEIRA** that the FBI was investigating how classified documents had been kept at The Mar-a-Lago Club, and the FBI asked **DE OLIVEIRA** questions about the location and movement of **TRUMP**'s boxes and other items. **DE OLIVEIRA** was advised by the FBI that the interview was voluntary and that he could tell the agents to leave at any time. The FBI also advised **DE OLIVEIRA** that it was a criminal offense to lie to the FBI. The interview was recorded.

119. On or about January 13, 2023, in Palm Beach County, in the Southern District of Florida, and elsewhere, the defendant,

CARLOS DE OLIVEIRA,

in a matter within the jurisdiction of the executive branch of the United States government, did knowingly and willfully make a materially false, fictitious, and fraudulent statement and representation; that is—in a voluntary interview during a federal criminal investigation being conducted by the FBI, **DE OLIVEIRA** was asked the following questions and gave the following false answers:

Question: When—after the end of the presidency, boxes arrived to Mar-a-Lago. Were you part of any group to help—

Answer: **No.**

Question: —unload them and move them?

Answer: **No.**

* * *

Question: Do you—were you—do you even know, like, or were you even there or aware that boxes were—

Answer: **No.**

Question: —like, all this stuff was being moved in?

Answer: **Never saw anything.**

Question: Okay.

Answer: Yeah. And then—

Question: Even his personal stuff, like, his clothes—

Answer: **Never.**

Question: —and furniture, nothing?

Answer: **Never saw nothing.**

Question: Okay. So you don't know where items would have been stored, as soon as he moved back to Mar-a-Lago?

Answer: **No.**

120. The underscored statements and representations above were false, as **DE OLIVEIRA** knew, because **DE OLIVEIRA** had personally observed and helped move **TRUMP**'s boxes when they arrived at The Mar-a-Lago Club in January 2021.

All in violation of Title 18, United States Code, Sections 1001(a)(2).

JACK SMITH
SPECIAL COUNSEL
UNITED STATES
DEPARTMENT OF JUSTICE

UNITED STATES DISTRICT COURT
SOUTHERN DISTRICT OF FLORIDA

UNITED STATES OF AMERICA
v.
Donald J. Trump,
Waltine Nauta, and
Carlos De Oliveira, ______________/

Defendants.

Court Division (select one)
☐ Miami ☐ Key West ☐ FTP ☐ FTL ☑ WPB

CASE NO.: 23-CR-80101-AMC(s)

CERTIFICATE OF TRIAL ATTORNEY

Superseding Case Information:
New Defendant(s) (Yes or No) Yes
Number of New Defendants 1
Total number of counts 42

I do hereby certify that:

1. I have carefully considered the allegations of the indictment, the number of defendants, the number of probable witnesses and the legal complexities of the Indictment/Information attached hereto.
2. I am aware that the information supplied on this statement will be relied upon by the Judges of this Court in setting their calendars and scheduling criminal trials under the mandate of the Speedy Trial Act, Title 28 U.S.C. §3161.
3. Interpreter: (Yes or No) **No;** List language and/or dialect: __________
4. This case will take **21** days for the parties to try.
5. Please check appropriate category and type of offense listed below (Check only one):

I	☐ 0 to 5 days	☐ Petty
II	☐ 6 to 10 days	☐ Minor
III	☐ 11 to 20 days	☐ Misdemeanor
IV	☑ 21 to 60 days	☑ Felony
V	☐ 61 days and over	☐

6. Has this case been previously filed in this District Court? (Yes or No) **Yes**
   If yes, Judge Cannon Case No. 23-cr-80101
7. Has a complaint been filed in this matter? (Yes or No) **No**
   If yes, Magistrate Case No. __________
8. Does this case relate to a previously filed matter in this District Court? (Yes or No) **No**
   If yes, Judge __________ Case No. __________
9. Defendant(s) in federal custody as of __________
10. Defendant(s) in state custody as of N/A
11. Rule 20 from the __________ District of __________
12. Is this a potential death penalty case? (Yes or No) **No**
13. Does this case originate from a matter pending in the Northern Region of the U.S. Attorney's Office prior to August 8, 2014 (Mag. Judge Shaniek Maynard? (Yes or No) **No**
14. Does this case originate from a matter pending in the Central Region of the U.S. Attorney's Office prior to October 3, 2019 (Mag. Judge Jared Strauss? (Yes or No) **No**
15. Did this matter involve the participation of or consultation with now Magistrate Judge Eduardo I. Sanchez during his tenure at the U.S. Attorney's Office, which concluded on January 22, 2023? **No**

By: ______________________
Jay I. Bratt
Assistant Special Counsel
Court ID No. A5502946

UNITED STATES DISTRICT COURT
SOUTHERN DISTRICT OF FLORIDA

PENALTY SHEET

Defendant's Name: Donald J. Trump

Case No: 23-CR-80101-AMC(s)

Counts #: 1–32

Willful Retention of National Defense Information, 18 U.S.C. § 793(e)

* **Max. Term of Imprisonment: 10 years**
* **Mandatory Min. Term of Imprisonment (if applicable): N/A**
* **Max. Supervised Release: 3 years**
* **Max. Fine: $250,000**

Count #: 33

Conspiracy to Obstruct Justice, 18 U.S.C. § 1512(k)

* **Max. Term of Imprisonment: 20 years**
* **Mandatory Min. Term of Imprisonment (if applicable): N/A**
* **Max. Supervised Release: 3 years**
* **Max. Fine: $250,000**

Count #: 34

Withholding a Document or Record, 18 U.S.C. § 1512(c)(1)

* **Max. Term of Imprisonment: 20 years**
* **Mandatory Min. Term of Imprisonment (if applicable): N/A**
* **Max. Supervised Release: 3 years**
* **Max. Fine: $250,000**

Count #: 35

Corruptly Concealing a Document or Record, 18 U.S.C. §§ 1512(c)(1), 2

* **Max. Term of Imprisonment: 20 years**
* **Mandatory Min. Term of Imprisonment (if applicable): N/A**
* **Max. Supervised Release: 3 years**
* **Max. Fine: $250,000**

***Refers only to possible term of incarceration, supervised release and fines. It does not include restitution, special assessments, parole terms, or forfeitures that may be applicable.**

Count #: 36

Concealing a Document in a Federal Investigation, 18 U.S.C. §§ 1519, 2

---

* **Max. Term of Imprisonment: 20 years**
* **Mandatory Min. Term of Imprisonment (if applicable): N/A**
* **Max. Supervised Release: 3 years**
* **Max. Fine: $250,000**

Count #: 37

Scheme to Conceal, 18 U.S.C. §§ 1001(a)(1), 2

---

* **Max. Term of Imprisonment: 5 years**
* **Mandatory Min. Term of Imprisonment (if applicable): N/A**
* **Max. Supervised Release: 3 years**
* **Max. Fine: $250,000**

Count #: 38

False Statements and Representations, 18 U.S.C. §§ 1001(a)(2), 2

---

* **Max. Term of Imprisonment: 5 years**
* **Mandatory Min. Term of Imprisonment (if applicable): N/A**
* **Max. Supervised Release: 3 years**
* **Max. Fine: $250,000**

***Refers only to possible term of incarceration, supervised release and fines. It does not include restitution, special assessments, parole terms, or forfeitures that may be applicable.**

UNITED STATES DISTRICT COURT
SOUTHERN DISTRICT OF FLORIDA

PENALTY SHEET

Defendant's Name: Waltine Nauta

Case No: 23-CR-80101-AMC(s)

Count #: 33

Conspiracy to Obstruct Justice, 18 U.S.C. § 1512(k)

* **Max. Term of Imprisonment: 20 years**
* **Mandatory Min. Term of Imprisonment (if applicable): N/A**
* **Max. Supervised Release: 3 years**
* **Max. Fine: $250,000**

Count #: 34

Withholding a Document or Record, 18 U.S.C. § 1512(b)(2)(A)

* **Max. Term of Imprisonment: 20 years**
* **Mandatory Min. Term of Imprisonment (if applicable): N/A**
* **Max. Supervised Release: 3 years**
* *** Max. Fine: $250,000**

Count #: 34

Corruptly Concealing a Document or Record, 18 U.S.C. § 1512(c)(1)

* **Max. Term of Imprisonment: 20 years**
* **Mandatory Min. Term of Imprisonment (if applicable): N/A**
* **Max. Supervised Release: 3 years**
* **Max. Fine: $250,000**

Count #: 35

Corruptly Concealing a Document or Record, 18 U.S.C. §§ 1512(c)(1), 2

* **Max. Term of Imprisonment: 20 years**
* **Mandatory Min. Term of Imprisonment (if applicable): N/A**
* **Max. Supervised Release: 3 years**
* **Max. Fine: $250,000**

***Refers only to possible term of incarceration, supervised release and fines. It does not include restitution, special assessments, parole terms, or forfeitures that may be applicable.**

Count #: 36

Concealing a Document in a Federal Investigation, 18 U.S.C. §§ 1519, 2

---

* **Max. Term of Imprisonment: 20 years**
* **Mandatory Min. Term of Imprisonment (if applicable): N/A**
* **Max. Supervised Release: 3 years**
* **Max. Fine: $250,000**

Count #: 37

Scheme to Conceal, 18 U.S.C. §§ 1001(a)(1), 2

---

* **Max. Term of Imprisonment: 5 years**
* **Mandatory Min. Term of Imprisonment (if applicable): N/A**
* **Max. Supervised Release: 3 years**
* **Max. Fine: $250,000**

Count #: 39

False Statements and Representations, 18 U.S.C. § 1001(a)(2)

---

* **Max. Term of Imprisonment: 5 years**
* **Mandatory Min. Term of Imprisonment (if applicable): N/A**
* **Max. Supervised Release: 3 years**
* **Max. Fine: $250,000**

Count #: 40

Altering, Destroying, Mutilating, or Concealing an Object, 18 U.S.C. §§ 1512(b)(2)(B), 2

---

* **Max. Term of Imprisonment: 20 years**
* **Mandatory Min. Term of Imprisonment (if applicable): N/A**
* **Max. Supervised Release: 3 years**
* **Max. Fine: $250,000**

Count #: 41

Corruptly Altering, Destroying, Mutilating, or Concealing a Document, Record, or Other Object, 18 U.S.C. §§ 1512(c)(1), 2

---

* **Max. Term of Imprisonment: 20 years**
* **Mandatory Min. Term of Imprisonment (if applicable): N/A**
* **Max. Supervised Release: 3 years**
* **Max. Fine: $250,000**

***Refers only to possible term of incarceration, supervised release and fines. It does not include restitution, special assessments, parole terms, or forfeitures that may be applicable.**

3.

THE STATE OF GEORGIA v. DONALD JOHN TRUMP, ET AL.

INDICTMENT
Clerk No. 23SC188947
FULTON SUPERIOR COURT

THE STATE OF GEORGIA

v.

DONALD JOHN TRUMP
Counts 1, 5, 9, 11, 13, 15, 17, 19, 27–29, 38–39

RUDOLPH WILLIAM LOUIS GIULIANI
Counts 1–3, 6–7, 9, 11, 13, 15, 17, 19, 23–24

JOHN CHARLES EASTMAN
Counts 1–2, 9, 11, 13, 15, 17, 19, 27

MARK RANDALL MEADOWS
Counts 1, 28

KENNETH JOHN CHESEBRO
Counts 1, 9, 11, 13, 15, 17, 19

JEFFREY BOSSERT CLARK
Counts 1, 22

JENNA LYNN ELLIS
Counts 1–2

RAY STALLINGS SMITH III
Counts 1–2, 4, 6, 9, 11, 13, 15, 17, 19, 23, 25

ROBERT DAVID CHEELEY
Counts 1, 9, 11, 13, 15, 17, 19, 23, 26, 41

MICHAEL A. ROMAN
Counts 1, 9, 11, 13, 15, 17, 19

DAVID JAMES SHAFER
Counts 1, 8, 10, 12, 14, 16, 18, 40

SHAWN MICAH TRESHER STILL
Counts 1, 8, 10, 12, 14, 16, 18

STEPHEN CLIFFGARD LEE
Counts 1, 20–21, 30–31

HARRISON WILLIAM PRESCOTT FLOYD
Counts 1, 30–31

TREVIAN C. KUTTI
Counts 1, 30–31

SIDNEY KATHERINE POWELL
Counts 1, 32–37

CATHLEEN ALSTON LATHAM
Counts 1, 8, 10, 12, 14, 32–37

SCOTT GRAHAM HALL
Counts 1, 32–37

MISTY HAMPTON AKA EMILY MISTY HAYES
Counts 1, 32–37

COUNT 1 OF 41

The Grand Jurors aforesaid, in the name and behalf of the citizens of Georgia, do hereby charge and accuse:

DONALD JOHN TRUMP,
RUDOLPH WILLIAM LOUIS GIULIANI,
JOHN CHARLES EASTMAN,
MARK RANDALL MEADOWS,
KENNETH JOHN CHESEBRO,
JEFFREY BOSSERT CLARK,
JENNA LYNN ELLIS,
RAY STALLINGS SMITH III,
ROBERT DAVID CHEELEY,
MICHAEL A. ROMAN,
DAVID JAMES SHAFER,
SHAWN MICAH TRESHER STILL,
STEPHEN CLIFFGARD LEE,
HARRISON WILLIAM PRESCOTT FLOYD,
TREVIAN C. KUTTI,
SIDNEY KATHERINE POWELL,
CATHLEEN ALSTON LATHAM,
SCOTT GRAHAM HALL, and
MISTY HAMPTON

with the offense of **VIOLATION OF THE GEORGIA RICO (RACKETEER INFLUENCED AND CORRUPT ORGANIZATIONS) ACT, O.C.G.A. § 16-14-4(c),** for the said accused, individually and as persons concerned in the commission of a crime, and together with unindicted co-conspirators, in the State of Georgia and County of Fulton, on and between the **4th day of November 2020 and the 15th**

day of September 2022, while associated with an enterprise, unlawfully conspired and endeavored to conduct and participate in, directly and indirectly, such enterprise through a pattern of racketeering activity in violation of **O.C.G.A. § 16-14-4(b),** as described below and incorporated by reference as if fully set forth herein, contrary to the laws of said State, the good order, peace, and dignity thereof;

INTRODUCTION

Defendant Donald John Trump lost the United States presidential election held on November 3, 2020. One of the states he lost was Georgia. Trump and the other Defendants charged in this Indictment refused to accept that Trump lost, and they knowingly and willfully joined a conspiracy to unlawfully change the outcome of the election in favor of Trump. That conspiracy contained a common plan and purpose to commit two or more acts of racketeering activity in Fulton County, Georgia, elsewhere in the State of Georgia, and in other states.

THE ENTERPRISE

At all times relevant to this Count of the Indictment, the Defendants, as well as others not named as defendants, unlawfully conspired and endeavored to conduct and participate in a criminal enterprise in Fulton County, Georgia, and elsewhere. Defendants Donald John Trump, Rudolph William Louis Giuliani, John Charles Eastman, Mark Randall Meadows, Kenneth John Chesebro, Jeffrey Bossert Clark, Jenna Lynn Ellis, Ray Stallings Smith III, Robert David Cheeley, Michael A. Roman, David James Shafer, Shawn Micah Tresher Still, Stephen Cliffgard Lee, Harrison William Prescott Floyd, Trevian C. Kutti, Sidney Katherine Powell, Cathleen Alston Latham, Scott Graham Hall, Misty Hampton, unindicted co-conspirators Individual 1 through Individual 30, and others known and unknown to the Grand Jury, constituted a criminal organization whose members and associates engaged in various related criminal activities including, but not limited to, false statements and writings, impersonating a public officer, forgery, filing false documents, influencing witnesses, computer theft, computer trespass, computer invasion of privacy, conspiracy to defraud the state, acts involving theft, and perjury.

This criminal organization constituted an enterprise as that term is defined in O.C.G.A. § 16-14-3(3), that is, a group of individuals associated in fact. The Defendants and other members and associates of the enterprise had connections and relationships with one another and with the enterprise. The enterprise constituted an ongoing organization whose members and associates functioned as a continuing unit for a common purpose of achieving the objectives of the enterprise. The enterprise operated in Fulton County, Georgia, elsewhere in the State of Georgia, in other states, including, but not limited to, Arizona, Michigan, Nevada, New Mexico, Pennsylvania, and Wisconsin, and in the District of Columbia. The enterprise operated for a period of time sufficient to permit its members and associates to pursue its objectives.

MANNER AND METHODS OF THE ENTERPRISE

The manner and methods used by the Defendants and other members and associates of the enterprise to further the goals of the enterprise and to achieve its purposes included, but were not limited to, the following:

1. False Statements to and Solicitation of State Legislatures

Members of the enterprise, including several of the Defendants, appeared at hearings in Fulton County, Georgia, before members of the Georgia General Assembly on December 3, 2020, December 10, 2020, and December 30, 2020. At these hearings, members of the enterprise made false statements concerning fraud in the November 3, 2020, presidential election. The purpose of these false statements was to persuade Georgia legislators to reject lawful electoral votes cast by the duly elected and qualified presidential electors from Georgia. Members of the enterprise corruptly solicited Georgia legislators instead to unlawfully appoint their own presidential electors for the purpose of casting electoral votes for Donald Trump. Members of the enterprise also made false statements to state legislators during hearings and meetings in Arizona, Michigan, and Pennsylvania in November and December 2020 to persuade legislators in those states to unlawfully appoint their own presidential electors.

2. False Statements to and Solicitation of High-Ranking State Officials

Members of the enterprise, including several of the Defendants, made false statements in Fulton County and elsewhere in the State of Georgia to Georgia officials, including the Governor, the Secretary of State, and the Speaker of the House of Representatives. Members of the enterprise also corruptly solicited Georgia officials, including the Secretary of State and the Speaker of the House of Representatives, to violate their oaths to the Georgia Constitution and to the United States Constitution by unlawfully changing the outcome of the November 3, 2020, presidential election in Georgia in favor of Donald Trump. Members of the enterprise also made false statements to and solicited state officials in Arizona, Michigan, and Pennsylvania.

3. Creation and Distribution of False Electoral College Documents

Members of the enterprise, including several of the Defendants, created false Electoral College documents and recruited individuals to convene and cast false Electoral College votes at the Georgia State Capitol, in Fulton County, on December 14, 2020. After the false Electoral College votes were cast, members of the enterprise transmitted the votes to the President of the United States Senate, the Archivist of the United States, the Georgia Secretary of State, and the Chief Judge of the United States District Court for the Northern District of Georgia. The false documents were intended to disrupt and delay the joint session of Congress on January 6, 2021, in order to unlawfully change the outcome of the November 3, 2020, presidential election in favor of Donald Trump. Similar schemes were executed by members of the enterprise in Arizona, Michigan, Nevada, New Mexico, Pennsylvania, and Wisconsin.

4. Harassment and Intimidation of Fulton County Election Worker Ruby Freeman

Members of the enterprise, including several of the Defendants, falsely accused Fulton County election worker Ruby Freeman of committing election crimes in Fulton County, Georgia. These false accusations were repeated to Georgia legislators and other Georgia officials in an effort to persuade them to unlawfully change the outcome of the November 3, 2020, presidential election in favor of Donald Trump. In furtherance of this scheme, members of the enterprise traveled from out of state to harass Freeman, intimidate her, and solicit her to falsely confess to election crimes that she did not commit.

5. Solicitation of High-Ranking United States Department of Justice Officials

Members of the enterprise, including several of the Defendants, corruptly solicited high-ranking United States Department of Justice officials to make false statements to government officials in Fulton County, Georgia, including the Governor, the Speaker of the House of Representatives, and the President Pro Tempore of the Senate. In one instance, Donald Trump stated to the Acting United States Attorney General, "Just say that the election was corrupt, and leave the rest to me and the Republican congressmen."

6. Solicitation of the Vice President of the United States

Members of the enterprise, including several of the Defendants, corruptly solicited the Vice President of the United States to violate the United States Constitution and federal law by unlawfully rejecting Electoral College votes cast in Fulton County, Georgia, by the duly elected and qualified presidential electors from Georgia. Members of the enterprise also corruptly solicited the Vice President to reject votes cast by the duly elected and qualified presidential electors from several other states.

7. Unlawful Breach of Election Equipment in Georgia and Elsewhere

Members of the enterprise, including several of the Defendants, corruptly conspired in Fulton County, Georgia, and elsewhere to unlawfully access secure voting equipment and voter data. In Georgia, members of the enterprise stole data, including ballot images, voting equipment software, and personal voter information. The stolen data was then distributed to other members of the enterprise, including members in other states.

8. Obstructive Acts in Furtherance of the Conspiracy and the Cover Up

Members of the enterprise, including several of the Defendants, filed false documents, made false statements to government investigators, and committed perjury in judicial proceedings in Fulton County, Georgia, and elsewhere in furtherance of and to cover up the conspiracy.

ACTS OF RACKETEERING ACTIVITY AND OVERT ACTS IN FURTHERANCE OF THE CONSPIRACY

As part of and on behalf of the criminal enterprise detailed above, the Defendants and other members and associates of the enterprise committed overt acts to effect the objectives of the enterprise, including but not limited to:

Act 1.

On or about the **4th day of November 2020, DONALD JOHN TRUMP** made a nationally televised speech falsely declaring victory in the 2020 presidential election. Approximately four days earlier, on or about October 31, 2020, **DONALD JOHN TRUMP** discussed a draft speech with unindicted co-conspirator Individual 1, whose identity is known to the Grand Jury, that falsely declared victory and falsely claimed voter fraud. The speech was an overt act in furtherance of the conspiracy.

Act 2.

On or about the **15th day of November 2020, RUDOLPH WILLIAM LOUIS GIULIANI** placed a telephone call to unindicted co-conspirator Individual 2, whose identity is known to the Grand Jury, and left an approximately 83-second-long voicemail message for unindicted co-conspirator Individual 2 making statements concerning fraud in the November 3, 2020, election in Fulton County, Georgia. This telephone call was an overt act in furtherance of the conspiracy.

Act 2.

On or about the **19th day of November 2020, RUDOLPH WILLIAM LOUIS GIULIANI, JENNA LYNN ELLIS, SIDNEY KATHERINE POWELL,** and unindicted co-conspirator Individual 3, whose identity is known to the Grand Jury, appeared at a press conference at the Republican National Committee Headquarters on behalf of **DONALD JOHN TRUMP** and Donald J. Trump for President, Inc. (the "Trump Campaign") and made false statements concerning fraud in the November 3, 2020, presidential election in Georgia and elsewhere. These were overt acts in furtherance of the conspiracy.

Act 4.

On or about the **20th day of November 2020, DAVID JAMES SHAFER** sent an e-mail to unindicted co-conspirator Individual 4, whose identity is known to the Grand Jury, and other individuals. In the e-mail, **DAVID JAMES SHAFER** stated that **SCOTT GRAHAM HALL,** a Georgia bail bondsman, "has been looking into the election on behalf of the President at the request of David Bossie" and asked unindicted co-conspirator Individual 4 to exchange contact information with **SCOTT GRAHAM HALL** and to "help him as needed." This was an overt act in furtherance of the conspiracy.

Act 5.

On or about the **20th day of November 2020, DONALD JOHN TRUMP** and **MARK RANDALL MEADOWS** met with Majority Leader of the Michigan Senate Michael Shirkey, Speaker of the Michigan House of Representatives Lee Chatfield, and other Michigan legislators in the Oval Office at the White House, and **DONALD JOHN TRUMP** made false statements concerning fraud in the November 3, 2020, presidential election in Michigan. **RUDOLPH WILLIAM LOUIS GIULIANI** joined the meeting by telephone. This meeting was an overt act in furtherance of the conspiracy.

Act 6.

On or about the **21st day of November 2020, MARK RANDALL MEADOWS** sent a text message to United States Representative Scott Perry from Pennsylvania and stated, "Can you send me the number for the speaker and the leader of PA Legislature. POTUS wants to chat with them." This was an overt act in furtherance of the conspiracy.

Act 7.

On or about the **22nd day of November 2020, DONALD JOHN TRUMP** and **RUDOLPH WILLIAM LOUIS GIULIANI** placed a telephone call to Speaker of the Arizona House of Representatives Russell "Rusty" Bowers. During the telephone call, **RUDOLPH WILLIAM LOUIS GIULIANI** made false statements concerning fraud in the November 3, 2020, presidential election in Arizona and solicited, requested, and importuned Bowers to unlawfully appoint presidential electors from Arizona. Bowers declined and later testified to the United States House of Representatives Select Committee to Investigate the January 6th Attack on the United States Capitol that he told **DONALD JOHN TRUMP,** "I would not break my oath." The false statements and solicitations were overt acts in furtherance of the conspiracy.

Act 8.

On or about the **25th day of November 2020, RUDOLPH WILLIAM LOUIS GIULIANI** and **JENNA LYNN ELLIS** appeared, spoke, and presented witnesses at a meeting of Pennsylvania legislators in Gettysburg, Pennsylvania. During the meeting, **RUDOLPH WILLIAM LOUIS GIULIANI** made false statements concerning fraud in the November 3, 2020, presidential election in Pennsylvania and solicited, requested, and importuned the Pennsylvania legislators present at the meeting to unlawfully appoint presidential electors from Pennsylvania. During the meeting, **JENNA LYNN ELLIS** solicited, requested, and importuned the Pennsylvania legislators present at the meeting to unlawfully appoint presidential electors from Pennsylvania. **DONALD JOHN TRUMP** joined the meeting by telephone, made false statements concerning fraud in the November 3, 2020, presidential election in Pennsylvania, and solicited, requested, and importuned the Pennsylvania legislators present at the meeting to unlawfully appoint presidential electors from Pennsylvania. These were overt acts in furtherance of the conspiracy.

Act 9.

On or about the **25th day of November 2020,** immediately after the meeting of Pennsylvania legislators in Gettysburg, Pennsylvania, where **RUDOLPH WILLIAM LOUIS GIULIANI** and **JENNA LYNN ELLIS** appeared, spoke, and presented witnesses, **DONALD JOHN TRUMP** invited a group of the Pennsylvania legislators and others to meet with him at the White House. Later that day, **DONALD JOHN TRUMP, MARK RANDALL MEADOWS, RUDOLPH WILLIAM LOUIS GIULIANI, JENNA LYNN ELLIS** and unindicted co-conspirators Individual 5 and Individual 6, whose identities are known to the Grand Jury, met with the group of Pennsylvania legislators at the

White House and discussed holding a special session of the Pennsylvania General Assembly. These were overt acts in furtherance of the conspiracy.

Act 10.

On or about the **26th day of November 2020, RUDOLPH WILLIAM LOUIS GIULIANI** and **JENNA LYNN ELLIS** placed a telephone call to Speaker of the Pennsylvania House of Representatives Bryan Cutler and left Cutler a voicemail message for the purpose of soliciting, requesting, and importuning him to unlawfully appoint presidential electors from Pennsylvania. This was an overt act in furtherance of the conspiracy.

Act 11.

On or about the **26th day of November 2020, RUDOLPH WILLIAM LOUIS GIULIANI** placed a telephone call to President Pro Tempore of the Pennsylvania Senate Jacob "Jake" Corman for the purpose of soliciting, requesting, and importuning Corman to unlawfully appoint presidential electors from Pennsylvania. This was an overt act in furtherance of the conspiracy.

Act 12.

On or about the **27th day of November 2020, RUDOLPH WILLIAM LOUIS GIULIANI** and **JENNA LYNN ELLIS** placed a telephone call to Speaker of the Pennsylvania House of Representatives Bryan Cutler and left Cutler a voicemail message for the purpose of soliciting, requesting, and importuning him to unlawfully appoint presidential electors from Pennsylvania. This was an overt act in furtherance of the conspiracy.

Act 12.

On or about the **27th day of November 2020, RUDOLPH WILLIAM LOUIS GIULIANI** and **JENNA LYNN ELLIS** placed a telephone call to President Pro Tempore of the Pennsylvania Senate Jake Corman for the purpose of soliciting, requesting, and importuning Corman to unlawfully appoint presidential electors from Pennsylvania. This was an overt act in furtherance of the conspiracy.

Act 14.

On or about the **27th day of November 2020, DONALD JOHN TRUMP** placed a telephone call to President Pro Tempore of the Pennsylvania Senate Jake Corman for the purpose of soliciting, requesting, and importuning Corman to unlawfully appoint presidential electors from Pennsylvania. This was an overt act in furtherance of the conspiracy.

Act 15.

On or about the **28th day of November 2020, RUDOLPH WILLIAM LOUIS GIULIANI** placed a telephone call to Speaker of the Pennsylvania House of Representatives Bryan Cutler and left Cutler a voicemail message for the purpose of soliciting, requesting, and importuning him to unlawfully appoint presidential electors from Pennsylvania. This was an overt act in furtherance of the conspiracy.

Act 16.

On or about the **29th day of November 2020, RUDOLPH WILLIAM LOUIS GIULIANI** placed a telephone call to Speaker of the Pennsylvania House of Representatives Bryan Cutler and left Cutler a voicemail message for the purpose of soliciting, requesting, and importuning him to unlawfully appoint presidential electors from Pennsylvania. This was an overt act in furtherance of the conspiracy.

Act 17.

On or about the **30th day of November 2020, RUDOLPH WILLIAM LOUIS GIULIANI** and **JENNA LYNN ELLIS** appeared, spoke, and presented witnesses at a meeting of Arizona legislators in Phoenix, Arizona. Unindicted co-conspirators Individual 5 and Individual 6, whose identities are known to the Grand Jury, were also present. During the meeting, **RUDOLPH WILLIAM LOUIS GIULIANI** made false statements concerning fraud in the November 3, 2020, presidential election in Arizona and solicited, requested, and importuned the Arizona legislators present at the meeting to unlawfully appoint presidential electors from Arizona. During the meeting, **JENNA LYNN ELLIS** solicited, requested, and importuned the Arizona legislators present at the meeting to unlawfully appoint presidential electors from Arizona. **DONALD JOHN TRUMP** joined the meeting by telephone and made false statements concerning fraud in the November 3, 2020, presidential election in Arizona. These were overt acts in furtherance of the conspiracy.

Act 18.

On or about the **30th day of November 2020, MICHAEL A. ROMAN** instructed unindicted co-conspirator Individual 7, whose identity is known to the Grand Jury, to coordinate with individuals associated with the Trump Campaign to contact state legislators in Georgia and elsewhere on behalf of **DONALD JOHN TRUMP** and to encourage them to unlawfully appoint presidential electors from their respective states. This was an overt act in furtherance of the conspiracy.

Act 19.

On or between the **1st day of December 2020 and the 31st day of December 2020, DONALD JOHN TRUMP** and **MARK RANDALL MEADOWS** met with John McEntee and requested that McEntee prepare a memorandum outlining a strategy for disrupting and delaying the joint session of Congress on January 6, 2021, the day prescribed by law for counting votes cast by the duly elected and qualified presidential electors from Georgia and the other states. The strategy included having Vice President Michael R. "Mike" Pence count only half of the electoral votes from certain states and then return the remaining electoral votes to state legislatures. The request was an overt act in furtherance of the conspiracy.

Act 20.

On or about the **1st day of December 2020, RUDOLPH WILLIAM LOUIS GIULIANI** and **JENNA LYNN ELLIS** met with Speaker of the Arizona House of Representatives Rusty Bowers, President of the Arizona Senate Karen Fann, and other Arizona legislators in Phoenix, Arizona. Unindicted co-conspirator Individual 5, whose identity is known to the Grand Jury, was also present. During the meeting, **RUDOLPH WILLIAM LOUIS GIULIANI** made false statements concerning fraud in the November 3, 2020, presidential election in Arizona and solicited, requested, and importuned the legislators present to call a special session of the Arizona State Legislature. These were overt acts in furtherance of the conspiracy.

Act 21.

On or about the **2nd day of December 2020, RUDOLPH WILLIAM LOUIS GIULIANI** and **JENNA LYNN ELLIS** appeared, spoke, and presented witnesses at a meeting of the Michigan House of Representatives Oversight Committee. During the meeting, **RUDOLPH WILLIAM LOUIS GIULIANI** made false statements concerning fraud in the November 3, 2020, presidential election in Michigan and solicited, requested, and importuned the Michigan legislators present at the meeting to unlawfully appoint presidential electors from Michigan. During the meeting, **JENNA LYNN ELLIS** solicited, requested, and importuned the Michigan legislators present at the meeting to unlawfully appoint presidential electors from Michigan. These were overt acts in furtherance of the conspiracy.

Act 22.

On or about the **3rd day of December 2020, DONALD JOHN TRUMP** caused to be tweeted from the Twitter account @RealDonaldTrump, "Georgia hearings now on @OANN. Amazing!" This was an overt act in furtherance of the conspiracy.

Act 23.

On or about the **3rd day of December 2020, RUDOLPH WILLIAM LOUIS GIULIANI, JOHN CHARLES EASTMAN, JENNA LYNN ELLIS,** and **RAY STALLINGS SMITH III** committed the felony offense of **SOLICITATION OF VIOLATION OF OATH BY PUBLIC OFFICER,** in violation of **O.C.G.A. §§ 16-4-7 & 16-10-1,** in Fulton County, Georgia, by unlawfully soliciting, requesting, and importuning certain public officers then serving as elected members of the Georgia Senate and present at a Senate Judiciary Subcommittee meeting, including unindicted co-conspirator Individual 8, whose identity is known to the Grand Jury, Senators Lee Anderson, Brandon Beach, Matt Brass, Greg Dolezal, Steve Gooch, Tyler Harper, Bill Heath, Jen Jordan, John F. Kennedy, William Ligon, Elena Parent, Michael Rhett, Carden

Summers, and Blake Tillery, to engage in conduct constituting the felony offense of Violation of Oath by Public Officer, O.C.G.A. § 16-10-1, by unlawfully appointing presidential electors from Georgia, in willful and intentional violation of the terms of the oath of said persons as prescribed by law, with intent that said persons engage in said conduct. This was an overt act in furtherance of the conspiracy.

Act 24.

On or about the **3rd day of December 2020, RUDOLPH WILLIAM LOUIS GIULIANI** committed the felony offense of **FALSE STATEMENTS AND WRITINGS,** in violation of **O.C.G.A. § 16-10-20,** in Fulton County, Georgia, by knowingly, willfully, and unlawfully making at least one of the following false statements and representations to members of the Georgia Senate present at a Senate Judiciary Subcommittee meeting:

1. That at least 96,600 mail-in ballots were counted in the November 3, 2020, presidential election in Georgia, despite there being no record of those ballots having been returned to a county elections office;

2. That Dominion Voting Systems equipment used in the November 3, 2020, presidential election in Antrim County, Michigan, mistakenly recorded 6,000 votes for Joseph R. Biden when the votes were actually cast for Donald John Trump;

said statements being within the jurisdiction of the Office of the Georgia Secretary of State and the Georgia Bureau of Investigation, departments and agencies of state government, and county and city law enforcement agencies. This was an act of racketeering activity under O.C.G.A. § 16-14-3(5)(A)(xxii) and an overt act in furtherance of the conspiracy.

Act 25.

On or about the **3rd day of December 2020, RAY STALLINGS SMITH III** committed the felony offense of **FALSE STATEMENTS AND WRITINGS,** in violation of **O.C.G.A. § 16-10-20,** in Fulton County, Georgia, by knowingly, willfully, and unlawfully making at least one of the following false statements and representations to members of the Georgia Senate present at a Senate Judiciary Subcommittee meeting:

1. That 2,506 felons voted illegally in the November 3, 2020, presidential election in Georgia;

2. That 66,248 underage people illegally registered to vote before their seventeenth birthday prior to the November 3, 2020, presidential election in Georgia;

3. That at least 2,423 people voted in the November 3, 2020, presidential election in Georgia who were not listed as registered to vote;

4. That 1,043 people voted in the November 3, 2020, presidential election in Georgia who had illegally registered to vote using a post office box;

5. That 10,315 or more dead people voted in the November 3, 2020, presidential election in Georgia;

6. That Fulton County election workers at State Farm Arena ordered poll watchers and members of the media to leave the tabulation area on the night of November 3, 2020, and continued to operate after ordering everyone to leave;

said statements being within the jurisdiction of the Office of the Georgia Secretary of State and the Georgia Bureau of Investigation, departments and agencies of state government, and county and city law enforcement agencies. This was an act of racketeering activity under O.C.G.A. § 16-14-3(5)(A)(xxii) and an overt act in furtherance of the conspiracy.

Act 26.

On or about the **3rd day of December 2020, DONALD JOHN TRUMP** caused to be tweeted from the Twitter account @RealDonaldTrump, "Wow! Blockbuster testimony taking place right now in Georgia. Ballot stuffing by Dems when Republicans were forced to leave the large counting room. Plenty more coming, but this alone leads to an easy win of the State!" This was an overt act in furtherance of the conspiracy.

Act 27.

On or about the **3rd day of December 2020, DONALD JOHN TRUMP** caused to be tweeted from the Twitter account @RealDonaldTrump, "People in Georgia got caught cold bringing in massive numbers of ballots and putting them in 'voting' machines. Great job @ BrianKempGA!" This was an overt act in furtherance of the conspiracy.

Act 28.

On or about the **3rd day of December 2020, DONALD JOHN TRUMP** met with Speaker of the Pennsylvania House of Representatives Bryan Cutler in the Oval Office at the White House and discussed holding a special session of the Pennsylvania General Assembly. This was an overt act in furtherance of the conspiracy.

Act 29.

On or between the **3rd day of December 2020** and the **26th day of December 2020, RUDOLPH WILLIAM LOUIS GIULIANI** placed a telephone call to President Pro Tempore of the Georgia Senate Cecil Terrell "Butch" Miller for the purpose of making false statements concerning fraud in the November 3, 2020, presidential election in Georgia. This was an overt act in furtherance of the conspiracy.

Act 30.

On or between the **3rd day of December 2020** and the **26th day of December 2020, DONALD JOHN TRUMP** placed a telephone call to President Pro Tempore of the Georgia Senate Butch Miller. This was an overt act in furtherance of the conspiracy.

Act 31.

On or about the **5th day of December 2020, DONALD JOHN TRUMP** placed a telephone call to Georgia Governor Brian Kemp and solicited, requested, and importuned Kemp to call a special session of the Georgia General Assembly. This was an overt act in furtherance of the conspiracy.

Act 32.

On or about the **6th day of December 2020, DONALD JOHN TRUMP** caused to be tweeted from the Twitter account @RealDonaldTrump, "Gee, what a surprise. Has anyone informed the so-called (says he has no power to do anything!) Governor @BrianKempGA & his puppet Lt. Governor @GeoffDuncanGA, that they could easily solve this mess, & WIN. Signature verification & call a Special Session. So easy! https://t.co/5cb4QdYzpU." This was an overt act in furtherance of the conspiracy.

Act 33.

On or about the **6th day of December 2020, SIDNEY KATHERINE POWELL** entered into a written engagement agreement with SullivanStrickler LLC, a forensic data firm located in Fulton County, Georgia, for the performance of computer forensic collections and analytics on Dominion Voting Systems equipment in Michigan and elsewhere. The unlawful breach of election equipment in Coffee County, Georgia, was subsequently performed under this agreement. This was an overt act in furtherance of the conspiracy.

Act 34.

On or about the **6th day of December 2020, ROBERT DAVID CHEELEY** sent an e-mail to **JOHN CHARLES EASTMAN,** unindicted co-conspirator Individual 8, whose identity is known to the Grand Jury, and Georgia Senator Brandon Beach that stated, "I am working on setting up a call for you with the Speaker and the President Pro Tempore tomorrow. I am also making the leadership aware of the importance for Trump electors to meet on December 14. Please provide the citation to the requirements of the duties which they must comply with." This was an overt act in furtherance of the conspiracy.

Act 35.

On or about the **6th day of December 2020, JOHN CHARLES EASTMAN** sent an e-mail to **ROBERT DAVID CHEELEY,** unindicted co-conspirator Individual 8, whose identity is known to the Grand Jury, and Georgia Senator Brandon Beach that stated that the Trump presidential elector nominees in Georgia needed to meet on December 14, 2020, sign six sets of certificates of vote, and mail them "to the President of the Senate and to other officials." This was an overt act in furtherance of the conspiracy.

Act 36.

On or about the **6th day of December 2020, ROBERT DAVID CHEELEY** sent an e-mail to unindicted co-conspirator Individual 2, whose identity is known to the Grand Jury, that stated he had been speaking with **JOHN CHARLES EASTMAN** and was attempting to set up a call with Speaker of the Georgia House of Representatives David Ralston and President Pro Tempore of the Georgia Senate Butch Miller to encourage them to call a special session of the Georgia General Assembly. In the e-mail, **ROBERT DAVID CHEELEY** stated, "Professor Eastman told me tonight that it is critical that the 16 Electors for President Trump meet next Monday and vote in accordance with 3 U.S.C. § 7." In the e-mail, **ROBERT DAVID CHEELEY** further stated, "I assume you can make sure this happens." This was an overt act in furtherance of the conspiracy.

Act 37.

On or about the **7th day of December 2020,** unindicted co-conspirator Individual 2, whose identity is known to the Grand Jury, sent an e-mail to **ROBERT DAVID CHEELEY** and **DAVID JAMES SHAFER** that stated, "Bob, can u get on a call with David Shafer, state GOP chair and I later this morning to discuss. David has been on top of a lot of efforts in the state. I get off of a board call around 10:30." This was an overt act in furtherance of the conspiracy.

Act 38.

On or about the **7th day of December 2020, RUDOLPH WILLIAM LOUIS GIULIANI** caused to be tweeted from the Twitter account @RudyGiuliani a retweet of unindicted co-conspirator Individual 8, whose identity is known to the Grand Jury, that stated, "Georgia Patriot Call to Action: today is the day we need you to call your state Senate & House Reps & ask them to sign the petition for a special session. We must have free & fair elections in GA & a this is our only path to ensuring every legal vote is counted. @realDonaldTrump." This was an overt act in furtherance of the conspiracy.

Act 39.

On or about the **7th day of December 2020, JOHN CHARLES EASTMAN** sent an e-mail to **RUDOLPH WILLIAM LOUIS GIULIANI** with an attached memorandum titled "The Real Deadline for Settling a State's Electoral Votes." The body of the e-mail stated, "Here's the memo we discussed." The memorandum was written by **KENNETH JOHN CHESEBRO** to James R. Troupis, an attorney associated with the Trump Campaign, and advocates for the position that Trump presidential elector nominees in Wisconsin should meet and cast electoral votes for **DONALD JOHN TRUMP** on December 14, 2020, despite the fact that **DONALD JOHN TRUMP** lost the November 3, 2020, presidential election in Wisconsin. This e-mail was an overt act in furtherance of the conspiracy.

Act 40.

On or about the **7th day of December 2020, DONALD JOHN TRUMP** requested that Bill White, an individual associated with the

Trump Campaign then residing in Fulton County, Georgia, provide him with certain information, including contact information for Majority Leader of the Georgia Senate Mike Dugan and President Pro Tempore of the Georgia Senate Butch Miller. The following day, White sent an e-mail containing the requested information to **RUDOLPH WILLIAM LOUIS GIULIANI,** unindicted co-conspirator Individual 5, whose identity is known to the Grand Jury, and others. This request was an overt act in furtherance of the conspiracy.

Act 41.

On or about the **7th day of December 2020, RUDOLPH WILLIAM LOUIS GIULIANI** placed a telephone call to Speaker of the Georgia House of Representatives David Ralston and discussed holding a special session of the Georgia General Assembly. This was an overt act in furtherance of the conspiracy.

Act 42.

On or about the **7th day of December 2020, DONALD JOHN TRUMP** committed the felony offense of **SOLICITATION OF VIOLATION OF OATH BY PUBLIC OFFICER,** in violation of **O.C.G.A. §§ 16-4-7 & 16-10-1,** in Fulton County, Georgia, by unlawfully soliciting, requesting, and importuning Speaker of the Georgia House of Representatives David Ralston, a public officer, to engage in conduct constituting the felony offense of Violation of Oath by Public Officer, O.C.G.A. § 16-10-1, by calling a special session of the Georgia General Assembly for the purpose of unlawfully appointing presidential electors from Georgia, in willful and intentional violation of the terms of the oath of said person as prescribed by law, with intent that said person engage in said conduct. This was an overt act in furtherance of the conspiracy.

Act 43.

On or about the **8th day of December 2020, DONALD JOHN TRUMP** placed a telephone call to Georgia Attorney General Chris Carr for the purpose of making false statements concerning fraud in the November 3, 2020, presidential election in Georgia and elsewhere. During the telephone call, **DONALD JOHN TRUMP** asked Carr not to discourage other state attorneys general from joining a federal lawsuit filed by the State of Texas contesting the administration of the November 3, 2020, presidential election in Georgia, Michigan, Pennsylvania, and Wisconsin. This was an overt act in furtherance of the conspiracy.

Act 44.

On or about the **8th day of December 2020, DONALD JOHN TRUMP** and **JOHN CHARLES EASTMAN** placed a telephone call to Republican National Committee Chairwoman Ronna McDaniel to request her assistance gathering certain individuals to meet and cast electoral votes for **DONALD JOHN TRUMP** on December 14, 2020, in certain states despite the fact that **DONALD JOHN TRUMP** lost the November 3, 2020, presidential election in those states. This was an overt act in furtherance of the conspiracy.

Act 45.

On or about the **8th day of December 2020, MICHAEL A. ROMAN** sent a text message to unindicted co-conspirator Individual 4, whose identity is known to the Grand Jury, stated that he had spoken to **MISTY HAMPTON,** and asked unindicted co-conspirator Individual 4 to "get" **MISTY HAMPTON** to attend the hearing before the Georgia House of Representatives Governmental Affairs Committee on December 10, 2020. This was an overt act in furtherance of the conspiracy.

Act 46.

On or about the **9th day of December 2020, KENNETH JOHN CHESEBRO** wrote a memorandum titled "Statutory Requirements for December 14 Electoral Votes" to James R. Troupis, an attorney associated with the Trump Campaign. The memorandum provides detailed, state-specific instructions for how Trump presidential elector nominees in Georgia, Arizona, Michigan, Nevada, Pennsylvania, and Wisconsin would meet and cast electoral votes for **DONALD JOHN TRUMP** on December 14, 2020, despite the fact that **DONALD JOHN TRUMP** lost the November 3, 2020, presidential election in those states. This was an overt act in furtherance of the conspiracy.

Act 47.

On or about the **10th day of December 2020, KENNETH JOHN CHESEBRO** sent an e-mail to Georgia Republican Party Chairman **DAVID JAMES SHAFER** and unindicted co-conspirator Individual 9, whose identity is known to the Grand Jury. **KENNETH JOHN CHESEBRO** stated in the e-mail that certain individuals associated with the Trump Campaign asked him "to help coordinate with the other 5 contested States, to help with logistics of the electors in other States hopefully joining in casting their votes on Monday." This was an overt act in furtherance of the conspiracy.

Act 48.

On or about the **10th day of December 2020, KENNETH JOHN CHESEBRO** sent an e-mail with attached documents to **DAVID JAMES SHAFER** and unindicted co-conspirators Individual 9, Individual 10, and Individual 11, whose identities are known to the Grand Jury. The documents were to be used by Trump presidential elector nominees in Georgia for the purpose of casting electoral votes for **DONALD JOHN TRUMP** on December 14, 2020, despite the fact that **DONALD JOHN TRUMP** lost the November 3, 2020, presidential election in Georgia. This was an overt act in furtherance of the conspiracy.

Act 49.

On or about the **10th day of December 2020, KENNETH JOHN CHESEBRO** sent an e-mail with attached documents to Arizona Republican Party Executive Director Greg Safsten and others. The documents were to be used by Trump presidential elector nominees in Arizona for the purpose of casting electoral votes for **DONALD JOHN TRUMP** on December 14, 2020, despite the fact that **DONALD JOHN TRUMP** lost the November 3, 2020, presidential election in Arizona. This was an overt act in furtherance of the conspiracy.

Act 50.

On or about the **10th day of December 2020, KENNETH JOHN CHESEBRO** sent an e-mail to Republican Party of Wisconsin Chairman Brian Schimming with proposed language for documents to be used by Trump presidential elector nominees in Wisconsin for the purpose of casting electoral votes for **DONALD JOHN TRUMP** on December 14, 2020, despite the fact that **DONALD JOHN TRUMP** lost the November 3, 2020, presidential election in Wisconsin. This was an overt act in furtherance of the conspiracy.

Act 51.

On or about the **10th day of December 2020, KENNETH JOHN CHESEBRO** sent an e-mail to Nevada Republican Party Vice Chairman Jim DeGraffenreid. **KENNETH JOHN CHESEBRO** stated in the e-mail that **RUDOLPH WILLIAM LOUIS GIULIANI** and other individuals associated with the Trump Campaign asked him "to reach out to you and the other Nevada electors to run point on the plan to have all Trump-Pence electors in all six contested States meet and transmit their votes to Congress on Monday, Dec. 14." This was an overt act in furtherance of the conspiracy.

Act 52.

On or about the **10th day of December 2020, KENNETH JOHN CHESEBRO** sent an e-mail with attached documents to Jim DeGraffenreid. The documents were to be used by Trump presidential elector nominees in Nevada for the purpose of casting electoral votes for **DONALD JOHN TRUMP** on December 14, 2020, despite the fact that **DONALD JOHN TRUMP** lost the November 3, 2020, presidential election in Nevada. This was an overt act in furtherance of the conspiracy.

Act 52.

On or about the **10th day of December 2020, KENNETH JOHN CHESEBRO** sent an e-mail with attached documents to Republican Party of Pennsylvania General Counsel Thomas W. King III. The documents were to be used by Trump presidential elector nominees in Pennsylvania for the purpose of casting electoral votes for **DONALD JOHN TRUMP** on December 14, 2020, despite the fact that **DONALD JOHN TRUMP** lost the November 3, 2020, presidential election in Pennsylvania. This was an overt act in furtherance of the conspiracy.

Act 54.

On or between the **10th day of December 2020 and the 14th day of December 2020, DAVID JAMES SHAFER** contacted unindicted co-conspirator Individual 2, whose identity is known to the Grand Jury, by telephone and discussed unindicted co-conspirator Individual 2's attendance at the December 14, 2020, meeting of Trump presidential elector nominees in Fulton County, Georgia. This was an overt act in furtherance of the conspiracy.

Act 55.

On or about the **10th day of December 2020, RUDOLPH WILLIAM LOUIS GIULIANI** and **RAY STALLINGS SMITH III** committed the felony offense of **SOLICITATION OF VIOLATION OF OATH BY PUBLIC OFFICER,** in violation of **O.C.G.A. §§ 16-4-7 & 16-10-1,** in Fulton County, Georgia, by unlawfully soliciting, requesting, and importuning certain public officers then serving as elected members of the Georgia House of Representatives and present at a House Governmental Affairs Committee meeting, including Representatives Shaw Blackmon, Jon Burns, Barry Fleming, Todd Jones, Bee Nguyen, Mary Margaret Oliver, Alan Powell, Renitta Shannon, Robert Trammell, Scot Turner, and Bruce Williamson, to engage in conduct constituting the felony offense of Violation of Oath by Public Officer, O.C.G.A. § 16-10-1, by unlawfully appointing presidential electors from Georgia, in willful and intentional violation of the terms of the oath of said persons as prescribed by law, with intent that said persons engage in said conduct. This was an overt act in furtherance of the conspiracy.

Act 56.

On or about the **10th day of December 2020, RUDOLPH WILLIAM LOUIS GIULIANI** committed the felony offense of **FALSE STATEMENTS AND WRITINGS,** in violation of **O.C.G.A. § 16-10-20,** in Fulton County, Georgia, by knowingly, willfully, and unlawfully making at least one of the following false statements and representations to members of the Georgia House of Representatives present at a House Governmental Affairs Committee meeting:

1. That it is quite clear from the State Farm Arena video from November 3, 2020, that Fulton County election workers were stealing votes and that Georgia officials were covering up a crime in plain sight;

2. That at State Farm Arena on November 3, 2020, Democratic officials "got rid of all of the reporters, all the observers, anyone that couldn't be trusted," used the excuse of a watermain break, cleared out the voting area and then "went about their dirty, crooked business";

3. That between 12,000 and 24,000 ballots were illegally counted by Fulton County election workers at State Farm Arena on November 3, 2020;

4. That in Michigan, there were 700,000 more ballots counted than were sent out to voters in the November 3, 2020, presidential election, which was accounted for by quadruple counting ballots;

5. That Ruby Freeman, Shaye Moss, and an unidentified man were "quite obviously surreptitiously passing around USB ports as if they're vials of heroin or cocaine" at State Farm Arena to be used to "infiltrate the crooked Dominion voting machines";

6. That 96,600 mail-in ballots were counted in the November 3, 2020, presidential election in Georgia, despite there being no record of those ballots having been returned to a county elections office;

said statements being within the jurisdiction of the Office of the Georgia Secretary of State and the Georgia Bureau of Investigation, departments and agencies of state government, and county and city law enforcement agencies. This was an act of racketeering activity under O.C.G.A. § 16-14-3(5)(A)(xxii) and an overt act in furtherance of the conspiracy.

Act 57.

On or about the **11th day of December 2020, DAVID JAMES SHAFER** reserved Room 216 at the Georgia State Capitol in Fulton County, Georgia, for the December 14, 2020, meeting of Trump presidential elector nominees in Fulton County, Georgia. This was an overt act in furtherance of the conspiracy.

Act 58.

On or about the **11th day of December 2020, KENNETH JOHN CHESEBRO** sent an e-mail to Jim DeGraffenreid and stated that "the purpose of having the electoral votes sent in to Congress is to provide the opportunity to debate the election irregularities in Congress, and to keep alive the possibility that the votes could be flipped to Trump." This was an overt act in furtherance of the conspiracy.

Act 59.

On or about the **11th day of December 2020, KENNETH JOHN CHESEBRO** sent an e-mail with attached documents to Greg Safsten and others. The documents were to be used by Trump presidential elector nominees in Arizona for the purpose of casting electoral votes for **DONALD JOHN TRUMP** on December 14, 2020, despite the fact that **DONALD JOHN TRUMP** lost the November 3, 2020, presidential election in Arizona. This was an overt act in furtherance of the conspiracy.

Act 60.

On or about the **11th day of December 2020, KENNETH JOHN CHESEBRO** sent an e-mail with attached documents to **MICHAEL A. ROMAN** and other individuals associated with the Trump Campaign. The documents were to be used by Trump presidential elector nominees in Nevada for the purpose of casting electoral votes for **DONALD JOHN TRUMP** on December 14, 2020, despite the fact that **DONALD JOHN TRUMP** lost the November 3, 2020, presidential election in Nevada. This was an overt act in furtherance of the conspiracy.

Act 61.

On or about the **11th day of December 2020, KENNETH JOHN CHESEBRO** sent an e-mail with attached documents to **MICHAEL A. ROMAN,** unindicted co-conspirator Individual 5, whose identity is known to the Grand Jury, and others. The documents were to be used by Trump presidential elector nominees in Georgia for the purpose of casting electoral votes for **DONALD JOHN TRUMP** on December 14, 2020, despite the fact that **DONALD JOHN TRUMP** lost the November 3, 2020, presidential election in Georgia. This was an overt act in furtherance of the conspiracy.

Act 62.

On or about the **12th day of December 2020, DAVID JAMES SHAFER** contacted unindicted co-conspirator Individual 12, whose identity is known to the Grand Jury, and discussed unindicted co-conspirator Individual 12's attendance at the December 14, 2020, meeting of Trump presidential elector nominees in Fulton County, Georgia. This was an overt act in furtherance of the conspiracy.

Act 63.

On or about the **12th day of December 2020, MICHAEL A. ROMAN** sent an e-mail to unindicted co-conspirators Individual 4 and Individual 7, whose identities are known to the Grand Jury, and other individuals associated with the Trump Campaign. In the e-mail, **MICHAEL A. ROMAN** stated, "I need a tracker for the electors," and instructed individuals associated with the Trump Campaign to populate entries on a shared spreadsheet listing Trump presidential elector nominees in Georgia, Arizona, Michigan, Nevada, Pennsylvania, and Wisconsin. The entries on the spreadsheet included contact information for the Trump presidential elector nominees, whether the Trump presidential elector nominees had been contacted, and whether the Trump presidential elector nominees had confirmed that they would attend the December 14, 2020, meetings of Trump presidential elector nominees in their respective states, despite the fact that **DONALD JOHN TRUMP** lost the November 3, 2020, presidential election in those states. This was an overt act in furtherance of the conspiracy.

Act 64.

On or about the **12th day of December 2020, KENNETH JOHN CHESEBRO** met with Brian Schimming and discussed the December 14, 2020, meeting of Trump presidential elector nominees in Wisconsin. **RUDOLPH WILLIAM LOUIS GIULIANI** joined the meeting by telephone and stated that the media should not be notified of the December 14, 2020, meeting of Trump presidential elector nominees in Wisconsin. These were overt acts in furtherance of the conspiracy.

Act 65.

On or about the **12th day of December 2020, MICHAEL A. ROMAN** instructed an individual associated with the Trump Campaign to distribute certain information related to the December 14, 2020, meetings of Trump presidential elector nominees in Georgia, Arizona, Michigan, Nevada, New Mexico, Pennsylvania, and Wisconsin to unindicted co-conspirator Individual 4, whose identity is known to the Grand Jury, and to other individuals associated with the Trump Campaign. This was an overt act in furtherance of the conspiracy.

Act 66.

On or about the **12th day of December 2020,** unindicted co-conspirator Individual 4, whose identity is known to the Grand Jury, sent an e-mail to **MICHAEL A. ROMAN** and **DAVID JAMES SHAFER** with updates on the progress of organizing the December 14, 2020, meeting of Trump presidential elector nominees in Fulton County, Georgia.

The e-mail stated which elector nominees had confirmed they would attend the meeting, that other individuals had been secured in case some of the elector nominees refused to participate in the meeting, that Georgia legislators had been contacted to ensure access to the Georgia Capitol, and that **DAVID JAMES SHAFER** had reserved Room 216 for the meeting. This was an overt act in furtherance of the conspiracy.

Act 67.

On or about the **12th day of December 2020, DAVID JAMES SHAFER** sent an e-mail to unindicted co-conspirator Individual 4, whose identity is known to the Grand Jury, advising them to "touch base" with each of the Trump presidential elector nominees in Georgia in advance of the December 14, 2020, meeting to confirm their attendance. This was an overt act in furtherance of the conspiracy.

Act 68.

On or about the **12th day of December 2020,** unindicted co-conspirator Individual 4, whose identity is known to the Grand Jury, sent a text message with contact information for unindicted co-conspirator Individual 8, whose identity is known to the Grand Jury, and Georgia Senator Brandon Beach to **MICHAEL A. ROMAN** for the purpose of providing the contact information to **RUDOLPH WILLIAM LOUIS GIULIANI.** This was an overt act in furtherance of the conspiracy.

Act 69.

On or about the **13th day of December 2020, KENNETH JOHN CHESEBRO** sent an e-mail with attached documents to **MICHAEL A. ROMAN.** The documents were to be used by Trump presidential elector nominees in New Mexico for the purpose of casting electoral votes for **DONALD JOHN TRUMP** on December 14, 2020, despite the fact that **DONALD JOHN TRUMP** lost the November 3, 2020, presidential election in New Mexico. This was an overt act in furtherance of the conspiracy.

Act 70.

On or about the **13th day of December 2020, KENNETH JOHN CHESEBRO** sent an e-mail to **RUDOLPH WILLIAM LOUIS GIULIANI** with the subject "PRIVILEGED AND CONFIDENTIAL—Brief notes on 'President of the Senate' strategy." In the e-mail, **KENNETH JOHN CHESEBRO** outlined multiple strategies for disrupting and delaying the joint session of Congress on January 6, 2021, the day prescribed by law for counting votes cast by the duly elected and qualified presidential electors from Georgia and the other states. In the e-mail, **KENNETH JOHN CHESEBRO** stated that the strategies outlined by him were "preferable to allowing the Electoral Count Act to operate by its terms." This was an overt act in furtherance of the conspiracy.

Act 71.

On or about the **13th day of December 2020, KENNETH JOHN CHESEBRO** sent an e-mail with attached documents to **MICHAEL A. ROMAN** and unindicted co-conspirator Individual 4, whose identity is known to the Grand Jury. The documents were to be used by Trump presidential elector nominees in Georgia for the purpose of casting electoral votes for **DONALD JOHN TRUMP** on December 14, 2020, despite the fact that **DONALD JOHN TRUMP** lost the November 3, 2020, presidential election in Georgia. This was an overt act in furtherance of the conspiracy.

Act 72.

On or about the **13th day of December 2020, KENNETH JOHN CHESEBRO** sent an e-mail to **MICHAEL A. ROMAN** and unindicted co-conspirator Individual 4, whose identity is known to the Grand Jury, and stated that **RUDOLPH WILLIAM LOUIS GIULIANI** "wants to keep this quiet until after all the voting is done," in reference to the December 14, 2020, meeting of Trump presidential elector nominees in Fulton County, Georgia. This was an overt act in furtherance of the conspiracy.

Act 73.

On or about the **13th day of December 2020, DAVID JAMES SHAFER** sent a text message to unindicted co-conspirator Individual 4, whose identity is known to the Grand Jury, and stated that unindicted co-conspirator Individual 8, whose identity is known to the Grand Jury, would attend the December 14, 2020, meeting of Trump presidential elector nominees in Fulton County, Georgia, in the place of a Trump presidential elector nominee who refused to participate in the meeting. This was an overt act in furtherance of the conspiracy.

Act 74.

On or about the **13th day of December 2020,** unindicted co-conspirator Individual 9, whose identity is known to the Grand Jury, sent a text message to **DAVID JAMES SHAFER** and confirmed that he and unindicted co-conspirator Individual 13, whose identity is known to the Grand Jury, would attend the December 14, 2020, meeting of Trump presidential elector nominees in Fulton County, Georgia. This was an overt act in furtherance of the conspiracy.

Act 75.

On or about the **14th day of December 2020, DONALD JOHN TRUMP** caused to be tweeted from the Twitter account @ RealDonaldTrump, "What a fool Governor @BrianKempGA of Georgia is. Could have been so easy, but now we have to do it the hard way. Demand this clown call a Special Session and open up signature verification, NOW. Otherwise, could be a bad day for two GREAT Senators on January 5th." This was an overt act in furtherance of the conspiracy.

Act 76.

On or about the **14th day of December 2020, DAVID JAMES SHAFER** sent a text message to unindicted co-conspirator Individual 4, whose identity is known to the Grand Jury that stated, "Listen. Tell them to go straight to Room 216 to avoid drawing attention to what we are doing," in reference to the December 14, 2020, meeting of Trump presidential elector nominees in Fulton County, Georgia. This was an overt act in furtherance of the conspiracy.

Act 77.

On or about the **14th day of December 2020, MICHAEL A. ROMAN** sent an e-mail to unindicted co-conspirators Individual 4 and Individual 7, whose identities are known to the Grand Jury, and stated, "Please send me an update as soon as the State Electoral College has adjourned and all paperwork is secured." This was an overt act in furtherance of the conspiracy.

Act 78.

On or about the **14th day of December 2020, RAY STALLINGS SMITH III** and **DAVID JAMES SHAFER** encouraged certain individuals present at the December 14, 2020, meeting of Trump presidential elector nominees in Fulton County, Georgia, to sign the document titled "CERTIFICATE OF THE VOTES OF THE 2020 ELECTORS FROM GEORGIA." This was an overt act in furtherance of the conspiracy.

Act 79.

On or about the **14th day of December 2020, DAVID JAMES SHAFER, SHAWN MICAH TRESHER STILL, CATHLEEN ALSTON LATHAM,** and unindicted co-conspirators Individual 2, Individual 8, Individual 9, Individual 10, Individual 11, Individual 12, Individual 13, Individual 14, Individual 15, Individual 16, Individual 17, Individual 18, and Individual 19, whose identities are known to the Grand Jury, committed the felony offense of **IMPERSONATING A PUBLIC OFFICER,** in violation of **O.C.G.A. § 16-10-23,** in Fulton County, Georgia, by unlawfully falsely holding themselves out as the duly elected and qualified presidential electors from the State of Georgia, public officers, with intent to mislead the President of the United States Senate, the Archivist of the United States, the Georgia Secretary of State, and the Chief Judge of the United States District Court for the Northern District of Georgia into believing that they actually were such officers by placing in the United States mail to said persons a document titled "CERTIFICATE OF THE VOTES OF THE 2020 ELECTORS FROM GEORGIA." This was an act of racketeering activity under O.C.G.A. § 16-14-3(5)(A)(xxiii) and an overt act in furtherance of the conspiracy.

Act 80.

On or about the **14th day of December 2020, DAVID JAMES SHAFER, SHAWN MICAH TRESHER STILL, CATHLEEN ALSTON LATHAM,** and unindicted co-conspirators Individual 2, Individual 8, Individual 9, Individual 10, Individual 11, Individual 12, Individual 13, Individual 14, Individual 15, Individual 16, Individual 17, Individual 18, and Individual 19, whose identities are known to the Grand Jury, committed the felony offense of **FORGERY IN THE FIRST DEGREE,** in violation of **O.C.G.A. § 16-9-1(b),** in Fulton County, Georgia, by, with the intent to defraud, knowingly making a document titled "CERTIFICATE OF THE VOTES OF THE 2020 ELECTORS FROM GEORGIA," a writing other than a check, in such manner that the writing as made purports to have been made by authority of the duly elected and qualified presidential electors from the State of Georgia, who did not give such authority, and uttered and delivered said document to the Archivist of the United States. This was an act of racketeering activity under O.C.G.A. § 16-14-3(5)(A)(xvi) and an overt act in furtherance of the conspiracy.

Act 81.

On or about the **14th day of December 2020, DAVID JAMES SHAFER, SHAWN MICAH TRESHER STILL, CATHLEEN ALSTON LATHAM,** and unindicted co-conspirators Individual 2, Individual 8, Individual 9, Individual 10, Individual 11, Individual 12, Individual 13, Individual 14, Individual 15, Individual 16, Individual 17, Individual 18, and Individual 19, whose identities are known to the Grand Jury, committed the felony offense of **FALSE STATEMENTS AND WRITINGS,** in violation of **O.C.G.A. § 16-10-20,** in Fulton County, Georgia, by knowingly, willfully, and unlawfully making and using a false document titled "CERTIFICATE OF THE VOTES OF THE 2020 ELECTORS FROM GEORGIA," with knowledge that said document contained the false statement, "WE, THE UNDERSIGNED, being the duly elected and qualified Electors for President and Vice President of the United States of America from the State of Georgia, do hereby certify the following," said document being within the jurisdiction of the Office of the Georgia Secretary of State and the Office of the Governor of Georgia, departments and agencies of state government. This was an act of racketeering activity under O.C.G.A. § 16-14-3(5)(A)(xxii) and an overt act in furtherance of the conspiracy.

Act 82.

On or about the **14th day of December 2020, DAVID JAMES SHAFER, SHAWN MICAH TRESHER STILL, CATHLEEN ALSTON LATHAM,** and unindicted co-conspirators Individual 2, Individual 8, Individual 9, Individual 10, Individual 11, Individual 12, Individual 13, Individual 14, Individual 15, Individual 16, Individual 17, Individual 18, and Individual 19, whose identities are known to the Grand Jury, attempted to commit the felony offense of **FILING FALSE DOCUMENTS,** in violation of **O.C.G.A. § 16-10-20.1(b)(1),** in Fulton County, Georgia, by placing in the United States mail a document titled "CERTIFICATE OF THE VOTES OF THE 2020 ELECTORS FROM GEORGIA," addressed to Chief Judge, U.S. District Court, Northern District of Georgia, 2188 Richard D. Russell Federal Office Building and U.S. Courthouse, 75 Ted Turner Drive, SW, Atlanta, GA 30303, with intent to knowingly file, enter, and record said document in a court of the United States, having reason to know that said document contained the materially false statement, "WE, THE UNDERSIGNED, being the duly elected and qualified Electors for President and Vice President of the United States of America from the State of Georgia, do hereby certify the following." This was an act of racketeering activity under O.C.G.A. § 16-14-3(5)(A)(xxii) and an overt act in furtherance of the conspiracy.

Act 83.

On or about the **14th day of December 2020, DAVID JAMES SHAFER** and **SHAWN MICAH TRESHER STILL** committed the felony offense of **FORGERY IN THE FIRST DEGREE,** in violation of **O.C.G.A. § 16-9-1(b),** in Fulton County, Georgia, by, with the intent to defraud, knowingly making a document titled "RE: Notice of Filling of Electoral College Vacancy," a writing other than a check, in such manner that the writing as made purports to have been made by the authority of the duly elected and qualified presidential electors from the State of Georgia, who did not give such authority, and uttered and delivered said document to the Archivist of the United States. This was an act of racketeering activity under O.C.G.A. § 16-14-3(5)(A)(xvi) and an overt act in furtherance of the conspiracy.

Act 84.

On or about the **14th day of December 2020, DAVID JAMES SHAFER** and **SHAWN MICAH TRESHER STILL** committed the felony offense of **FALSE STATEMENTS AND WRITINGS,** in violation of **O.C.G.A. § 16-10-20,** in Fulton County, Georgia, by knowingly, willfully, and unlawfully making and using a false document titled "RE: Notice of Filling of Electoral College Vacancy," with knowledge that said document contained the false statements that **DAVID JAMES SHAFER** was Chairman of the 2020 Georgia Electoral College Meeting and **SHAWN MICAH TRESHER STILL** was Secretary of the 2020 Georgia Electoral College Meeting, said document being within the jurisdiction of the Office of the Georgia Secretary of State and the Office of the Governor of Georgia, departments and agencies of state government. This was an act of racketeering activity under O.C.G.A. § 16-14-3(5)(A)(xxii) and an overt act in furtherance of the conspiracy.

Act 85.

On or about the **14th day of December 2020, DAVID JAMES SHAFER** instructed unindicted co-conspirator Individual 15, whose identity is known to the Grand Jury, to deliver to the Office of the Governor of Georgia a document signed by **DAVID JAMES SHAFER** and **SHAWN MICAH TRESHER STILL** titled "RE: Notice of Filling of Electoral College Vacancy." The document contained multiple false statements. This was an overt act in furtherance of the conspiracy.

Act 86.

On or about the **14th day of December 2020,** unindicted co-conspirator Individual 4, whose identity is known to the Grand Jury, sent an e-mail to **MICHAEL A. ROMAN,** unindicted co-conspirator Individual 7, whose identity is known to the Grand Jury, and others that stated, "All votes cast, paperwork complete, being mailed now. Ran pretty smoothly," in reference to the December 14, 2020, meeting of Trump presidential elector nominees in Fulton County, Georgia. This was an overt act in furtherance of the conspiracy.

Act 87.

On or about the **14th day of December 2020, STEPHEN CLIFFGARD LEE** attempted to commit the felony offense of **INFLUENCING WITNESSES,** in violation of **O.C.G.A. § 16-10-93(b)(1)(A),** in

Fulton County, Georgia, by traveling to the home of Ruby Freeman, a Fulton County, Georgia, election worker, and speaking to her neighbor, with intent to knowingly engage in misleading conduct toward Ruby Freeman, by purporting to offer her help, and with intent to influence her testimony in an official proceeding in Fulton County, Georgia, concerning events at State Farm Arena in the November 3, 2020, presidential election in Georgia. This was an act of racketeering activity pursuant to O.C.G.A. § 16-14-3(5)(A)(xxvii) and an overt act in furtherance of the conspiracy.

Act 88.

On or about the **15th day of December 2020, STEPHEN CLIFFGARD LEE** attempted to commit the felony offense of **INFLUENCING WITNESSES,** in violation of **O.C.G.A. § 16-10-93(b)(1)(A),** in Fulton County, Georgia, by traveling to the home of Ruby Freeman, a Fulton County, Georgia, election worker, and knocking on her door, with intent to knowingly engage in misleading conduct toward Ruby Freeman, by purporting to offer her help, and with intent to influence her testimony in an official proceeding in Fulton County, Georgia, concerning events at State Farm Arena in the November 3, 2020, presidential election in Georgia. This was an act of racketeering activity pursuant to O.C.G.A. § 16-14-3(5)(A)(xxvii) and an overt act in furtherance of the conspiracy.

Act 89.

On or between the **15th day of December 2020 and the 4th day of January 2021, STEPHEN CLIFFGARD LEE** solicited **HARRISON WILLIAM PRESCOTT FLOYD,** an individual associated with the organization Black Voices for Trump, to assist with his effort to speak to Ruby Freeman, a Fulton County, Georgia, election worker. **STEPHEN CLIFFGARD LEE** stated to **HARRISON WILLIAM PRESCOTT FLOYD** that Freeman was afraid to talk to **STEPHEN CLIFFGARD LEE** because he was a white man. These were overt acts in furtherance of the conspiracy.

Act 90.

On or about the **18th day of December 2020, DONALD JOHN TRUMP** met with **RUDOLPH WILLIAM LOUIS GIULIANI, SIDNEY KATHERINE POWELL,** unindicted co-conspirator Individual 20, whose identity is known to the Grand Jury, and others at the White House. The individuals present at the meeting discussed certain strategies and theories intended to influence the outcome of the November 3, 2020, presidential election, including seizing voting equipment and appointing **SIDNEY KATHERINE POWELL** as special counsel with broad authority to investigate allegations of voter fraud in Georgia and elsewhere. This was an overt act in furtherance of the conspiracy.

Act 91.

On or about the **21st day of December 2020, SIDNEY KATHERINE POWELL** sent an e-mail to the Chief Operations Officer of Sullivan-Strickler LLC and instructed him that she and unindicted co-conspirators Individual 6, Individual 21, and Individual 22, whose identities are known to the Grand Jury, were to immediately "receive a copy of all data" obtained by SullivanStrickler LLC from Dominion Voting Systems equipment in Michigan. This was an overt act in furtherance of the conspiracy.

Act 92.

On or about the **22nd day of December 2020, MARK RANDALL MEADOWS** traveled to the Cobb County Civic Center in Cobb County, Georgia, and attempted to observe the signature match audit being performed there by law enforcement officers from the Georgia Bureau of Investigation and the Office of the Georgia Secretary of State, despite the fact that the audit process was not open to the public. While present at the center, **MARK RANDALL MEADOWS** spoke to Georgia Deputy Secretary of State Jordan Fuchs, Office of the Georgia Secretary of State Chief Investigator Frances Watson, Georgia Bureau of Investigation Special Agent in Charge Bahan Rich, and others, who prevented **MARK RANDALL MEADOWS** from entering into the space where the audit was being conducted. This was an overt act in furtherance of the conspiracy.

Act 93.

On or about the **23rd day of December 2020, DONALD JOHN TRUMP** placed a telephone call to Office of the Georgia Secretary of State Chief Investigator Frances Watson that had been previously arranged by **MARK RANDALL MEADOWS.** During the phone call, **DONALD JOHN TRUMP** falsely stated that he had won the November 3, 2020, presidential election in Georgia "by hundreds of thousands of votes" and stated to Watson that "when the right answer comes out you'll be praised." This was an overt act in furtherance of the conspiracy.

Act 94.

On or about the **23rd day of December 2020, JOHN CHARLES EASTMAN** sent an e-mail to **KENNETH JOHN CHESEBRO** and unindicted co-conspirator Individual 3, whose identity is known to the Grand Jury, with the subject "FW: Draft 2, with edits." In the e-mail, **JOHN CHARLES EASTMAN** attached a memorandum titled "PRIVILEGED AND CONFIDENTIAL—Dec 23 memo on Jan 6 scenario .docx" and stated, "As for hearings, I think both are unnecessary. The fact that we have multiple slates of electors demonstrates the uncertainty of either. That should be enough. And I agree with Ken that Judiciary Committee hearings on the constitutionality of the Electoral Count Act could invite counter views that we do not believe should constrain Pence (or Grassley) in the exercise of power they have under the 12th Amendment. Better for them just to act boldly and be challenged, since the challenge would likely lead to the Court denying review on nonjusticiable political question grounds." This was an overt act in furtherance of the conspiracy.

Act 95.

On or about the **25th day of December 2020, DONALD JOHN TRUMP** placed a telephone call to Speaker of the Arizona House of Representatives Rusty Bowers for the purpose of soliciting, requesting, and importuning Bowers to unlawfully appoint presidential electors from Arizona. During the call, Bowers stated to Trump, "I voted for you. I worked for you. I campaigned for you. I just won't do anything illegal for you." This telephone call was an overt act in furtherance of the conspiracy.

Act 96.

On or about the **27th day of December 2020, MARK RANDALL MEADOWS** sent a text message to Office of the Georgia Secretary of State Chief Investigator Frances Watson that stated in part, "Is there a way to speed up Fulton county signature verification in order to have results before Jan 6 if the trump campaign assist financially." This was an overt act in furtherance of the conspiracy.

Act 97.

On or about the **27th day of December 2020, DONALD JOHN TRUMP** solicited Acting United States Attorney General Jeffrey Rosen and Acting United States Deputy Attorney General Richard Donoghue to make a false statement by stating, "Just say that the election was corrupt, and leave the rest to me and the Republican congressmen." This was an overt act in furtherance of the conspiracy.

Act 98.

On or about the **28th day of December 2020, JEFFREY BOSSERT CLARK** attempted to commit the felony offense of **FALSE STATEMENTS AND WRITINGS,** in violation of **O.C.G.A. § 16-10-20,** in Fulton County, Georgia, by knowingly and willfully making a false writing and document knowing the same to contain the false statement that the United States Department of Justice had "identified significant concerns that may have impacted the outcome of the election in multiple States, including the State of Georgia," said statement being within the jurisdiction of the Office of the Georgia Secretary of State and the Georgia Bureau of Investigation, departments and agencies of state government, and county and city law enforcement agencies;

And on or about the **28th day of December 2020, JEFFREY BOSSERT CLARK** sent an e-mail to Acting United States Attorney General Jeffrey Rosen and Acting United States Deputy Attorney General Richard Donoghue and requested authorization to send said false writing and document to Georgia Governor Brian Kemp, Speaker of the Georgia House of Representatives David Ralston, and President Pro Tempore of the Georgia Senate Butch Miller, which constitutes a substantial step toward the commission of False Statements and Writings, O.C.G.A. § 16-10-20. This was an act of racketeering activity under O.C.G.A. § 16-14-3(5)(A)(xxii) and an overt act in furtherance of the conspiracy.

Act 99.

On or about the **28th day of December 2020, JEFFREY BOSSERT CLARK** solicited Acting United States Attorney General Jeffrey Rosen and Acting United States Deputy Attorney General Richard Donoghue to sign and send a document that falsely stated that the United States Department of Justice had "identified significant concerns that may have impacted the outcome of the election in multiple States, including the State of Georgia," to Georgia Governor Brian Kemp, Speaker of the Georgia House of Representatives David Ralston, and President Pro Tempore of the Georgia Senate Butch Miller. This was an overt act in furtherance of the conspiracy.

Act 100.

On or about the **30th day of December 2020, DONALD JOHN TRUMP** caused to be tweeted from the Twitter account @RealDonaldTrump, "Hearings from Atlanta on the Georgia Election overturn now being broadcast. Check it out. @OANN @newsmax and many more. @BrianKempGA should resign from office. He is an obstructionist who refuses to admit that we won Georgia, BIG! Also won the other Swing States." This was an overt act in furtherance of the conspiracy.

Act 101.

On or about the **30th day of December 2020, DONALD JOHN TRUMP** caused to be tweeted from the Twitter account @RealDonaldTrump, "Hearings from Atlanta on the Georgia Election overturn now being broadcast LIVE via @RSBNetwork! https://t.co/ogBvLbKfqG." This was an overt act in furtherance of the conspiracy.

Act 102.

On or about the **30th day of December 2020, RUDOLPH WILLIAM LOUIS GIULIANI, RAY STALLINGS SMITH III,** and **ROBERT DAVID CHEELEY** committed the felony offense of **SOLICITATION OF VIOLATION OF OATH BY PUBLIC OFFICER,** in violation of **O.C.G.A. §§ 16-4-7 & 16-10-1,** in Fulton County, Georgia, by soliciting, requesting, and importuning certain public officers then serving as elected members of the Georgia Senate and present at a Senate Judiciary Subcommittee meeting, including unindicted co-conspirator Individual 8, whose identity is known to the Grand Jury, Senators Brandon Beach, Bill Heath, William Ligon, Michael Rhett, and Blake Tillery, to engage in conduct constituting the felony offense of Violation of Oath by Public Officer, O.C.G.A. § 16-10-1, by unlawfully appointing presidential electors from the State of Georgia, in willful and intentional violation of the terms of the oath of said persons as prescribed by law, with intent that said persons engage in said conduct. This was an overt act in furtherance of the conspiracy.

Act 103.

On or about the **30th day of December 2020, RUDOLPH WILLIAM LOUIS GIULIANI** committed the felony offense of **FALSE STATEMENTS AND WRITINGS,** in violation of **O.C.G.A. § 16-10-20,** in Fulton County, Georgia, by knowingly, willfully, and unlawfully making at least one of the following false statements and representations to members of the Georgia Senate present at a Senate Judiciary Subcommittee meeting:

1. That Fulton County election workers fraudulently counted certain ballots as many as five times at State Farm Arena on November 3, 2020;

2. That 2,560 felons voted illegally in the November 3, 2020, presidential election in Georgia;

3. That 10,315 dead people voted in the November 3, 2020, presidential election in Georgia;

said statements being within the jurisdiction of the Office of the Georgia Secretary of State and the Georgia Bureau of Investigation, departments and agencies of state government, and county and city law enforcement agencies. This was an act of racketeering activity under O.C.G.A. § 16-14-3(5)(A)(xxii) and an overt act in furtherance of the conspiracy.

Act 104.

On or about the **30th day of December 2020, RAY STALLINGS SMITH III** committed the felony offense of **FALSE STATEMENTS AND WRITINGS,** in violation of **O.C.G.A. § 16-10-20,** in Fulton County, Georgia, by knowingly, willfully, and unlawfully making at least one of the following false statements and representations to members of the Georgia Senate present at a Senate Judiciary Subcommittee meeting:

1. That Georgia Secretary of State General Counsel Ryan Germany stated that his office had sent letters to 8,000 people who voted illegally in the November 3, 2020, presidential election and told them not to vote in the January 5, 2021, runoff election;

2. That the Georgia Secretary of State admitted "that they had a 90% accuracy rate" in the November 3, 2020, presidential election and that "there's still a 10% margin that's not accurate";

said statements being within the jurisdiction of the Office of the Georgia Secretary of State and the Georgia Bureau of Investigation, departments and agencies of state government, and county and city law enforcement agencies. This was an act of racketeering activity under O.C.G.A. § 16-14-3(5)(A)(xxii) and an overt act in furtherance of the conspiracy.

Act 105.

On or about the **30th day of December 2020, ROBERT DAVID CHEELEY** committed the felony offense of **FALSE STATEMENTS AND WRITINGS,** in violation of **O.C.G.A. § 16-10-20,** in Fulton County, Georgia, by knowingly, willfully, and unlawfully making at least one of the following false statements and representations to members of the Georgia Senate present at a Senate Judiciary Subcommittee meeting:

1. That poll watchers and media at State Farm Arena were told late in the evening of November 3, 2020, that the vote count was being suspended until the next morning and to go home because of "a major watermain break";

2. That Fulton County election workers at State Farm Arena "voted" the same ballots "over and over again" on November 3, 2020;

said statements being within the jurisdiction of the Office of the Georgia Secretary of State and the Georgia Bureau of Investigation, departments and agencies of state government, and county and city law enforcement agencies. This was an act of racketeering activity under O.C.G.A. § 16-14-3(5)(A)(xxii) and an overt act in furtherance of the conspiracy.

Act 106.

On or about the **30th day of December 2020, DONALD JOHN TRUMP** caused to be tweeted from the Twitter account @RealDonaldTrump, "We now have far more votes than needed to flip Georgia in the Presidential race. Massive VOTER FRAUD took place. Thank you to the Georgia Legislature for today's revealing meeting!" This was an overt act in furtherance of the conspiracy.

Act 107.

On or about the **31st day of December 2020, JENNA LYNN ELLIS** wrote a memorandum titled "Memorandum Re: Constitutional Analysis of Vice President Authority for January 6, 2021 Electoral College Vote Count" to **DONALD JOHN TRUMP.** The memorandum outlined a strategy for disrupting and delaying the joint session of Congress on January 6, 2021, the day prescribed by law for counting votes cast by the duly elected and qualified presidential electors from Georgia and the other states, and stated, "the Vice President should therefore not open any of the votes" from six states, including Georgia, that were falsely characterized as having "electoral delegates in dispute." This was an overt act in furtherance of the conspiracy.

Act 108.

On or about the **31st day of December 2020, DONALD JOHN TRUMP** and **JOHN CHARLES EASTMAN** committed the felony offense of **FILING FALSE DOCUMENTS,** in violation of **O.C.G.A. § 16-10-20.1(b)(1),** in Fulton County, Georgia, by knowingly filing a document titled "VERIFIED COMPLAINT FOR EMERGENCY INJUNCTIVE AND DECLARATORY RELIEF" in the matter of Trump

v. Kemp, Case 1:20-cv-05310-MHC, in the United States District Court for the Northern District of Georgia, a court of the United States having reason to know that said document contained at least one of the following materially false statements:

1. That "as many as 2,506 felons with an uncompleted sentence" voted illegally in the November 3, 2020, presidential election in Georgia;

2. That "at least 66,247 underage" people voted illegally in the November 3, 2020, presidential election in Georgia;

3. That "at least 2,423 individuals" voted illegally in the November 3, 2020, presidential election in Georgia "who were not listed in the State's records as having been registered to vote";

4. That "at least 1,043 individuals" voted illegally in the November 3, 2020, presidential election "who had illegally registered to vote using a postal office box as their habitation";

5. That "as many as 10,315 or more" dead people voted in the November 3, 2020, presidential election in Georgia;

6. That "[d]eliberate misinformation was used to instruct Republican poll watchers and members of the press to leave the premises for the night at approximately 10:00 p.m. on November 3, 2020" at State Farm Arena in Fulton County, Georgia;

Earlier on the same day, **JOHN CHARLES EASTMAN** sent an e-mail to attorneys associated with the Trump Campaign admitting his knowledge that at least some of the allegations in the verified complaint were not accurate. This filing was an act of racketeering activity under O.C.G.A. § 16-14-3(5)(A)(xxii) and an overt act in furtherance of the conspiracy.

Act 109.

On or about the **1st day of January 2021, KENNETH JOHN CHESEBRO** sent an e-mail to **JOHN CHARLES EASTMAN** and unindicted co-conspirator Individual 3, whose identity is known to the Grand Jury. In the e-mail, **KENNETH JOHN CHESEBRO** outlined a strategy for disrupting and delaying the joint session of Congress on January 6, 2021, the day prescribed by law for counting votes cast by the duly elected and qualified presidential electors from Georgia and the other states. This was an overt act in furtherance of the conspiracy.

Act 110.

On or about the **2nd day of January 2021, SCOTT GRAHAM HALL,** a Georgia bail bondsman, placed a telephone call to **JEFFREY BOSSERT CLARK** and discussed the November 3, 2020, presidential election in Georgia. The telephone call was 63 minutes in duration. This was an overt act in furtherance of the conspiracy.

Act 111.

On or about the **2nd day of January 2021, JEFFREY BOSSERT CLARK** solicited Acting United States Attorney General Jeffrey Rosen and Acting United States Deputy Attorney General Richard Donoghue to sign and send a document that falsely stated that the United States Department of Justice had "identified significant concerns that may have impacted the outcome of the election in multiple States, including the State of Georgia," to Georgia Governor Brian Kemp, Speaker of the Georgia

House of Representatives David Ralston, and President Pro Tempore of the Georgia Senate Butch Miller. This was an overt act in furtherance of the conspiracy.

Act 112.

On or about the **2nd day of January 2021, DONALD JOHN TRUMP** and **MARK RANDALL MEADOWS** committed the felony offense of **SOLICITATION OF VIOLATION OF OATH BY PUBLIC OFFICER,** in violation of **O.C.G.A. §§ 16-4-7 & 16-10-1,** in Fulton County, Georgia, by unlawfully soliciting, requesting, and importuning Georgia Secretary of State Brad Raffensperger, a public officer, to engage in conduct constituting the felony offense of Violation of Oath by Public Officer, O.C.G.A. § 16-10-1, by unlawfully altering, unlawfully adjusting, and otherwise unlawfully influencing the certified returns for presidential electors for the November 3, 2020, presidential election in Georgia, in willful and intentional violation of the terms of the oath of said person as prescribed by law, with intent that said person engage in said conduct. This was an overt act in furtherance of the conspiracy.

Act 113.

On or about the **2nd day of January 2021, DONALD JOHN TRUMP** committed the felony offense of **FALSE STATEMENTS AND WRITINGS,** in violation of **O.C.G.A. § 16-10-20,** in Fulton County, Georgia, by knowingly, willfully, and unlawfully making at least one of the following false statements and representations to Georgia Secretary of State Brad Raffensperger, Georgia Deputy Secretary of State Jordan Fuchs, and Georgia Secretary of State General Counsel Ryan Germany:

1. That anywhere from 250,000 to 300,000 ballots were dropped mysteriously into the rolls in the November 3, 2020, presidential election in Georgia;

2. That thousands of people attempted to vote in the November 3, 2020, presidential election in Georgia and were told they could not because a ballot had already been cast in their name;

3. That 4,502 people voted in the November 3, 2020, presidential election in Georgia who were not on the voter registration list;

4. That 904 people voted in the November 3, 2020, presidential election in Georgia who were registered at an address that was a post office box;

5. That Ruby Freeman was a professional vote scammer and a known political operative;

6. That Ruby Freeman, her daughter, and others were responsible for fraudulently awarding at least 18,000 ballots to Joseph R. Biden at State Farm Arena in the November 3, 2020, presidential election in Georgia;

7. That close to 5,000 dead people voted in the November 3, 2020, presidential election in Georgia;

8. That 139% of people voted in the November 3, 2020, presidential election in Detroit;

9. That 200,000 more votes were recorded than the number of people who voted in the November 3, 2020, presidential election in Pennsylvania;

10. That thousands of dead people voted in the November 3, 2020, presidential election in Michigan;

11. That Ruby Freeman stuffed the ballot boxes;

12. That hundreds of thousands of ballots had been "dumped" into Fulton County and another county adjacent to Fulton County in the November 3, 2020, presidential election in Georgia;

13. That he won the November 3, 2020, presidential election in Georgia by 400,000 votes;

said statements being within the jurisdiction of the Office of the Georgia Secretary of State and the Georgia Bureau of Investigation, departments and agencies of state government. This was an act of racketeering activity under O.C.G.A. § 16-14-3(5)(A)(xxii) and an overt act in furtherance of the conspiracy.

Act 114.

On or about the **3rd day of January 2021, DONALD JOHN TRUMP** caused to be tweeted from the Twitter account @RealDonaldTrump, "I spoke to Secretary of State Brad Raffensperger yesterday about Fulton County and voter fraud in Georgia. He was unwilling, or unable, to answer questions such as the 'ballots under table' scam, ballot destruction, out of state 'voters', dead voters, and more. He has no clue!" This was an overt act in furtherance of the conspiracy.

Act 115.

On or about the **3rd day of January 2021, STEPHEN CLIFFGARD LEE, HARRISON WILLIAM PRESCOTT FLOYD, and TREVIAN C. KUTTI** placed multiple telephone calls and sent text messages to each other and to other individuals involved in the conspiracy. They include the following:

1. At 7:48 p.m., **HARRISON WILLIAM PRESCOTT FLOYD** placed a telephone call to Ruby Freeman, a Fulton County, Georgia, election worker, that was unsuccessful.

2. At 7:49 p.m., **HARRISON WILLIAM PRESCOTT FLOYD** placed a telephone call to Ruby Freeman that was unsuccessful.

3. At 7:49 p.m., **HARRISON WILLIAM PRESCOTT FLOYD** placed a telephone call to **TREVIAN C. KUTTI.**

4. At 7:53 p.m., **HARRISON WILLIAM PRESCOTT FLOYD** sent a text message to Ruby Freeman.

5. At 8:03 p.m., **TREVIAN C. KUTTI** placed a telephone call to **HARRISON WILLIAM PRESCOTT FLOYD.**

6. At 8:11 p.m., **HARRISON WILLIAM PRESCOTT FLOYD** placed a telephone call to unindicted co-conspirator Individual 23, whose identity is known to the Grand Jury.

7. At 8:18 p.m., **HARRISON WILLIAM PRESCOTT FLOYD** placed a telephone call to **STEPHEN CLIFFGARD LEE.**

8. At 8:48 p.m., **HARRISON WILLIAM PRESCOTT FLOYD** placed a telephone call to **TREVIAN C. KUTTI.**

9. At 9:16 p.m., **HARRISON WILLIAM PRESCOTT FLOYD** placed a telephone call to **TREVIAN C. KUTTI.**

10. At 9:33 p.m., **HARRISON WILLIAM PRESCOTT FLOYD** placed a telephone call to **TREVIAN C. KUTTI.**

11. At 9:50 p.m., **HARRISON WILLIAM PRESCOTT FLOYD** placed a telephone call to **STEPHEN CLIFFGARD LEE.**

These were overt acts in furtherance of the conspiracy.

Act 116.

On or about the **4th day of January 2021, TREVIAN C. KUTTI,** having been recruited by **HARRISON WILLIAM PRESCOTT FLOYD,** traveled from Chicago, Illinois, to Atlanta, Georgia, and caused a certain individual, whose identity is known to the Grand Jury, to pick her up from a train station in Fulton County, Georgia, for the purpose of attempting to contact Ruby Freeman, a Fulton County, Georgia, election worker. This was an overt act in furtherance of the conspiracy.

Act 117.

On or about the **4th day of January 2021, TREVIAN C. KUTTI** traveled to Ruby Freeman's home in Cobb County, Georgia, and attempted to contact her but was unsuccessful. **TREVIAN C. KUTTI** spoke with Freeman's neighbor and falsely stated that she was a crisis manager attempting to "help" Freeman before leaving Freeman's home. This was an overt act in furtherance of the conspiracy.

Act 118.

On or about the **4th day of January 2021, TREVIAN C. KUTTI,** while in Fulton County, Georgia, placed a telephone call to Ruby Freeman and stated that Freeman was in danger. **TREVIAN C. KUTTI** stated that she could "help" Freeman and requested that Freeman meet with and speak to her that night at a Cobb County Police Department precinct in Cobb County, Georgia. This was an overt act in furtherance of the conspiracy.

Act 119.

On or about the **4th day of January 2021, TREVIAN C. KUTTI** traveled to a Cobb County Police Department precinct in Cobb County, Georgia, and met with and spoke to Ruby Freeman for approximately one hour. **HARRISON WILLIAM PRESCOTT FLOYD** joined the meeting by telephone. **TREVIAN C. KUTTI** and **HARRISON WILLIAM PRESCOTT FLOYD** stated to Freeman that she needed protection and purported to offer her help. This was an overt act in furtherance of the conspiracy.

Act 120.

On or about the **4th day of January 2021 STEPHEN CLIFFGARD LEE, HARRISON WILLIAM PRESCOTT FLOYD,** and

TREVIAN C. KUTTI committed the felony offense of **SOLICITATION OF FALSE STATEMENTS AND WRITINGS,** in violation of **O.C.G.A. §§ 16-4-7 & 16-10-20,** in Cobb County, Georgia, by soliciting, requesting, and importuning Ruby Freeman, a Fulton County, Georgia, election worker, to engage in conduct constituting the felony offense of False Statements and Writings, O.C.G.A. § 16-10-20, by knowingly and willfully making a false statement and representation concerning events at State Farm Arena in the November 3, 2020, presidential election in Georgia, said statement and representation being within the jurisdiction of the Office of the Georgia Secretary of State and the Georgia Bureau of Investigation, departments and agencies of state government, and county and city law enforcement agencies, with intent that said person engage in said conduct. This was an act of racketeering activity under O.C.G.A. § 16-14-3(5)(A)(xxii) and an overt act in furtherance of the conspiracy.

Act 121.

On or about the **4th day of January 2021 STEPHEN CLIFFGARD LEE, HARRISON WILLIAM PRESCOTT FLOYD,** and **TREVIAN C. KUTTI** committed the felony offense of **INFLUENCING WITNESSES,** in violation of **O.C.G.A. § 16-10-93(b)(1)(A),** in Fulton County, Georgia, by knowingly and unlawfully engaging in misleading conduct toward Ruby Freeman, a Fulton County, Georgia, election worker, by stating that she needed protection and by purporting to offer her help, with intent to influence her testimony in an official proceeding in Fulton County, Georgia, concerning events at State Farm Arena in the November 3, 2020, presidential election in Georgia. This was an act of racketeering activity under O.C.G.A. § 16-14-3(5)(A)(xxvii) and an overt act in furtherance of the conspiracy.

Act 122.

On or about the **4th day of January 2021, STEPHEN CLIFFGARD LEE, HARRISON WILLIAM PRESCOTT FLOYD, and TREVIAN C. KUTTI** placed multiple telephone calls and sent text messages to each other and to other individuals involved in the conspiracy. They include the following:

1. At 9:41 a.m., STEPHEN CLIFFGARD LEE placed a telephone call to HARRISON WILLIAM PRESCOTT FLOYD.

2. At 11:24 a.m., HARRISON WILLIAM PRESCOTT FLOYD placed a telephone call to DAVID JAMES SHAFER.

3. At 12:25 p.m., STEPHEN CLIFFGARD LEE placed a telephone call to HARRISON WILLIAM PRESCOTT FLOYD.

4. At 12:32 p.m., STEPHEN CLIFFGARD LEE sent a text message to HARRISON WILLIAM PRESCOTT FLOYD.

5. At 8:10 p.m., HARRISON WILLIAM PRESCOTT FLOYD placed a telephone call to DAVID JAMES SHAFER.

6. At 10:00 p.m., HARRISON WILLIAM PRESCOTT FLOYD placed a telephone call to STEPHEN CLIFFGARD LEE.

7. At 10:19 p.m., HARRISON WILLIAM PRESCOTT FLOYD placed a telephone call to TREVIAN C. KUTTI.

8. At 10:43 p.m., TREVIAN C. KUTTI placed a telephone call to HARRISON WILLIAM PRESCOTT FLOYD.

9. At 11:10 p.m., TREVIAN C. KUTTI placed a telephone call to HARRISON WILLIAM PRESCOTT FLOYD.

10. At 12:12 a.m. on January 5, 2021, TREVIAN C. KUTTI placed a telephone call to HARRISON WILLIAM PRESCOTT FLOYD.

These were overt acts in furtherance of the conspiracy.

Act 123.

On or about the **4th day of January 2020, JOHN CHARLES EASTMAN** placed a telephone call to Speaker of the Arizona House of Representatives Rusty Bowers and solicited, requested, and importuned Bowers to unlawfully appoint presidential electors from Arizona. During the telephone call, Bowers declined to comply with Eastman's request and stated that he would not risk violating his oath of office. The request was an overt act in furtherance of the conspiracy.

Act 124.

On or about the **4th day of January 2021, KENNETH JOHN CHESEBRO** sent an e-mail to **JOHN CHARLES EASTMAN** with the subject "Fwd: Draft 2, with edits" and included within the body of the e-mail another e-mail that **KENNETH JOHN CHESEBRO** previously sent to **RUDOLPH WILLIAM LOUIS GIULIANI** with the subject "PRIVILEGED AND CONFIDENTIAL—Brief notes on 'President of the Senate' strategy." In the e-mail, **KENNETH JOHN CHESEBRO** outlined multiple strategies for disrupting and delaying the joint session of Congress on January 6, 2021, the day prescribed by law for counting votes cast by the duly elected and qualified presidential electors from Georgia and the other states, and stated that the outcomes of any of these strategies were "preferable to allowing the Electoral Count Act to operate by its terms." This was an overt act in furtherance of the conspiracy.

Act 123.

On or about the **4th day of January 2021, DONALD JOHN TRUMP** and **JOHN CHARLES EASTMAN** met with Vice President Mike Pence, Chief of Staff to the Vice President Marc Short, and Counsel to the Vice President Greg Jacob in the Oval Office at the White House. During the meeting, **DONALD JOHN TRUMP** and **JOHN CHARLES EASTMAN** argued to Pence that he could either reject electoral votes from certain states or delay the joint session of Congress on January 6, 2021, the day prescribed by law for counting votes cast by the duly elected and qualified presidential electors from Georgia and the other states, for the purpose of allowing certain state legislatures to unlawfully appoint presidential electors in favor of **DONALD JOHN TRUMP.** During the meeting, **JOHN CHARLES EASTMAN** admitted both options violated the Electoral Count Act. This was an overt act in furtherance of the conspiracy.

Act 126.

On or about the **5th day of January 2021, JENNA LYNN ELLIS** wrote a memorandum titled "Re: Vice President Authority in Counting Electors pursuant to U.S. Constitution and 3 U.S. Code §§ 5 and 15" to an attorney associated with **DONALD JOHN TRUMP.** The memorandum outlined a strategy for disrupting and delaying the joint session of Congress on January 6, 2021, the day prescribed by law for counting votes cast by the duly elected and qualified presidential electors from Georgia and the other states, and stated, "the Vice President should begin alphabetically in order of the states, and coming first to Arizona, not open the purported certification, but simply stop the count at that juncture." This was an overt act in furtherance of the conspiracy.

Act 127.

On or about the **5th day of January 2021, ROBERT DAVID CHEELEY, STEPHEN CLIFFGARD LEE, HARRISON WILLIAM PRESCOTT FLOYD, TREVIAN C. KUTTI, and SCOTT GRAHAM HALL** placed multiple telephone calls to each other and to other individuals involved in the conspiracy. They include the following:

1. At 11:32 a.m., **STEPHEN CLIFFGARD LEE** placed a telephone call to **TREVIAN C. KUTTI.**

2. At 12:14 p.m., **HARRISON WILLIAM PRESCOTT FLOYD, TREVIAN C. KUTTI, STEPHEN CLIFFGARD LEE,** and unindicted co-conspirator Individual 23, whose identity is known to the Grand Jury, participated in a four-way telephone call.

3. At 12:19 p.m., **SCOTT GRAHAM HALL** placed a telephone call to **ROBERT DAVID CHEELEY.**

4. At 12:34 p.m., **SCOTT GRAHAM HALL** placed a telephone call to **ROBERT DAVID CHEELEY.**

5. At 1:07 p.m., **ROBERT DAVID CHEELEY** placed a telephone call to **SCOTT GRAHAM HALL.**

6. At 1:09 p.m., **ROBERT DAVID CHEELEY** placed a telephone call to **SCOTT GRAHAM HALL.**

7. At 2:30 p.m., **ROBERT DAVID CHEELEY** placed a telephone call to **HARRISON WILLIAM PRESCOTT FLOYD.**

8. At 2:45 p.m., **HARRISON WILLIAM PRESCOTT FLOYD** placed a telephone call to **ROBERT DAVID CHEELEY.**

9. At 3:59 p.m., **ROBERT DAVID CHEELEY** placed a telephone call to **SCOTT GRAHAM HALL.**

10. At 4:42 p.m., **STEPHEN CLIFFGARD LEE** placed a telephone call to **ROBERT DAVID CHEELEY.**

11. At 4:50 p.m., **STEPHEN CLIFFGARD LEE** placed a telephone call to **HARRISON WILLIAM PRESCOTT FLOYD.**

12. At 5:05 p.m., **STEPHEN CLIFFGARD LEE** placed a telephone call to **HARRISON WILLIAM PRESCOTT FLOYD.**

13. At 7:19 p.m., **TREVIAN C. KUTTI** placed a telephone call to **ROBERT DAVID CHEELEY.**

14. At 7:48 p.m., **ROBERT DAVID CHEELEY** placed a telephone call to **TREVIAN C. KUTTI.**

15. At 8:27 p.m., **ROBERT DAVID CHEELEY** placed a telephone call to **TREVIAN C. KUTTI.**

16. At 8:49 p.m., **ROBERT DAVID CHEELEY** placed a telephone call to **STEPHEN CLIFFGARD LEE.**

17. At 9:18 p.m., **SCOTT GRAHAM HALL** placed a telephone call to **ROBERT DAVID CHEELEY.**

18. At 9:31 p.m., **TREVIAN C. KUTTI** placed a telephone call to **ROBERT DAVID CHEELEY.**

19. At 10:14 p.m., **ROBERT DAVID CHEELEY** placed a telephone call to **STEPHEN CLIFFGARD LEE.**

20. At 11:16 p.m., **ROBERT DAVID CHEELEY** placed a telephone call to **TREVIAN C. KUTTI.**

21. At 11:25 p.m., **SCOTT GRAHAM HALL** placed a telephone call to **ROBERT DAVID CHEELEY.**

22. At 11:35 p.m., **ROBERT DAVID CHEELEY, TREVIAN C. KUTTI,** and **SCOTT GRAHAM HALL** participated in a three-way telephone call.

23. At 12:09 a.m. on January 6, 2021, **TREVIAN C. KUTTI** placed a telephone call to **ROBERT DAVID CHEELEY.**

These were overt acts in furtherance of the conspiracy.

Act 128.

On or about the **5th day of January 2021, DONALD JOHN TRUMP** caused to be tweeted from the Twitter account @RealDonaldTrump, "The Vice President has the power to reject fraudulently chosen electors." This was an overt act in furtherance of the conspiracy.

Act 129.

On or about the **5th day of January 2021, JOHN CHARLES EASTMAN** met with Chief of Staff to the Vice President Marc Short and Counsel to the Vice President Greg Jacob for the purpose of requesting that Vice President Mike Pence reject slates of presidential electors from Georgia and certain other states during the joint session of Congress on January 6, 2021, the day prescribed by law for counting votes cast by the duly elected and qualified presidential electors from Georgia and the other states. This was an overt act in furtherance of the conspiracy.

Act 130.

On or about the **5th day of January 2021, DONALD JOHN TRUMP** met with Vice President Mike Pence in the Oval Office at the White House. During the meeting, **DONALD JOHN TRUMP** stated that Pence had the power to decertify the November 3, 2020, presidential election results, that people cheated, and that Pence wanted to "play by Marquess of Queensberry rules." When Pence stated that it was his duty to support and defend the Constitution and that only Congress had the power to decide to reject slates of presidential electors, **DONALD JOHN TRUMP** stated that Pence was naive, implied that he lacked courage, and stated that Pence was doing "a great disservice." This was an overt act in furtherance of the conspiracy.

Act 131.

On or about the **5th day of January 2021, DONALD JOHN TRUMP** placed a telephone call to Vice President Mike Pence. During the telephone call, **DONALD JOHN TRUMP** and **JOHN CHARLES EASTMAN** attempted to persuade Pence to reject slates of presidential electors or return the slates of presidential electors to state legislatures. This was an overt act in furtherance of the conspiracy.

Act 132.

On or about the **5th day of January 2021, DONALD JOHN TRUMP** placed a second telephone call to Vice President Mike Pence. During the telephone call, **DONALD JOHN TRUMP** asked Pence if he had received a copy of a letter from a group of Pennsylvania legislators urging Congress to return the state's electoral college votes and stated to Pence, "You gotta be tough tomorrow." This was an overt act in furtherance of the conspiracy.

Act 133.

On or about the **5th day of January 2021, DONALD JOHN TRUMP** issued a statement through the Trump Campaign that falsely stated, "The Vice President and I are in total agreement that the Vice President has the power to act. . . . Our Vice President has several options under the U.S. Constitution. He can decertify the results or send them back to the states for change and certification. He can also decertify the illegal and corrupt results and send them to the House of Representatives for the one vote for one state tabulation." This was an overt act in furtherance of the conspiracy.

Act 134.

On or about the **6th day of January 2021, CATHLEEN ALSTON LATHAM** placed a telephone call to **SCOTT GRAHAM HALL.** Several hours later, **SCOTT GRAHAM HALL** placed a telephone call to **CATHLEEN ALSTON LATHAM.** During at least one of the phone calls, they discussed **SCOTT GRAHAM HALL**'s request to assist with the unlawful breach of election equipment at the Coffee County Board of Elections & Registration Office in Coffee County, Georgia. These were overt acts in furtherance of the conspiracy.

Act 135.

On or about the **6th day of January 2021, DONALD JOHN TRUMP** appeared and spoke at a rally at the Ellipse in Washington, D.C. During the rally, **DONALD JOHN TRUMP** made false statements concerning fraud in the November 3, 2020, presidential election in Georgia and elsewhere, solicited Vice President Mike Pence to disrupt and delay the joint session of Congress on January 6, 2021, the day prescribed by law for counting votes cast by the duly elected and qualified presidential electors from Georgia and the other states, and encouraged those in attendance at the rally to march to the United States Capitol. This was an overt act in furtherance of the conspiracy.

Act 136.

On or about the **6th day of January 2021, RUDOLPH WILLIAM LOUIS GIULIANI** appeared and spoke at a rally at the Ellipse in Washington, D.C. During the rally, **RUDOLPH WILLIAM LOUIS GIULIANI** made false statements concerning fraud in the November 3, 2020, presidential election in Georgia and elsewhere and solicited Vice President Mike Pence to disrupt and delay the joint session of Congress on January 6, 2021, the day prescribed by law for counting votes cast by the duly elected and qualified presidential electors from Georgia and the other states. This was an overt act in furtherance of the conspiracy.

Act 137.

On or about the **6th day of January 2021, JOHN CHARLES EASTMAN** appeared and spoke at a rally at the Ellipse in Washington, D.C. During the rally, **JOHN CHARLES EASTMAN** made false statements concerning fraud in the November 3, 2020, presidential election and solicited Vice President Mike Pence to disrupt and delay the joint session of Congress on January 6, 2021, the day prescribed by law for counting votes cast by the duly elected and qualified presidential electors from Georgia and the other states. This was an overt act in furtherance of the conspiracy.

Act 138.

On or about the **6th day of January 2021, DONALD JOHN TRUMP** caused to be tweeted from the Twitter account @RealDonaldTrump, "If Vice President @Mike_Pence comes through for us, we will win the Presidency. Many States want to decertify the mistake they made in certifying incorrect & even fraudulent numbers in a process NOT approved by their State Legislatures (which it must be). Mike can send it back!" This was an overt act in furtherance of the conspiracy.

Act 139.

On or about the **6th day of January 2021, DONALD JOHN TRUMP** caused to be tweeted from the Twitter account @RealDonaldTrump, "States want to correct their votes, which they now know were based on irregularities and fraud, plus corrupt process never received legislative approval. All Mike Pence has to do is send them back to the States, AND WE WIN. Do it Mike, this is a time for extreme courage!" This was an overt act in furtherance of the conspiracy.

Act 140.

On or about the **6th day of January 2021, DONALD JOHN TRUMP** placed a telephone call to Vice President Mike Pence and solicited him to disrupt and delay the joint session of Congress on January 6, 2021, the day prescribed by law for counting votes cast by the duly elected and qualified presidential electors from Georgia and the other states. When Pence refused, **DONALD JOHN TRUMP** stated that Pence would "go down as a wimp" and that Pence was not protecting the United States. This was an overt act in furtherance of the conspiracy.

Act 141.

On or about the **6th day of January 2021, JOHN CHARLES EASTMAN** sent an e-mail to Counsel to the Vice President Greg Jacob that stated:

> "The Senate and House have both violated the Electoral Count Act this evening—they debated the Arizona objections for more than 2 hours. Violation of 3 USC 17. And the VP allowed further debate or statements by leadership after the question had been voted upon. Violation of 3 USC 17. And they had that debate upon motion approved by the VP, in violation of the requirements in 3 USC 15 that after the vote in the separate houses, 'they shall immediately again meet.'
>
> So now that the precedent has been set that the Electoral Count Act is not quite so sacrosanct as was previously claimed, I implore you to consider one more relatively minor violation and adjourn for 10 days to allow the legislatures to finish their investigations, as well as to allow a full forensic audit of the massive amount of illegal activity that

has occurred here. If none of that moves the needle, at least a good portion of the 75 million people who supported President Trump will have seen a process that allowed the illegality to be aired.

John"

This was an overt act in furtherance of the conspiracy.

Act 142.

On or about the **7th day of January 2021, CATHLEEN ALSTON LATHAM** sent a text message to the Chief Operations Officer of SullivanStrickler LLC with the address for the Douglas Municipal Airport in Coffee County, Georgia, to coordinate picking up **SCOTT GRAHAM HALL** from the airport and driving him to the Coffee County Board of Elections & Registration Office for the purpose of assisting with the unlawful breach of election equipment at the Coffee County Board of Elections & Registration Office. This was an act of racketeering activity under O.C.G.A. § 16-14-3(5)(B) and an overt act in furtherance of the conspiracy.

Act 143.

On or about the **7th day of January 2021, SCOTT GRAHAM HALL** and unindicted co-conspirator Individual 24, whose identity is known to the Grand Jury, flew from DeKalb-Peachtree Airport in DeKalb County, Georgia, to Douglas Municipal Airport in Coffee County, Georgia, for the purpose of assisting with the unlawful breach of election equipment at the Coffee County Board of Elections & Registration Office. This was an act of racketeering activity under O.C.G.A. § 16-14-3(5)(B) and an overt act in furtherance of the conspiracy.

Act 144.

On or about the **7th day of January 2021, SIDNEY KATHERINE POWELL, CATHLEEN ALSTON LATHAM, SCOTT GRAHAM HALL,** and **MISTY HAMPTON** committed the felony offense of **INTERFERENCE WITH PRIMARIES AND ELECTIONS,** in violation of **O.C.G.A. § 21-2-566,** in Coffee County, Georgia, by willfully and unlawfully tampering with electronic ballot markers and tabulating machines in Coffee County, Georgia. This was an overt act in furtherance of the conspiracy.

Act 145.

On or about the **7th day of January 2021, SIDNEY KATHERINE POWELL, CATHLEEN ALSTON LATHAM, SCOTT GRAHAM HALL,** and **MISTY HAMPTON** committed the felony offense of **UNLAWFUL POSSESSION OF BALLOTS,** in violation of **O.C.G.A. § 21-2-574,** in Coffee County, Georgia, by causing certain members of the conspiracy, who were not officers charged by law with the care of ballots and who were not persons entrusted by any such officer with the care of ballots for a purpose required by law, to possess official ballots outside of the polling place in Coffee County, Georgia. This was an overt act in furtherance of the conspiracy.

Act 146.

On or about the **7th day of January 2021, SIDNEY KATHERINE POWELL, CATHLEEN ALSTON LATHAM, SCOTT GRAHAM HALL,** and **MISTY HAMPTON** committed the felony offense of **COMPUTER THEFT,** in violation of **O.C.G.A. § 16-9-93(a),** in

Coffee County, Georgia, by using a computer with knowledge that such use was without authority and with the intention of taking and appropriating information, data, and software, the property of Dominion Voting Systems Corporation in Coffee County, Georgia. This was an act of racketeering activity under O.C.G.A. § 16-14-3(5)(A)(xix) and an overt act in furtherance of the conspiracy.

Act 147.

On or about the **7th day of January 2021, SIDNEY KATHERINE POWELL, CATHLEEN ALSTON LATHAM, SCOTT GRAHAM HALL,** and **MISTY HAMPTON** committed the felony offense of **COMPUTER TRESPASS,** in violation of **O.C.G.A § 16-9-93(b),** in Coffee County, Georgia, by using a computer with knowledge that such use was without authority and with the intention of removing voter data and Dominion Voting Systems Corporation data from said computer in Coffee County, Georgia. This was an act of racketeering activity under O.C.G.A § 16-14-3(5)(A)(xix) and an overt act in furtherance of the conspiracy.

Act 148.

On or about the **7th day of January 2021, SIDNEY KATHERINE POWELL, CATHLEEN ALSTON LATHAM, SCOTT GRAHAM HALL,** and **MISTY HAMPTON** committed the felony offense of **COMPUTER INVASION OF PRIVACY,** in violation of **O.C.G.A. § 16-9-93(c),** in Coffee County, Georgia, by using a computer with the intention of examining personal voter data with knowledge that such examination was without authority. This was an act of racketeering activity under O.C.G.A § 16-14-3(5)(A)(xix) and an overt act in furtherance of the conspiracy.

Act 149.

On and between the **6th day of December 2020 and the 7th day of January 2021, SIDNEY KATHERINE POWELL, CATHLEEN ALSTON LATHAM, SCOTT GRAHAM HALL,** and **MISTY HAMPTON** committed the felony offense of **CONSPIRACY TO DEFRAUD THE STATE,** in violation of **O.C.G.A. § 16-10-21,** in Coffee County, Georgia, by unlawfully conspiring and agreeing to commit theft of voter data, property which was under the control of Georgia Secretary of State Brad Raffensperger, a state officer, in his official capacity. This was an act of racketeering activity under O.C.G.A. § 16-14-3(5)(B) and an overt act in furtherance of the conspiracy.

Act 150.

On or about the **9th day of January 2021, the 10th day of January 2021, the 11th day of January 2021, and the 13th day of January 2021,** unindicted co-conspirator Individual 25, whose identity is known to the Grand Jury, unlawfully accessed certain data copied from Dominion Voting Systems equipment at the Coffee County Board of Elections & Registration Office in Coffee County, Georgia, by downloading said data from a server maintained by SullivanStrickler LLC. This was an act of racketeering activity under O.C.G.A. § 16-14-3(5)(B) and an overt act in furtherance of the conspiracy.

Act 151.

On or about the **9th day of January 2021, the 10th day of January 2021, the 11th day of January 2021, the 18th day of January 2021, and the 19th day of January 2021,** unindicted co-conspirator Individual 26, whose identity is unknown to the Grand Jury, unlawfully accessed certain data copied from Dominion Voting Systems equipment at the Coffee County Board of Elections & Registration Office in Coffee County, Georgia, by downloading said data from a server maintained by Sullivan-Strickler LLC. This was an act of racketeering activity under O.C.G.A. § 16-14-3(5)(B) and an overt act in furtherance of the conspiracy.

Act 152.

On or about the **10th day of January 2021, the 12th day of January 2021, the 13th day of January 2021, the 25th day of February 2021, and the 26th day of February 2021,** unindicted co-conspirator Individual 27, whose identity is unknown to the Grand Jury, unlawfully accessed certain data copied from Dominion Voting Systems equipment at the Coffee County Board of Elections & Registration Office in Coffee County, Georgia, by downloading said data from a server maintained by Sullivan-Strickler LLC. This was an act of racketeering activity under O.C.G.A. § 16-14-3(5)(B) and an overt act in furtherance of the conspiracy.

Act 153.

On or about the **13th day of January 2021,** unindicted co-conspirator Individual 28, whose identity is known to the Grand Jury, unlawfully accessed certain data copied from Dominion Voting Systems equipment at the Coffee County Board of Elections & Registration Office in Coffee County, Georgia, by downloading said data from a server maintained by Sullivan-Strickler LLC. This was an act of racketeering activity under O.C.G.A. § 16-14-3(5)(B) and an overt act in furtherance of the conspiracy.

Act 154.

On or about the **18th day of January 2021, MISTY HAMPTON** allowed unindicted co-conspirators Individual 25 and Individual 29, whose identities are known to the Grand Jury, to access non-public areas of the Coffee County Board of Elections & Registration Office in Coffee County, Georgia, and facilitated their access to Dominion Voting Systems equipment. This was an overt act in furtherance of the conspiracy.

Act 155.

On or about the **22nd day of April 2021,** unindicted co-conspirator Individual 28, whose identity is known to the Grand Jury, sent an e-mail to the Chief Operations Officer of SullivanStrickler LLC directing him to transmit all data copied from Dominion Voting Systems equipment at the Coffee County Board of Elections & Registration Office in Coffee County, Georgia, to unindicted co-conspirator Individual 30, whose identity is known to the Grand Jury, an attorney associated with **SIDNEY KATHERINE POWELL** and the Trump Campaign. This was an act of racketeering activity under O.C.G.A. § 16-14-3(5)(B) and an overt act in furtherance of the conspiracy.

Act 156.

On or about the **17th day of September 2021, DONALD JOHN TRUMP** committed the felony offense of **SOLICITATION OF VIOLATION OF OATH BY PUBLIC OFFICER,** in violation of **O.C.G.A. §§ 16-4-7 and 16-10-1,** in Fulton County, Georgia, by unlawfully soliciting, requesting, and importuning Georgia Secretary of State Brad Raffensperger, a public officer, to engage in conduct constituting the felony offense of Violation of Oath by Public Officer, O.C.G.A. § 16-10-1, by unlawfully "decertifying the Election, or whatever the correct legal remedy is, and announce the true winner," in willful and intentional violation of the terms of the oath of said person as prescribed by law, with intent that said person engage in said conduct. This was an overt act in furtherance of the conspiracy.

Act 157.

On or about the **17th day of September 2021, DONALD JOHN TRUMP** committed the felony offense of **FALSE STATEMENTS AND WRITINGS,** in violation of **O.C.G.A. § 16-10-20,** in Fulton County, Georgia, by knowingly, willfully, and unlawfully making the following false statement and representation to Georgia Secretary of State Brad Raffensperger:

1. "As stated to you previously, the number of false and/or irregular votes is far greater than needed to change the Georgia election result";

said statement being within the jurisdiction of the Office of the Georgia Secretary of State and the Georgia Bureau of Investigation, departments and agencies of state government, and county and city law enforcement agencies. This was an act of racketeering activity under O.C.G.A. § 16-14-3(5)(A)(xxii) and an overt act in furtherance of the conspiracy.

Act 158.

On or about the **25th day of April 2022, DAVID JAMES SHAFER** committed the felony offense of **FALSE STATEMENTS AND WRITINGS**, in violation of **O.C.G.A. § 16-10-20**, in Fulton County, Georgia, by knowingly, willfully, and unlawfully making at least one of the following false statements and representations in the presence of Fulton County District Attorney's Office investigators:

1. That he "attended and convened" the December 14, 2020, meeting of Trump presidential elector nominees in Fulton County, Georgia, but that he did not "call each of the individual members and notify them of the meeting or make any of the other preparations necessary for the meeting";

2. That a court reporter was not present at the December 14, 2020, meeting of Trump presidential elector nominees in Fulton County, Georgia;

said statements being within the jurisdiction of the Fulton County District Attorney's Office, a department and agency of the government of a county of this state. This was an act of racketeering activity under O.C.G.A. § 16-14-3(5)(A)(xxii) and an overt act in furtherance of the conspiracy.

Act 159.

On or about the **7th day of May 2022, SIDNEY KATHERINE POWELL** made at least one of the following false statements and representations in a sworn deposition with the United States House of Representatives Select Committee to Investigate the January 6th Attack on the United States Capitol:

1. That she "didn't have any role in really setting up" efforts to access voting machines in Coffee County, Georgia, or Antrim County, Michigan;

2. That she was aware there was an "effort by some people" to get access to voting machines in Georgia but that she did not "know

what happened with that" and did not "remember whether that was Rudy or other folks."

This was an overt act in furtherance of the conspiracy.

Act 160.

On or about the **1st day of September 2022, CATHLEEN ALSTON LATHAM** committed the felony offense of **PERJURY**, in violation of **O.C.G.A. § 16-10-70(a)**, in Houston County, Georgia, by knowingly, willfully, and unlawfully making at least one of the following false statements in a deposition in the matter of Curling v. Raffensperger, Case 1:17-cv-02989-AT in the United States District Court for the Northern District of Georgia, a judicial proceeding, after having been administered a lawful oath:

1. That she was only present at the Coffee County Board of Elections & Registration Office in Coffee County, Georgia, for "just a few minutes" on January 7, 2021;

2. That she only "walked into the front part" of the Coffee County Board of Elections & Registration Office on January 7, 2021, and "didn't go into the office";

3. That she had "no idea" if employees of SullivanStrickler met Eric Chaney at the Coffee County Board of Elections & Registration Office on January 7, 2021;

4. That she did not see Misty Hampton at the Coffee County Board of Elections & Registration Office on January 7, 2021;

5. That her only interaction with Scott Hall at the Coffee County Board of Elections & Registration Office on January 7, 2021, was meeting him, speaking to him outside of the office, and then leaving the office;

6. That she did not see Scott Hall speak to anyone other than herself at the Coffee County Board of Elections & Registration Office on January 7, 2021;

said statements being material to the accused's own involvement in the January 7, 2021, unlawful breach of election equipment at the Coffee County Board of Elections & Registration Office and to the accused's communications with others involved, the issues in question. This was an act of racketeering activity under O.C.G.A. § 16-14-3(5)(A)(xxv) and an overt act in furtherance of the conspiracy.

Act 161.

On or about the **15th day of September 2022, ROBERT DAVID CHEELEY** committed the felony offense of **PERJURY**, in violation of **O.C.G.A. § 16-10-70(a),** in Fulton County, Georgia, by knowingly, willfully, and unlawfully making at least one of the following false statements before the Fulton County Special Purpose Grand Jury, a judicial proceeding, after having been administered a lawful oath:

1. That he was unaware of the December 14, 2020, meeting of Trump presidential elector nominees in Fulton County, Georgia, until after the meeting had already taken place;

2. That he had no substantive conversations with anyone concerning the December 14, 2020, meeting of Trump presiden-

tial elector nominees in Fulton County, Georgia, until after the meeting had already taken place;

3. That he never suggested to anyone that the Trump presidential elector nominees in Georgia should meet on December 14, 2020;

4. That the only communication he had with John Eastman concerning the November 3, 2020, presidential election was for the purpose of connecting Eastman to Georgia Senator Brandon Beach and unindicted co-conspirator Individual 8, whose identity is known to the Grand Jury, for possible legal representation;

5. That he never worked to connect John Eastman with any Georgia legislators other than Georgia Senator Brandon Beach and unindicted co-conspirator Individual 8, whose identity is known to the Grand Jury;

said statements being material to the accused's own involvement in the December 14, 2020, meeting of Trump presidential elector nominees in Fulton County, Georgia, and to the accused's communications with others involved in the meeting, the issues in question. This was an act of racketeering activity under O.C.G.A. § 16-14-3(5)(A)(xxv) and an overt act in furtherance of the conspiracy.

* * *

The acts set forth above were committed in furtherance of the conspiracy alleged above and had the same and similar intents, results, accomplices, victims, and methods of commission and otherwise were interrelated by distinguishing characteristics and were not isolated acts.

COUNT 2 OF 41

And the Grand Jurors aforesaid, in the name and behalf of the citizens of Georgia, do charge and accuse **RUDOLPH WILLIAM LOUIS GIULIANI, JOHN CHARLES EASTMAN, JENNA LYNN ELLIS,** and **RAY STALLINGS SMITH III** with the offense of **SOLICITATION OF VIOLATION OF OATH BY PUBLIC OFFICER, O.C.G.A. §§ 16-4-7 & 16-10-1,** for the said accused, individually and as persons concerned in the commission of a crime, and together with unindicted co-conspirators, in the County of Fulton and State of Georgia, on the **3rd day of December 2020,** unlawfully solicited, requested, and importuned certain public officers then serving as elected members of the Georgia Senate and present at a Senate Judiciary Subcommittee meeting, including unindicted co-conspirator Individual 8, whose identity is known to the Grand Jury, Senators Lee Anderson, Brandon Beach, Matt Brass, Greg Dolezal, Steve Gooch, Tyler Harper, Bill Heath, Jen Jordan, John F. Kennedy, William Ligon, Elena Parent, Michael Rhett, Carden Summers, and Blake Tillery, to engage in conduct constituting the felony offense of Violation of Oath by Public Officer, O.C.G.A. § 16-10-1, by unlawfully appointing presidential electors from the State of Georgia, in willful and intentional violation of the terms of the oath of said persons as prescribed by law, with intent that said persons engage in said conduct, said date being a material element of the offense, contrary to the laws of said State, the good order, peace and dignity thereof;

COUNT 3 OF 41

And the Grand Jurors aforesaid, in the name and behalf of the citizens of Georgia, do charge and accuse **RUDOLPH WILLIAM LOUIS GIULIANI** with the offense of **FALSE STATEMENTS AND WRITINGS, O.C.G.A. § 16-10-20,** for the said accused, in the County of Fulton and State of Georgia, on or about the **3rd day of December 2020,** knowingly, willfully, and unlawfully made at least one of the following false statements and representations to members of the Georgia Senate present at a Senate Judiciary Subcommittee meeting:

1. That at least 96,600 mail-in ballots were counted in the November 3, 2020, presidential election in Georgia, despite there being no record of those ballots having been returned to a county elections office;

2. That a Dominion Voting Systems machine used in the November 3, 2020, presidential election in Antrim County, Michigan, mistakenly recorded 6,000 votes for Joseph R. Biden when the votes were actually cast for Donald Trump;

said statements being within the jurisdiction of the Office of the Georgia Secretary of State and the Georgia Bureau of Investigation, departments and agencies of state government, and county and city law enforcement agencies, contrary to the laws of said State, the good order, peace and dignity thereof;

COUNT 4 OF 41

And the Grand Jurors aforesaid, in the name and behalf of the citizens of Georgia, do charge and accuse **RAY STALLINGS SMITH III** with the offense of **FALSE STATEMENTS AND WRITINGS, O.C.G.A. § 16-10-20,** for the said accused, in the County of Fulton and State of Georgia, on or about the **3rd day of December 2020,** knowingly, willfully, and unlawfully made at least one of the following false statements and representations to members of the Georgia Senate present at a Senate Judiciary Subcommittee meeting:

1. That 2,506 felons voted illegally in the November 3, 2020, presidential election in Georgia;

2. That 66,248 underage people illegally registered to vote before their seventeenth birthday prior to the November 3, 2020, presidential election in Georgia;

3. That at least 2,423 people voted in the November 3, 2020, presidential election in Georgia who were not listed as registered to vote;

4. That 1,043 people voted in the November 3, 2020, presidential election in Georgia who had illegally registered to vote using a post office box;

5. That 10,315 or more dead people voted in the November 3, 2020, presidential election in Georgia;

6. That Fulton County election workers at State Farm Arena ordered poll watchers and members of the media to leave the tabulation area on the night of November 3, 2020, and continued to operate after ordering everyone to leave;

said statements being within the jurisdiction of the Office of the Georgia Secretary of State and the Georgia Bureau of Investigation, departments and agencies of state government, and county and city law enforcement agencies, contrary to the laws of said State, the good order, peace and dignity thereof;

COUNT 5 OF 41

And the Grand Jurors aforesaid, in the name and behalf of the citizens of Georgia, do charge and accuse **DONALD JOHN TRUMP** with the offense of **SOLICITATION OF VIOLATION OF OATH BY PUBLIC OFFICER, O.C.G.A. §§ 16-4-7 & 16-10-1,** for the said accused, in the County of Fulton and State of Georgia, on or about the **7th day of December 2020,** unlawfully solicited, requested, and importuned Speaker of the Georgia House of Representatives David Ralston, a public officer, to engage in conduct constituting the felony offense of Violation of Oath by Public Officer, O.C.G.A. § 16-10-1, by calling for a special session of the Georgia General Assembly for the purpose of unlawfully appointing presidential electors from the State of Georgia, in willful and intentional violation of the terms of the oath of said person as prescribed by law, with intent that said person engage in said conduct, contrary to the laws of said State, the good order, peace and dignity thereof;

COUNT 6 OF 41

And the Grand Jurors aforesaid, in the name and behalf of the citizens of Georgia, do charge and accuse **RUDOLPH WILLIAM LOUIS GIULIANI** and **RAY STALLINGS SMITH III** with the offense of **SOLICITATION OF VIOLATION OF OATH BY PUBLIC OFFICER, O.C.G.A. §§ 16-4-7 & 16-10-1,** for the said accused, individually and as persons concerned in the commission of a crime, and together with unindicted co-conspirators, in the County of Fulton and State of Georgia, on the **10th day of December 2020,** unlawfully solicited, requested, and importuned certain public officers then serving as elected members of the Georgia House of Representatives and present at a House Governmental Affairs Committee meeting, including Representatives Shaw Blackmon, Jon Burns, Barry Fleming, Todd Jones, Bee Nguyen, Mary Margaret Oliver, Alan Powell, Renitta Shannon, Robert Trammell, Scot Turner, and Bruce Williamson, to engage in conduct constituting the felony offense of Violation of Oath by Public Officer, O.C.G.A. § 16-10-1, by unlawfully appointing presidential electors from the State of Georgia, in willful and intentional violation of the terms of the oath of said persons as prescribed by law, with intent that said persons engage in said conduct, said date being a material element of the offense, contrary to the laws of said State, the good order, peace and dignity thereof;

COUNT 7 OF 41

And the Grand Jurors aforesaid, in the name and behalf of the citizens of Georgia, do charge and accuse **RUDOLPH WILLIAM LOUIS GIULIANI** with the offense of **FALSE STATEMENTS AND WRITINGS, O.C.G.A. § 16-10-20,** for the said accused, in the County of Fulton and State of Georgia, on or about the **10th day of December 2020,** knowingly, willfully, and unlawfully made at least one of the following false statements and representations to members of the Georgia House of Representatives present at a House Governmental Affairs Committee meeting:

1. That it is quite clear from the State Farm Arena video from November 3, 2020, that Fulton County election workers were stealing votes and that Georgia officials were covering up a crime in plain sight;

2. That at State Farm Arena on November 3, 2020, Democratic officials "got rid of all of the reporters, all the observers, anyone that couldn't be trusted," used the excuse of a watermain break, cleared out the voting area and then "went about their dirty, crooked business";

3. That between 12,000 and 24,000 ballots were illegally counted by Fulton County election workers at State Farm Arena on November 3, 2020;

4. That in Michigan, there were 700,000 more ballots counted than were sent out to voters in the November 3, 2020, presidential election, which was accounted for by quadruple counting ballots;

5. That Ruby Freeman, Shaye Moss, and an unidentified man were "quite obviously surreptitiously passing around USB ports as if they're vials of heroin or cocaine" at State Farm Arena to be used to "infiltrate the crooked Dominion voting machines";

6. That 96,600 mail-in ballots were counted in the November 3, 2020, presidential election in Georgia, despite there being no record of those ballots having been returned to a county elections office;

said statements being within the jurisdiction of the Office of the Georgia Secretary of State and the Georgia Bureau of Investigation, departments and agencies of state government, and county and city law enforcement agencies, contrary to the laws of said State, the good order, peace and dignity thereof;

COUNT 8 OF 41

And the Grand Jurors aforesaid, in the name and behalf of the citizens of Georgia, do charge and accuse **DAVID JAMES SHAFER, SHAWN MICAH TRESHER STILL,** and **CATHLEEN ALSTON LATHAM** with the offense of **IMPERSONATING A PUBLIC OFFICER, O.C.G.A. § 16-10-23,** for the said accused, individually and as persons concerned in the commission of a crime, and together with unindicted co-conspirators, in the County of Fulton and State of Georgia, on or about the **14th day of December 2020,** unlawfully falsely held themselves out as the duly elected and qualified presidential electors from the State of Georgia, public officers, with intent to mislead the President of the United States Senate, the Archivist of the United States, the Georgia Secretary of State, and the Chief Judge of the United States District Court for the Northern District of Georgia into believing that they actually were such officers by placing in the United States mail to said persons a document titled "CERTIFICATE OF THE VOTES OF THE 2020 ELECTORS FROM GEORGIA," contrary to the laws of said State, the good order, peace and dignity thereof;

COUNT 9 OF 41

And the Grand Jurors aforesaid, in the name and behalf of the citizens of Georgia, do charge and accuse **DONALD JOHN TRUMP, RUDOLPH WILLIAM LOUIS GIULIANI, JOHN CHARLES EASTMAN, KENNETH JOHN CHESEBRO, RAY STALLINGS SMITH III, ROBERT DAVID CHEELEY,** and **MICHAEL A. ROMAN** with the offense of **CONSPIRACY TO COMMIT IMPERSONATING A PUBLIC OFFICER, O.C.G.A. §§ 16-4-8 & 16-10-23,** for the said accused, individually and as persons concerned in the commission of a crime, and together with indicted and unindicted co-conspirators, in the County of Fulton and State of Georgia, on and between the **6th day of December 2020 and the 14th day of December 2020,** unlawfully conspired to cause certain individuals to falsely hold themselves out as the duly elected and qualified presidential electors from the State of Georgia, public officers, with intent to mislead the President of the United States Senate, the Archivist of the United States, the Georgia Secretary of State, and the Chief Judge of the United States District Court for the Northern District of Georgia into believing that they actually were such officers;

And the Defendants named in Count 8, acting as co-conspirators, as described above and incorporated by reference as if fully set forth herein, falsely held themselves out as said public officers by placing in the United States mail to said persons a document titled "CERTIFICATE OF THE VOTES OF THE 2020 ELECTORS FROM GEORGIA" in Fulton County, Georgia, which was an overt act to effect the object of the conspiracy, contrary to the laws of said State, the good order, peace and dignity thereof;

COUNT 10 OF 41

And the Grand Jurors aforesaid, in the name and behalf of the citizens of Georgia, do charge and accuse **DAVID JAMES SHAFER, SHAWN MICAH TRESHER STILL,** and **CATHLEEN ALSTON LATHAM** with the offense of **FORGERY IN THE FIRST DEGREE, O.C.G.A. § 16-9-1(b),** for the said accused, individually and as persons concerned in the commission of a crime, and together with unindicted co-conspirators, in the County of Fulton and State of Georgia, on or about the **14th day of December 2020,** unlawfully and with the intent to defraud, knowingly made a document titled "CERTIFICATE OF THE VOTES OF THE 2020 ELECTORS FROM GEORGIA," a writing other than a check, in such manner that the writing as made purports to have been made by authority of the duly elected and qualified presidential electors from the State of Georgia, who did not give such authority, and uttered and delivered said document to the Archivist of the United States, contrary to the laws of said State, the good order, peace and dignity thereof;

COUNT 11 OF 41

And the Grand Jurors aforesaid, in the name and behalf of the citizens of Georgia, do charge and accuse **DONALD JOHN TRUMP, RUDOLPH WILLIAM LOUIS GIULIANI, JOHN CHARLES**

EASTMAN, KENNETH JOHN CHESEBRO, RAY STALLINGS SMITH III, ROBERT DAVID CHEELEY, and **MICHAEL A. ROMAN** with the offense of **CONSPIRACY TO COMMIT FORGERY IN THE FIRST DEGREE, O.C.G.A. §§ 16-4-8 & 16-9-1(b),** for the said accused, individually and as persons concerned in the commission of a crime, and together with indicted and unindicted co-conspirators, in the County of Fulton and State of Georgia, on and between the **6th day of December 2020 and the 14th day of December 2020**, unlawfully conspired, with the intent to defraud, to knowingly make a document titled "CERTIFICATE OF THE VOTES OF THE 2020 ELECTORS FROM GEORGIA," a writing other than a check, in such manner that the writing as made purports to have been made by authority of the duly elected and qualified presidential electors from the State of Georgia, who did not give such authority, and to utter and deliver said document to the Archivist of the United States;

And the Defendants named in Count 10, acting as co-conspirators, as described above and incorporated by reference as if fully set forth herein, made said document in Fulton County, Georgia, and uttered and delivered said document to the Archivist of the United States in Fulton County, Georgia, which were overt acts to effect the object of the conspiracy, contrary to the laws of said State, the good order, peace and dignity thereof;

COUNT 12 OF 41

And the Grand Jurors aforesaid, in the name and behalf of the citizens of Georgia, do charge and accuse **DAVID JAMES SHAFER, SHAWN MICAH TRESHER STILL,** and **CATHLEEN ALSTON LATHAM** with the offense of **FALSE STATEMENTS AND WRITINGS, O.C.G.A. § 16-10-20,** for the said accused, individually and as persons concerned in the commission of a crime, and together with unindicted co-

conspirators, in the County of Fulton and State of Georgia, on or about the **14th day of December 2020,** knowingly, willfully, and unlawfully made and used a false document titled "CERTIFICATE OF THE VOTES OF THE 2020 ELECTORS FROM GEORGIA," with knowledge that said document contained the false statement, "WE, THE UNDERSIGNED, being the duly elected and qualified Electors for President and Vice President of the United States of America from the State of Georgia, do hereby certify the following," said document being within the jurisdiction of the Office of the Georgia Secretary of State and the Office of the Governor of Georgia, departments and agencies of state government, contrary to the laws of said State, the good order, peace and dignity thereof;

COUNT 13 OF 41

And the Grand Jurors aforesaid, in the name and behalf of the citizens of Georgia, do charge and accuse **DONALD JOHN TRUMP, RUDOLPH WILLIAM LOUIS GIULIANI, JOHN CHARLES EASTMAN, KENNETH JOHN CHESEBRO, RAY STALLINGS SMITH III, ROBERT DAVID CHEELEY,** and **MICHAEL A. ROMAN** with the offense of **CONSPIRACY TO COMMIT FALSE STATEMENTS AND WRITINGS, O.C.G.A. §§ 16-4-8 & 16-10-20,** for the said accused, individually and as persons concerned in the commission of a crime, and together with indicted and unindicted co-conspirators, in the County of Fulton and State of Georgia, on and between the **6th day of December 2020 and the 14th day of December 2020,** unlawfully conspired to knowingly and willfully make and use a false document titled "CERTIFICATE OF THE VOTES OF THE 2020 ELECTORS FROM GEORGIA," with knowledge that said document contained the false statement, "WE, THE UNDERSIGNED, being the duly elected and qualified Electors for President and Vice President of the United States of America from the State of Georgia, do hereby certify the following," said document being within the jurisdiction of the Office of the Georgia Secretary of State and the Office of the Governor of Georgia, departments and agencies of state government;

And the Defendants named in Count 12, acting as co-conspirators, as described above and incorporated by reference as if fully set forth herein, made and used said document in Fulton County, Georgia, which were overt acts to effect the object of the conspiracy, contrary to the laws of said State, the good order, peace and dignity thereof;

COUNT 14 OF 41

And the Grand Jurors aforesaid, in the name and behalf of the citizens of Georgia, do charge and accuse **DAVID JAMES SHAFER, SHAWN MICAH TRESHER STILL,** and **CATHLEEN ALSTON LATHAM** with the offense of **CRIMINAL ATTEMPT TO COMMIT FILING FALSE DOCUMENTS, O.C.G.A. §§ 16-4-1 & 16-10-20.1(b)(1),** for the said accused, individually and as persons concerned in the commission of a crime, and together with unindicted co-conspirators, in the County of Fulton and State of Georgia, on or about the **14th day of December 2020,** unlawfully, with intent to commit the crime of Filing False Documents, O.C.G.A. § 16-10-20.1(b)(1), placed in the United States mail a document titled "CERTIFICATE OF THE VOTES OF THE 2020 ELECTORS FROM GEORGIA," addressed to Chief Judge, U.S. District Court, Northern District of Georgia, 2188 Richard D. Russell Federal Office Building and U.S. Courthouse, 75 Ted Turner Drive, SW, Atlanta, GA 30303, a substantial step toward the commission of Filing False Documents, O.C.G.A. § 16-10-20.1(b)(1), with intent to knowingly file, enter, and record said document in a court of the United States, having reason to know that said document contained the materially false statement, "WE, THE UNDERSIGNED, being the duly elected and qualified Electors for President and Vice President of the United States of

America from the State of Georgia, do hereby certify the following," contrary to the laws of said State, the good order, peace and dignity thereof;

COUNT 15 OF 41

And the Grand Jurors aforesaid, in the name and behalf of the citizens of Georgia, do charge and accuse **DONALD JOHN TRUMP, RUDOLPH WILLIAM LOUIS GIULIANI, JOHN CHARLES EASTMAN, KENNETH JOHN CHESEBRO, RAY STALLINGS SMITH III, ROBERT DAVID CHEELEY,** and **MICHAEL A. ROMAN** with the offense of **CONSPIRACY TO COMMIT FILING FALSE DOCUMENTS, O.C.G.A. §§ 16-4-8 & 16-10-20.1(b)(1),** for the said accused, individually and as persons concerned in the commission of a crime, and together with indicted and unindicted co-conspirators, in the County of Fulton and State of Georgia, on and between the **6th day of December 2020 and the 14th day of December 2020,** unlawfully conspired to knowingly file, enter, and record a document titled "CERTIFICATE OF THE VOTES OF THE 2020 ELECTORS FROM GEORGIA," in a court of the United States, having reason to know that said document contained the materially false statement, "WE, THE UNDERSIGNED, being the duly elected and qualified Electors for President and Vice President of the United States of America from the State of Georgia, do hereby certify the following";

And the Defendants named in Count 14, acting as co-conspirators, as described above and incorporated by reference as if fully set forth herein, placed in the United States mail said document, addressed to Chief Judge, U.S. District Court, Northern District of Georgia, 2188 Richard D. Russell Federal Office Building and U.S. Courthouse, 75 Ted Turner Drive, SW, Atlanta, GA 30303, in Fulton County, Georgia, which was an overt act to effect the object of the conspiracy, contrary to the laws of said State, the good order, peace and dignity thereof;

COUNT 16 OF 41

And the Grand Jurors aforesaid, in the name and behalf of the citizens of Georgia, do charge and accuse **DAVID JAMES SHAFER** and **SHAWN MICAH TRESHER STILL** with the offense of **FORGERY IN THE FIRST DEGREE, O.C.G.A. § 16-9-1(b),** for the said accused, individually and as persons concerned in the commission of a crime, and together with unindicted co-conspirators, in the County of Fulton and State of Georgia, on or about the **14th day of December 2020,** unlawfully and with the intent to defraud, knowingly made a document titled "RE: Notice of Filling of Electoral College Vacancy," a writing other than a check, in such manner that the writing as made purports to have been made by the authority of the duly elected and qualified presidential electors from the State of Georgia, who did not give such authority, and uttered and delivered said document to the Archivist of the United States and the Office of the Governor of Georgia, contrary to the laws of said State, the good order, peace and dignity thereof;

COUNT 17 OF 41

And the Grand Jurors aforesaid, in the name and behalf of the citizens of Georgia, do charge and accuse **DONALD JOHN TRUMP, RUDOLPH WILLIAM LOUIS GIULIANI, JOHN CHARLES EASTMAN, KENNETH JOHN CHESEBRO, RAY STALLINGS SMITH III, ROBERT DAVID CHEELEY,** and **MICHAEL A. ROMAN** with the offense of **CONSPIRACY TO COMMIT FORGERY IN THE FIRST DEGREE, O.C.G.A. §§ 16-4-8 & 16-9-1(b),** for the said accused, individually and as persons concerned in the commission of a crime, and together with indicted and unindicted co-conspirators, in the County of Fulton and State of Georgia, on and between the **6th day of December 2020 and the 14th day of December 2020,** unlawfully conspired, with the intent to defraud, to knowingly make a document titled "RE: Notice of Filling of Electoral College Vacancy," a writing other than a check, in such manner that the writing as made purports to have been made by the authority of the duly elected and qualified presidential electors from the State of Georgia, who did not give such authority, and to utter and deliver said document to the Archivist of the United States and the Office of the Governor of Georgia;

And the Defendants named in Count 16, acting as co-conspirators, as described above and incorporated by reference as if fully set forth herein, made said document in Fulton County, Georgia, and uttered and delivered said document to the Archivist of the United States and the Office of the Governor of Georgia in Fulton County, Georgia, which were overt acts to effect the object of the conspiracy, contrary to the laws of said State, the good order, peace and dignity thereof;

COUNT 18 OF 41

And the Grand Jurors aforesaid, in the name and behalf of the citizens of Georgia, do charge and accuse **DAVID JAMES SHAFER** and **SHAWN MICAH TRESHER STILL** with the offense of **FALSE STATEMENTS AND WRITINGS, O.C.G.A. § 16-10-20,** for the said accused, individually and as persons concerned in the commission of a crime, and together with unindicted co-conspirators, in the County of Fulton and State of Georgia, on or about the **14th day of December 2020,** knowingly, willfully, and unlawfully made and used a false document titled "RE: Notice of Filling of Electoral College Vacancy," with knowledge that said document contained the false statements that **DAVID JAMES SHAFER** was Chairman of the 2020 Georgia Electoral College Meeting and **SHAWN MICAH TRESHER STILL** was Secretary of the 2020 Georgia Electoral College Meeting, said document being within the jurisdiction of the Office of the Georgia Secretary of State and the Office of the Governor of Georgia, departments and agencies of state government, contrary to the laws of said State, the good order, peace and dignity thereof;

COUNT 19 OF 41

And the Grand Jurors aforesaid, in the name and behalf of the citizens of Georgia, do charge and accuse **DONALD JOHN TRUMP, RUDOLPH WILLIAM LOUIS GIULIANI, JOHN CHARLES EASTMAN, KENNETH JOHN CHESEBRO, RAY STALLINGS SMITH III, ROBERT DAVID CHEELEY** and **MICHAEL A. ROMAN** with the offense of **CONSPIRACY TO COMMIT FALSE STATEMENTS AND WRITINGS, O.C.G.A. §§ 16-4-8 & 16-10-20,** for the said accused, individually and as persons concerned in the commission of a crime, and together with indicted and unindicted co-conspirators, in the County of Fulton and State of Georgia, on and between the **6th day of December 2020 and the 14th day of December 2020,** unlawfully conspired to knowingly and willfully make and use a false document titled "RE: Notice of Filling of Electoral College Vacancy," with knowledge that said document contained the false statements that **DAVID JAMES SHAFER** was Chairman of the 2020 Georgia Electoral College Meeting and **SHAWN MICAH TRESHER STILL** was Secretary of the 2020 Georgia Electoral College Meeting, said document being within the jurisdiction of the Office of the Georgia Secretary of State and the Office of the Governor of Georgia, departments and agencies of state government;

And the Defendants named in Count 18, acting as co-conspirators, as described above and incorporated by reference as if fully set forth herein, made and used said document in Fulton County, Georgia, which were overt acts to effect the object of the conspiracy, contrary to the laws of said State, the good order, peace and dignity thereof;

COUNT 20 OF 41

And the Grand Jurors aforesaid, in the name and behalf of the citizens of Georgia, do charge and accuse **STEPHEN CLIFFGARD LEE** with the offense of **CRIMINAL ATTEMPT TO COMMIT INFLUENCING WITNESSES, O.C.G.A. §§ 16-4-1 & 16-10-93(b)(1)(A),** for the said accused, in the County of Fulton and State of Georgia, on the **14th day of December 2020,** unlawfully, with intent to commit the crime of Influencing Witnesses, O.C.G.A. § 16-10-93(b)(1)(A), traveled to the home of Ruby Freeman, a Fulton County, Georgia, election worker, and spoke to her neighbor, a substantial step toward the commission of Influencing Witnesses, O.C.G.A. § 16-10-93(b)(1)(A), with intent to knowingly engage in misleading conduct toward Ruby Freeman, by purporting to offer her help, and with intent to influence her testimony in an official proceeding in Fulton County, Georgia, concerning events at State Farm Arena in the November 3, 2020, presidential election in Georgia, said date being a material element of the offense, contrary to the laws of said State, the good order, peace and dignity thereof;

COUNT 21 OF 41

And the Grand Jurors aforesaid, in the name and behalf of the citizens of Georgia, do charge and accuse **STEPHEN CLIFFGARD LEE** with the offense of **CRIMINAL ATTEMPT TO COMMIT INFLUENCING WITNESSES, O.C.G.A. §§ 16-4-1 & 16-10-93(b)(1)(A),** for the said accused, in the County of Fulton and State of Georgia, on the **15th day of December 2020,** unlawfully, with intent to commit the crime of Influencing Witnesses, O.C.G.A. § 16-10-93(b)(1)(A), traveled to the home of Ruby Freeman, a Fulton County, Georgia, election worker, and knocked on her door, a substantial step toward the commission of Influencing Witnesses, O.D.G.A. § 16-10-93(b)(1)(A), with intent to knowingly engage in misleading conduct toward Ruby Freeman, by purporting to offer her help, and with intent to influence her testimony in an official proceeding in Fulton County, Georgia, concerning events at State Farm Arena in the November 3, 2020, presidential election in Georgia, said date being a material element of the offense, contrary to the laws of said State, the good order, peace and dignity thereof;

COUNT 22 OF 41

And the Grand Jurors aforesaid, in the name and behalf of the citizens of Georgia, do charge and accuse **JEFFREY BOSSERT CLARK** with the offense of **CRIMINAL ATTEMPT TO COMMIT FALSE STATEMENTS AND WRITINGS, O.C.G.A. §§ 16-4-1 & 16-10-20,** for the said accused, individually and as a person concerned in the commission of a crime, and together with unindicted co-conspirators, in the County of Fulton and State of Georgia, on and between the **28th day of December 2020 and the 2nd day of January 2021,** unlawfully, with intent to commit the crime of False Statements and Writings, O.C.G.A. § 16-10-20, knowingly and willfully made a false writing and document knowing the same to contain the false statement that the United States Department of Justice had "identified significant concerns that may have impacted the outcome of the election in multiple States, including the State of Georgia," said statement being within the jurisdiction of the Office of the Georgia Secretary of State and the Georgia Bureau of Investigation, departments and agencies of state government, and county and city law enforcement agencies;

And, on or about the **28th day of December 2020,** the said accused sent an e-mail to Acting United States Attorney General Jeffrey Rosen and Acting United States Deputy Attorney General Richard Donoghue and requested authorization to send said false writing and document to Georgia Governor Brian Kemp, Speaker of the Georgia House of Representatives David Ralston, and President Pro Tempore of the Georgia Senate Butch Miller;

And, on or about the **2nd day of January 2021,** the said accused met with Acting United States Attorney General Jeffrey Rosen and Acting United States Deputy Attorney General Richard Donoghue and requested authorization to send said false writing and document to Georgia Governor Brian Kemp, Speaker of the Georgia House of Representatives David Ralston, and President Pro Tempore of the Georgia Senate Butch Miller;

And said acts constituted substantial steps toward the commission of False Statements and Writings, O.C.G.A. § 16-10-20, and said conduct committed outside the state of Georgia constituted an attempt to commit a crime within the state of Georgia, pursuant to O.C.G.A. § 17-2-1(b)(2), contrary to the laws of said State, the good order, peace and dignity thereof;

COUNT 23 OF 41

And the Grand Jurors aforesaid, in the name and behalf of the citizens of Georgia, do charge and accuse **RUDOLPH WILLIAM LOUIS GIULIANI, RAY STALLINGS SMITH III,** and **ROBERT DAVID CHEELEY** with the offense of **SOLICITATION OF VIOLATION OF OATH BY PUBLIC OFFICER, O.C.G.A. §§ 16-4-7 & 16-10-1,** for the said accused, individually and as persons concerned in the commission of a crime, and together with unindicted co-conspirators, in the County of Fulton and State of Georgia, on the **30th day of December 2020,** unlawfully solicited, requested, and importuned certain public officers then serving as elected members of the Georgia Senate and present at a Senate Judiciary Subcommittee meeting, including unindicted co-conspirator Individual 8, whose identity is known to the Grand Jury, Senators Brandon Beach, Bill Heath, William Ligon, Michael Rhett, and Blake Tillery, to engage in conduct constituting the felony offense of Violation of Oath by Public Officer, O.C.G.A. § 16-10-1, by unlawfully appointing presidential electors from the State of Georgia, in willful and intentional violation of the terms of the oath of said persons as prescribed by law, with intent that said persons engage in said conduct, said date being a material element of the offense, contrary to the laws of said State, the good order, peace and dignity thereof;

COUNT 24 OF 41

And the Grand Jurors aforesaid, in the name and behalf of the citizens of Georgia, do charge and accuse **RUDOLPH WILLIAM LOUIS GIULIANI** with the offense of **FALSE STATEMENTS AND WRITINGS, O.C.G.A. § 16-10-20,** for the said accused, in the County of Fulton and State of Georgia, on or about the **30th day of December 2020,** knowingly, willfully, and unlawfully made at least one of the following false statements and representations to members of the Georgia Senate present at a Senate Judiciary Subcommittee meeting:

1. That Fulton County election workers fraudulently counted certain ballots as many as five times at State Farm Arena on November 3, 2020;

2. That 2,560 felons voted illegally in the November 3, 2020, presidential election in Georgia;

3. That 10,315 dead people voted in the November 3, 2020, presidential election in Georgia;

said statements being within the jurisdiction of the Office of the Georgia Secretary of State and the Georgia Bureau of Investigation, departments and agencies of state government, and county and city law enforcement agencies, contrary to the laws of said State, the good order, peace and dignity thereof;

COUNT 25 OF 41

And the Grand Jurors aforesaid, in the name and behalf of the citizens of Georgia, do charge and accuse **RAY STALLINGS SMITH III** with the offense of **FALSE STATEMENTS AND WRITINGS, O.C.G.A. § 16-10-20,** for the said accused, in the County of Fulton and State of Georgia, on or about the **30th day of December 2020,** knowingly, willfully, and unlawfully made at least one of the following false statements and representations to members of the Georgia Senate present at a Senate Judiciary Subcommittee meeting:

1. That Georgia Secretary of State General Counsel Ryan Germany stated that his office had sent letters to 8,000 people who voted illegally in the November 3, 2020, presidential election and told them not to vote in the January 5, 2021, runoff election;

2. That the Georgia Secretary of State admitted "that they had a 90% accuracy rate" in the November 3, 2020, presidential election and that "there's still a 10% margin that's not accurate";

said statements being within the jurisdiction of the Office of the Georgia Secretary of State and the Georgia Bureau of Investigation, departments and agencies of state government, and county and city law enforcement agencies, contrary to the laws of said State, the good order, peace and dignity thereof;

COUNT 26 OF 41

And the Grand Jurors aforesaid, in the name and behalf of the citizens of Georgia, do charge and accuse **ROBERT DAVID CHEELEY** with the offense of **FALSE STATEMENTS AND WRITINGS, O.C.G.A. § 16-10-20,** for the said accused, in the County of Fulton and State of Georgia, on or about the **30th day of December 2020,** knowingly, willfully, and unlawfully made at least one of the following false statements and representations to members of the Georgia Senate present at a Senate Judiciary Subcommittee meeting:

1. That poll watchers and media at State Farm Arena were told late in the evening of November 3, 2020, that the vote count was being suspended until the next morning and to go home because of "a major watermain break";

2. That Fulton County election workers at State Farm Arena "voted" the same ballots "over and over again" on November 3, 2020;

said statements being within the jurisdiction of the Office of the Georgia Secretary of State and the Georgia Bureau of Investigation, departments and agencies of state government, and county and city law enforcement agencies, contrary to the laws of said State, the good order, peace and dignity thereof;

COUNT 27 OF 41

And the Grand Jurors aforesaid, in the name and behalf of the citizens of Georgia, do charge and accuse **DONALD JOHN TRUMP** and **JOHN CHARLES EASTMAN** with the offense of **FILING FALSE**

DOCUMENTS, O.C.G.A. § 16-10-20.1(b)(1), for the said accused, individually and as persons concerned in the commission of a crime, and together with unindicted co-conspirators, in the County of Fulton and State of Georgia, on or about the **31st day of December 2020,** knowingly and unlawfully filed a document titled "VERIFIED COMPLAINT FOR EMERGENCY INJUNCTIVE AND DECLARATORY RELIEF" in the matter of Trump v. Kemp, Case 1:20-cv-05310-MHC, in the United States District Court for the Northern District of Georgia, a court of the United States, having reason to know that said document contained at least one of the following materially false statements:

1. That "as many as 2,506 felons with an uncompleted sentence" voted illegally in the November 3, 2020, presidential election in Georgia;

2. That "at least 66,247 underage" people voted illegally in the November 3, 2020, presidential election in Georgia;

3. That "at least 2,423 individuals" voted illegally in the November 3, 2020, presidential election in Georgia "who were not listed in the State's records as having been registered to vote";

4. That "at least 1,043 individuals" voted illegally in the November 3, 2020, presidential election "who had illegally registered to vote using a postal office box as their habitation";

5. That "as many as 10,315 or more" dead people voted in the November 3, 2020, presidential election in Georgia;

6. That "[d]eliberate misinformation was used to instruct Republican poll watchers and members of the press to leave the prem-

ises for the night at approximately 10:00 p.m. on November 3, 2020" at State Farm Arena in Fulton County, Georgia;

contrary to the laws of said State, the good order, peace and dignity thereof;

COUNT 28 OF 41

And the Grand Jurors aforesaid, in the name and behalf of the citizens of Georgia, do charge and accuse **DONALD JOHN TRUMP** and **MARK RANDALL MEADOWS** with the offense of **SOLICITATION OF VIOLATION OF OATH BY PUBLIC OFFICER, O.C.G.A. §§ 16-4-7 & 16-10-1,** for the said accused, individually and as persons concerned in the commission of a crime, and together with unindicted co-conspirators, in the County of Fulton and State of Georgia, on or about the **2nd day of January 2021,** unlawfully solicited, requested, and importuned Georgia Secretary of State Brad Raffensperger, a public officer, to engage in conduct constituting the felony offense of Violation of Oath by Public Officer, O.C.G.A. § 16-10-1, by unlawfully altering, unlawfully adjusting, and otherwise unlawfully influencing the certified returns for presidential electors for the November 3, 2020, presidential election in Georgia, in willful and intentional violation of the terms of the oath of said person as prescribed by law, with intent that said person engage in said conduct, contrary to the laws of said State, the good order, peace and dignity thereof;

COUNT 29 OF 41

And the Grand Jurors aforesaid, in the name and behalf of the citizens of Georgia, do charge and accuse **DONALD JOHN TRUMP** with the offense of **FALSE STATEMENTS AND WRITINGS, O.C.G.A. § 16-10-20,** for the said accused, in the County of Fulton and State of

Georgia, on or about the **2nd day of January 2021,** knowingly, willfully, and unlawfully made at least one of the following false statements and representations to Georgia Secretary of State Brad Raffensperger, Georgia Deputy Secretary of State Jordan Fuchs, and Georgia Secretary of State General Counsel Ryan Germany:

1. That anywhere from 250,000 to 300,000 ballots were dropped mysteriously into the rolls in the November 3, 2020, presidential election in Georgia;

2. That thousands of people attempted to vote in the November 3, 2020, presidential election in Georgia and were told they could not because a ballot had already been cast in their name;

3. That 4,502 people voted in the November 3, 2020, presidential election in Georgia who were not on the voter registration list;

4. That 904 people voted in the November 3, 2020, presidential election in Georgia who were registered at an address that was a post office box;

5. That Ruby Freeman was a professional vote scammer and a known political operative;

6. That Ruby Freeman, her daughter, and others were responsible for fraudulently awarding at least 18,000 ballots to Joseph R. Biden at State Farm Arena in the November 3, 2020, presidential election in Georgia;

7. That close to 5,000 dead people voted in the November 3, 2020, presidential election in Georgia;

8. That 139% of people voted in the November 3, 2020, presidential election in Detroit;

9. That 200,000 more votes were recorded than the number of people who voted in the November 3, 2020, presidential election in Pennsylvania;

10. That thousands of dead people voted in the November 3, 2020, presidential election in Michigan;

11. That Ruby Freeman stuffed the ballot boxes;

12. That hundreds of thousands of ballots had been "dumped" into Fulton County and another county adjacent to Fulton County in the November 3, 2020, presidential election in Georgia;

13. That he won the November 3, 2020, presidential election in Georgia by 400,000 votes;

said statements being within the jurisdiction of the Office of the Georgia Secretary of State and the Georgia Bureau of Investigation, departments and agencies of state government, contrary to the laws of said State, the good order, peace and dignity thereof;

COUNT 30 OF 41

And the Grand Jurors aforesaid, in the name and behalf of the citizens of Georgia, do charge and accuse **STEPHEN CLIFFGARD LEE, HARRISON WILLIAM PRESCOTT FLOYD,** and **TREVIAN C. KUTTI** with the offense of **CONSPIRACY TO COMMIT SOLICITATION OF FALSE STATEMENTS AND WRITINGS, O.C.G.A.**

§§ 16-4-8, 16-4-7, & 16-10-20, for the said accused, individually and as persons concerned in the commission of a crime, and together with unindicted co-conspirators, in the County of Fulton and State of Georgia, on or about the **4th day of January 2021,** unlawfully conspired to solicit, request, and importune Ruby Freeman, a Fulton County, Georgia, election worker, to engage in conduct constituting the felony offense of False Statements and Writings, O.C.G.A. § 16-10-20, by knowingly and willfully making a false statement and representation concerning events at State Farm Arena in the November 3, 2020, presidential election in Georgia, said statement and representation being within the jurisdiction of the Office of the Georgia Secretary of State and the Georgia Bureau of Investigation, departments and agencies of state government, and county and city law enforcement agencies, with intent that said person engage in said conduct; and **TREVIAN C. KUTTI** traveled to Fulton County, Georgia, and placed a telephone call to Ruby Freeman while in Fulton County, Georgia, which were overt acts to effect the object of the conspiracy, contrary to the laws of said State, the good order, peace and dignity thereof;

COUNT 31 OF 41

And the Grand Jurors aforesaid, in the name and behalf of the citizens of Georgia, do charge and accuse **STEPHEN CLIFFGARD LEE, HARRISON WILLIAM PRESCOTT FLOYD** and **TREVIAN C. KUTTI** with the offense of **INFLUENCING WITNESSES, O.C.G.A. § 16-10-93(b)(1)(A),** for the said accused, individually and as persons concerned in the commission of a crime, and together with unindicted co-conspirators, in the County of Fulton and State of Georgia, on or about the **4th day of January 2021,** knowingly and unlawfully engaged in misleading conduct toward Ruby Freeman, a Fulton County, Georgia, election worker, by stating that she needed protection and by purporting to offer her help, with intent to influence her testimony in an official proceeding in Fulton County, Georgia, concerning events at State Farm Arena in the November 3, 2020, presidential election in Georgia, contrary to the laws of said State, the good order, peace and dignity thereof;

COUNT 32 OF 41

And the Grand Jurors aforesaid, in the name and behalf of the citizens of Georgia, do charge and accuse **SIDNEY KATHERINE POWELL, CATHLEEN ALSTON LATHAM, SCOTT GRAHAM HALL,** and **MISTY HAMPTON** with the offense of **CONSPIRACY TO COMMIT ELECTION FRAUD, O.C.G.A. §§ 21-2-603 & 21-2-566,** for the said accused, individually and as persons concerned in the commission of a crime, and together with unindicted co-conspirators, in the County of Fulton and State of Georgia, on and between the **1st day of December 2020 and the 7th day of January 2021,** unlawfully conspired and agreed to willfully tamper with electronic ballot markers and tabulating machines in the State of Georgia;

And **SIDNEY KATHERINE POWELL** entered into a contract with SullivanStrickler LLC in Fulton County, Georgia, delivered a payment to SullivanStrickler LLC in Fulton County, Georgia, and caused employees of SullivanStrickler LLC to travel from Fulton County, Georgia, to Coffee County, Georgia, for the purpose of willfully tampering with said electronic ballot markers and tabulating machines, which were overt acts to effect the object of the conspiracy;

And **CATHLEEN ALSTON LATHAM, SCOTT GRAHAM HALL,** and **MISTY HAMPTON** aided, abetted, and encouraged employees of SullivanStrickler LLC in willfully tampering with electronic ballot markers and tabulating machines while inside the Coffee County Elections & Registration Office in Coffee County, Georgia, which were overt acts to effect the object of the conspiracy, contrary to the laws of said State, the good order, peace and dignity thereof;

COUNT 33 OF 41

And the Grand Jurors aforesaid, in the name and behalf of the citizens of Georgia, do charge and accuse **SIDNEY KATHERINE POWELL, CATHLEEN ALSTON LATHAM, SCOTT GRAHAM HALL,** and **MISTY HAMPTON** with the offense of **CONSPIRACY TO COMMIT ELECTION FRAUD, O.C.G.A. §§ 21-2-603 & 21-2-574,** for the said accused, individually and as persons concerned in the commission of a crime, and together with unindicted co-conspirators, in the County of Fulton and State of Georgia, on and between the **1st day of December 2020 and the 7th day of January 2021,** unlawfully conspired and agreed to cause certain members of the conspiracy, who were not officers charged by law with the care of ballots and who were not persons entrusted by any such officer with the care of ballots for a purpose required by law, to possess official ballots outside of the polling place in the State of Georgia;

And **SIDNEY KATHERINE POWELL** entered into a contract with SullivanStrickler LLC in Fulton County, Georgia, delivered a payment to SullivanStrickler LLC in Fulton County, Georgia, and caused employees of SullivanStrickler LLC to travel from Fulton County, Georgia, to Coffee County, Georgia, for the purpose of causing certain members of the conspiracy, who were not officers charged by law with the care of ballots and who were not persons entrusted by any such officer with the care of ballots for a purpose required by law, to possess official ballots outside of the polling place, which were overt acts to effect the object of the conspiracy;

And **CATHLEEN ALSTON LATHAM, SCOTT GRAHAM HALL,** and **MISTY HAMPTON** aided, abetted, and encouraged employees of SullivanStrickler LLC in accessing election equipment while inside the Coffee County Elections & Registration Office in Coffee County, Georgia, for the purpose of causing certain members of the conspiracy, who were not officers charged by law with the care of ballots and who were not persons entrusted by any such officer with the care of ballots for a purpose required by law, to possess official ballots outside of the polling place, which were overt acts to effect the object of the conspiracy, contrary to the laws of said State, the good order, peace and dignity thereof;

COUNT 34 OF 41

And the Grand Jurors aforesaid, in the name and behalf of the citizens of Georgia, do charge and accuse **SIDNEY KATHERINE POWELL, CATHLEEN ALSTON LATHAM, SCOTT GRAHAM HALL,** and **MISTY HAMPTON** with the offense of **CONSPIRACY TO COMMIT COMPUTER THEFT, O.C.G.A. §§ 16-4-8 & 16-9-93(a),** for the said accused, individually and as persons concerned in the commission of a crime, and together with unindicted co-conspirators, in the County of Fulton and State of Georgia, on and between the **1st day of December 2020 and the 7th day of January 2021,** unlawfully conspired to use a computer with knowledge that such use was without authority and with the intention of taking and appropriating information, data, and software, the property of Dominion Voting Systems Corporation,

And **SIDNEY KATHERINE POWELL** entered into a contract with SullivanStrickler LLC in Fulton County, Georgia, delivered a payment to SullivanStrickler LLC in Fulton County, Georgia, and caused employees of SullivanStrickler LLC to travel from Fulton County, Georgia, to Coffee County, Georgia, for the purpose of using a computer with knowledge that such use was without authority and with the intention of taking and appropriating information, data, and software, the property of Dominion Voting Systems Corporation, which were overt acts to effect the object of the conspiracy;

And **CATHLEEN ALSTON LATHAM, SCOTT GRAHAM HALL,** and **MISTY HAMPTON** aided, abetted, and encouraged employees of SullivanStrickler LLC in using a computer with knowledge that such use was without authority and with the intention of taking and appropriating information, data, and software, the property of Dominion Voting Systems Corporation, while inside the Coffee County Elections & Registration Office in Coffee County, Georgia, which were overt acts to effect the object of the conspiracy, contrary to the laws of said State, the good order, peace and dignity thereof;

COUNT 35 OF 41

And the Grand Jurors aforesaid, in the name and behalf of the citizens of Georgia, do charge and accuse **SIDNEY KATHERINE POWELL, CATHLEEN ALSTON LATHAM, SCOTT GRAHAM HALL,** and **MISTY HAMPTON** with the offense of **CONSPIRACY TO COMMIT COMPUTER TRESPASS, O.C.G.A. §§ 16-4-8 & 16-9-93(b),** for the said accused, individually and as persons concerned in the commission of a crime, and together with unindicted co-conspirators, in the County of Fulton and State of Georgia, on and between the **1st day of December 2020 and the 7th day of January 2021,** unlawfully conspired to use a computer with knowledge that such use was without authority and with the intention of removing voter data and Dominion Voting Systems Corporation data from said computer;

And **SIDNEY KATHERINE POWELL** entered into a contract with SullivanStrickler LLC in Fulton County, Georgia, delivered a payment to SullivanStrickler LLC in Fulton County, Georgia, and caused employees of SullivanStrickler LLC to travel from Fulton County, Georgia, to Coffee County, Georgia, for the purpose of using a computer with knowledge that such use was without authority and with the intention of removing voter data and Dominion Voting Systems Corporation data from said computer, which were overt acts to effect the object of the conspiracy;

And **CATHLEEN ALSTON LATHAM, SCOTT GRAHAM HALL,** and **MISTY HAMPTON** aided, abetted, and encouraged employees of SullivanStrickler LLC in using a computer with knowledge that such use was without authority and with the intention of removing voter data and Dominion Voting Systems Corporation data from said computer, while inside the Coffee County Elections & Registration Office in Coffee County, Georgia, which were overt acts to effect the object of the conspiracy, contrary to the laws of said State, the good order, peace and dignity thereof;

COUNT 36 OF 41

And the Grand Jurors aforesaid, in the name and behalf of the citizens of Georgia, do charge and accuse **SIDNEY KATHERINE POWELL, CATHLEEN ALSTON LATHAM, SCOTT GRAHAM HALL,** and **MISTY HAMPTON** with the offense of **CONSPIRACY TO COMMIT COMPUTER INVASION OF PRIVACY, O.C.G.A. §§ 16-4-8 & 16-9-93(c),** for the said accused, individually and as persons concerned in the commission of a crime, and together with unindicted co-conspirators, in the County of Fulton and State of Georgia, on and between the **1st day of December 2020 and the 7th day of January 2021,** unlawfully conspired to use a computer with the intention of examining personal voter data with knowledge that such examination was without authority;

And **SIDNEY KATHERINE POWELL** entered into a contract with SullivanStrickler LLC in Fulton County, Georgia, delivered a payment to SullivanStrickler LLC in Fulton County, Georgia, and caused employees of SullivanStrickler LLC to travel from Fulton County, Georgia, to Coffee County, Georgia, for the purpose of using a computer with the intention of examining personal voter data with knowledge that such examination was without authority, which were overt acts to effect the object of the conspiracy;

And **CATHLEEN ALSTON LATHAM, SCOTT GRAHAM HALL,** and **MISTY HAMPTON** aided, abetted, and encouraged employees of SullivanStrickler LLC in using a computer with the intention of examining personal voter data with knowledge that such examination was without authority, while inside the Coffee County Elections & Registration Office in Coffee County, Georgia, which were overt acts to effect the object of the conspiracy, contrary to the laws of said State, the good order, peace and dignity thereof;

COUNT 37 OF 41

And the Grand Jurors aforesaid, in the name and behalf of the citizens of Georgia, do charge and accuse **SIDNEY KATHERINE POWELL, CATHLEEN ALSTON LATHAM, SCOTT GRAHAM HALL,** and **MISTY HAMPTON** with the offense of **CONSPIRACY TO DEFRAUD THE STATE, O.C.G.A. § 16-10-21,** for the said accused, individually and as persons concerned in the commission of a crime, and together with unindicted co-conspirators, in the County of Fulton and State of Georgia, on and between the **1st day of December 2020 and the 7th day of January 2021,** unlawfully conspired and agreed to commit theft of voter data, property which was under the control of Georgia Secretary of State Brad Raffensperger, a state officer, in his official capacity;

And **SIDNEY KATHERINE POWELL** entered into a contract with SullivanStrickler LLC in Fulton County, Georgia, delivered a payment to SullivanStrickler LLC in Fulton County, Georgia, and caused employees of SullivanStrickler LLC to travel from Fulton County, Georgia, to Coffee County, Georgia, for the purpose of committing theft of voter data, property which was under the control of Georgia Secretary of State Brad Raffensperger, a state officer, in his official capacity, which were overt acts to effect the object of the conspiracy;

And **CATHLEEN ALSTON LATHAM, SCOTT GRAHAM HALL,** and **MISTY HAMPTON** aided, abetted, and encouraged employees of SullivanStrickler LLC in accessing election equipment while inside the Coffee County Elections & Registration Office in Douglas, Georgia, for the purpose of committing theft of voter data, property which was under the control of Georgia Secretary of State Brad Raffensperger, a state officer, in his official capacity, which were overt acts to effect the object of the conspiracy, contrary to the laws of said State, the good order, peace and dignity thereof;

COUNT 38 OF 41

And the Grand Jurors aforesaid, in the name and behalf of the citizens of Georgia, do charge and accuse **DONALD JOHN TRUMP** with the offense of **SOLICITATION OF VIOLATION OF OATH BY PUBLIC OFFICER, O.C.G.A. §§ 16-4-7 and 16-10-1,** for the said accused, in the County of Fulton and State of Georgia, on or about the **17th day of September 2021,** unlawfully solicited, requested, and importuned Georgia Secretary of State Brad Raffensperger, a public officer, to engage in conduct constituting the felony offense of Violation of Oath by Public Officer, O.C.G.A. § 16-10-1, by unlawfully "decertifying the Election, or whatever the correct legal remedy is, and announce the true winner," in willful and intentional violation of the terms of the oath of said person as prescribed by law, with intent that said person engage in said conduct, contrary to the laws of said State, the good order, peace and dignity thereof;

COUNT 39 OF 41

And the Grand Jurors aforesaid, in the name and behalf of the citizens of Georgia, do charge and accuse **DONALD JOHN TRUMP** with the offense of **FALSE STATEMENTS AND WRITINGS, O.C.G.A.**

§ 16-10-20, for the said accused, in the County of Fulton and State of Georgia, on or about the **17th day of September 2021,** knowingly, willfully, and unlawfully made the following false statement and representation to Georgia Secretary of State Brad Raffensperger:

1. "As stated to you previously, the number of false and/or irregular votes is far greater than needed to change the Georgia election result";

said statement being within the jurisdiction of the Office of the Georgia Secretary of State and the Georgia Bureau of Investigation, departments and agencies of state government, and county and city law enforcement agencies, contrary to the laws of said State, the good order, peace and dignity thereof;

COUNT 40 OF 41

And the Grand Jurors aforesaid, in the name and behalf of the citizens of Georgia, do charge and accuse **DAVID JAMES SHAFER** with the offense of **FALSE STATEMENTS AND WRITINGS, O.C.G.A. § 16-10-20,** for the said accused, in the County of Fulton and State of Georgia, on or about the **25th day of April 2022,** knowingly, willfully, and unlawfully made at least one of the following false statements and representations in the presence of Fulton County District Attorney's Office investigators:

1. That he "attended and convened" the December 14, 2020, meeting of Trump presidential elector nominees in Fulton County, Georgia, but that he did not "call each of the individual members and notify them of the meeting or make any of the other preparations necessary for the meeting";

2. That a court reporter was not present at the December 14, 2020, meeting of Trump presidential elector nominees in Fulton County, Georgia;

said statements being within the jurisdiction of the Fulton County District Attorney's Office, a department and agency of the government of a county of this state, contrary to the laws of said State, the good order, peace and dignity thereof;

COUNT 41 OF 41

And the Grand Jurors aforesaid, in the name and behalf of the citizens of Georgia, do charge and accuse **ROBERT DAVID CHEELEY** with the offense of **PERJURY, O.C.G.A. § 16-10-70(a),** for the said accused, in the County of Fulton and State of Georgia, on or about the **15th day of September 2022,** knowingly, willfully, and unlawfully made at least one of the following false statements before the Fulton County Special Purpose Grand Jury, a judicial proceeding, after having been administered a lawful oath:

1. That he was unaware of the December 14, 2020, meeting of Trump presidential elector nominees in Fulton County, Georgia, until after the meeting had already taken place;

2. That he had no substantive conversations with anyone concerning the December 14, 2020, meeting of Trump presidential elector nominees in Fulton County, Georgia, until after the meeting had already taken place;

3. That he never suggested to anyone that the Trump presidential elector nominees in Georgia should meet on December 14, 2020;

4. That the only communication he had with John Eastman concerning the November 3, 2020, presidential election was for the purpose of connecting Eastman to Georgia Senator Brandon Beach and unindicted co-conspirator Individual 8, whose identity is known to the Grand Jury, for possible legal representation;

5. That he never worked to connect John Eastman with any Georgia legislators other than Georgia Senator Brandon Beach and unindicted co-conspirator Individual 8, whose identity is known to the Grand Jury;

said statements being material to the accused's own involvement in the December 14, 2020, meeting of Trump presidential elector nominees in Fulton County, Georgia, and to the accused's communications with others involved in said meeting, the issues in question, contrary to the laws of said State, the good order, peace and dignity thereof.

FANI T. WILLIS, District Attorney

4.

PEOPLE OF THE STATE OF NEW YORK v. TRUMP

SUPREME COURT OF THE STATE OF NEW YORK
COUNTY OF NEW YORK

THE PEOPLE OF THE STATE OF NEW YORK

-against-

DONALD J. TRUMP,

Defendant.

THE GRAND JURY OF THE COUNTY OF NEW YORK, by this indictment, accuses the defendant of the crime of **FALSIFYING BUSINESS RECORDS IN THE FIRST DEGREE**, in violation of Penal Law § 175.10, committed as follows:

The defendant, in the County of New York and elsewhere, on or about February 14, 2017, with intent to defraud and intent to commit another crime and aid and conceal the commission thereof, made and caused a false entry in the business records of an enterprise, to wit, an invoice from Michael Cohen dated February 14, 2017, marked as a record of the Donald J. Trump Revocable Trust, and kept and maintained by the Trump Organization.

SECOND COUNT

AND THE GRAND JURY AFORESAID, by this indictment, further accuses the defendant of the crime of **FALSIFYING BUSINESS RECORDS IN THE FIRST DEGREE**, in violation of Penal Law § 175.10, committed as follows:

The defendant, in the County of New York and elsewhere, on or about February 14, 2017, with intent to defraud and intent to commit another crime and aid and conceal the commission thereof, made and caused a false entry in the business records of an enterprise, to wit, an entry in the Detail General Ledger for the Donald J. Trump Revocable Trust, bearing voucher number 842457, and kept and maintained by the Trump Organization.

THIRD COUNT

AND THE GRAND JURY AFORESAID, by this indictment, further accuses the defendant of the crime of **FALSIFYING BUSINESS RECORDS IN THE FIRST DEGREE**, in violation of Penal Law § 175.10, committed as follows:

The defendant, in the County of New York and elsewhere, on or about February 14, 2017, with intent to defraud and intent to commit another crime and aid and conceal the commission thereof, made and caused a false entry in the business records of an enterprise, to wit, an entry in the Detail General Ledger for the Donald J. Trump Revocable Trust, bearing voucher number 842460, and kept and maintained by the Trump Organization.

FOURTH COUNT

AND THE GRAND JURY AFORESAID, by this indictment, further accuses the defendant of the crime of **FALSIFYING BUSINESS**

RECORDS IN THE FIRST DEGREE, in violation of Penal Law § 175.10, committed as follows:

The defendant, in the County of New York and elsewhere, on or about February 14, 2017, with intent to defraud and intent to commit another crime and aid and conceal the commission thereof, made and caused a false entry in the business records of an enterprise, to wit, a Donald J. Trump Revocable Trust Account check and check stub dated February 14, 2017, bearing check number 000138, and kept and maintained by the Trump Organization.

FIFTH COUNT

AND THE GRAND JURY AFORESAID, by this indictment, further accuses the defendant of the crime of **FALSIFYING BUSINESS RECORDS IN THE FIRST DEGREE**, in violation of Penal Law § 175.10, committed as follows:

The defendant, in the County of New York and elsewhere, on or about March 16, 2017 through March 17, 2017, with intent to defraud and intent to commit another crime and aid and conceal the commission thereof, made and caused a false entry in the business records of an enterprise, to wit, an invoice from Michael Cohen dated February 16, 2017 and transmitted on or about March 16, 2017, marked as a record of the Donald J. Trump Revocable Trust, and kept and maintained by the Trump Organization.

SIXTH COUNT

AND THE GRAND JURY AFORESAID, by this indictment, further accuses the defendant of the crime of **FALSIFYING BUSINESS RECORDS IN THE FIRST DEGREE**, in violation of Penal Law § 175.10, committed as follows:

The defendant, in the County of New York and elsewhere, on or about March 17, with intent to defraud and intent to commit another crime and aid and conceal the commission thereof, made and caused a false entry in the business records of an enterprise, to wit, an entry in the Detail General Ledger for the Donald J. Trump Revocable Trust, bearing voucher number 846907, and kept and maintained by the Trump Organization.

SEVENTH COUNT

AND THE GRAND JURY AFORESAID, by this indictment, further accuses the defendant of the crime of **FALSIFYING BUSINESS RECORDS IN THE FIRST DEGREE**, in violation of Penal Law § 175.10, committed as follows:

The defendant, in the County of New York and elsewhere, on or about March 17, 2017, with intent to defraud and intent to commit another crime and aid and conceal the commission thereof, made and caused a false entry in the business records of an enterprise, to wit, a Donald J. Trump Revocable Trust Account check and check stub dated March 17, 2017, bearing check number 000147, and kept and maintained by the Trump Organization.

EIGHTH COUNT

AND THE GRAND JURY AFORESAID, by this indictment, further accuses the defendant of the crime of **FALSIFYING BUSINESS RECORDS IN THE FIRST DEGREE**, in violation of Penal Law § 175.10, committed as follows:

The defendant, in the County of New York and elsewhere, on or about April 13, 2017 through June 19, 2017, with intent to defraud and intent to commit another crime and aid and conceal the commission thereof, made and caused a false entry in the business records of an enterprise, to wit, an invoice from Michael Cohen dated April 13, 2017, marked as a record of Donald J. Trump, and kept and maintained by the Trump Organization.

NINTH COUNT

AND THE GRAND JURY AFORESAID, by this indictment, further accuses the defendant of the crime of **FALSIFYING BUSINESS RECORDS IN THE FIRST DEGREE,** in violation of Penal Law § 175.10, committed as follows:

The defendant, in the County of New York and elsewhere, on or about June 19, 2017, with intent to defraud and intent to commit another crime and aid and conceal the commission thereof, made and caused a false entry in the business records of an enterprise, to wit, an entry in the Detail General Ledger for Donald J. Trump, bearing voucher number 858770, and kept and maintained by the Trump Organization.

TENTH COUNT

AND THE GRAND JURY AFORESAID, by this indictment, further accuses the defendant of the crime of **FALSIFYING BUSINESS RECORDS IN THE FIRST DEGREE**, in violation of Penal Law § 175.10, committed as follows:

The defendant, in the County of New York and elsewhere, on or about June 19, 2017, with intent to defraud and intent to commit another crime and aid and conceal the commission thereof, made and caused a false entry in the business records of an enterprise, to wit, a Donald J. Trump account check and check stub dated June 19, 2017, bearing check number 002740, and kept and maintained by the Trump Organization.

ELEVENTH COUNT

AND THE GRAND JURY AFORESAID, by this indictment, further accuses the defendant of the crime of **FALSIFYING BUSINESS RECORDS IN THE FIRST DEGREE**, in violation of Penal Law § 175.10, committed as follows:

The defendant, in the County of New York and elsewhere, on or about May 22, 2017, with intent to defraud and intent to commit another crime and aid and conceal the commission thereof, made and caused a false entry in the business records of an enterprise, to wit, an invoice from Michael Cohen dated May 22, 2017, marked as a record of Donald J. Trump, and kept and maintained by the Trump Organization.

TWELFTH COUNT

AND THE GRAND JURY AFORESAID, by this indictment, further accuses the defendant of the crime of **FALSIFYING BUSINESS RECORDS IN THE FIRST DEGREE**, in violation of Penal Law § 175.10, committed as follows:

The defendant, in the County of New York and elsewhere, on or about May 22, 2017, with intent to defraud and intent to commit another crime and aid and conceal the commission thereof, made and caused a false entry in the business records of an enterprise, to wit, an entry in the Detail General Ledger for Donald J. Trump, bearing voucher number 855331, and kept and maintained by the Trump Organization.

THIRTEENTH COUNT

AND THE GRAND JURY AFORESAID, by this indictment, further accuses the defendant of the crime of **FALSIFYING BUSINESS**

RECORDS IN THE FIRST DEGREE, in violation of Penal Law § 175.10, committed as follows:

The defendant, in the County of New York and elsewhere, on or about May 23, 2017, with intent to defraud and intent to commit another crime and aid and conceal the commission thereof, made and caused a false entry in the business records of an enterprise, to wit, a Donald J. Trump account check and check stub dated May 23, 2017, bearing check number 002700, and kept and maintained by the Trump Organization.

FOURTEENTH COUNT

AND THE GRAND JURY AFORESAID, by this indictment, further accuses the defendant of the crime of **FALSIFYING BUSINESS RECORDS IN THE FIRST DEGREE**, in violation of Penal Law § 175.10, committed as follows:

The defendant, in the County of New York and elsewhere, on or about June 16, 2017 through June 19, 2017, with intent to defraud and intent to commit another crime and aid and conceal the commission thereof, made and caused a false entry in the business records of an enterprise, to wit, an invoice from Michael Cohen dated June 16, 2017, marked as a record of Donald J. Trump, and kept and maintained by the Trump Organization.

FIFTEENTH COUNT

AND THE GRAND JURY AFORESAID, by this indictment, further accuses the defendant of the crime of **FALSIFYING BUSINESS RECORDS IN THE FIRST DEGREE**, in violation of Penal Law § 175.10, committed as follows:

The defendant, in the County of New York and elsewhere, on or about June 19, 2017, with intent to defraud and intent to commit another crime and aid and conceal the commission thereof, made and caused a false entry in the business records of an enterprise, to wit, an entry in the Detail General Ledger for Donald J. Trump, bearing voucher number 858772, and kept and maintained by the Trump Organization.

SIXTEENTH COUNT

AND THE GRAND JURY AFORESAID, by this indictment, further accuses the defendant of the crime of **FALSIFYING BUSINESS RECORDS IN THE FIRST DEGREE**, in violation of Penal Law § 175.10, committed as follows:

The defendant, in the County of New York and elsewhere, on or about June 19, 2017, with intent to defraud and intent to commit another crime and aid and conceal the commission thereof, made and caused a false entry in the business records of an enterprise, to wit, a Donald J. Trump account check and check stub dated June 19, 2017, bearing check number 002741, and kept and maintained by the Trump Organization.

SEVENTEENTH COUNT

AND THE GRAND JURY AFORESAID, by this indictment, further accuses the defendant of the crime of **FALSIFYING BUSINESS RECORDS IN THE FIRST DEGREE**, in violation of Penal Law § 175.10, committed as follows:

The defendant, in the County of New York and elsewhere, on or about July 11, 2017, with intent to defraud and intent to commit another crime and aid and conceal the commission thereof, made and caused a false entry in the business records of an enterprise, to wit, an invoice from Michael Cohen dated July 11, 2017, marked as a record of Donald J. Trump, and kept and maintained by the Trump Organization.

EIGHTEENTH COUNT

AND THE GRAND JURY AFORESAID, by this indictment, further accuses the defendant of the crime of **FALSIFYING BUSINESS RECORDS IN THE FIRST DEGREE**, in violation of Penal Law § 175.10, committed as follows:

The defendant, in the County of New York and elsewhere, on or about July 11, 2017, with intent to defraud and intent to commit another crime and aid and conceal the commission thereof, made and caused a false entry in the business records of an enterprise, to wit, an entry in the Detail General Ledger for Donald J. Trump, bearing voucher number 861096, and kept and maintained by the Trump Organization.

NINETEENTH COUNT

AND THE GRAND JURY AFORESAID, by this indictment, further accuses the defendant of the crime of **FALSIFYING BUSINESS RECORDS IN THE FIRST DEGREE**, in violation of Penal Law § 175.10, committed as follows:

The defendant, in the County of New York and elsewhere, on or about July 11, 2017, with intent to defraud and intent to commit another crime and aid and conceal the commission thereof, made and caused a false entry in the business records of an enterprise, to wit, a Donald J. Trump account check and check stub dated July 11, 2017, bearing check number 002781, and kept and maintained by the Trump Organization.

TWENTIETH COUNT

AND THE GRAND JURY AFORESAID, by this indictment, further accuses the defendant of the crime of **FALSIFYING BUSINESS RECORDS IN THE FIRST DEGREE**, in violation of Penal Law § 175.10, committed as follows:

The defendant, in the County of New York and elsewhere, on or about August 1, 2017, with intent to defraud and intent to commit another crime and aid and conceal the commission thereof, made and caused a false entry in the business records of an enterprise, to wit, an invoice from Michael Cohen dated August 1, 2017, marked as a record of Donald J. Trump, and kept and maintained by the Trump Organization.

TWENTY-FIRST COUNT

AND THE GRAND JURY AFORESAID, by this indictment, further accuses the defendant of the crime of **FALSIFYING BUSINESS RECORDS IN THE FIRST DEGREE**, in violation of Penal Law § 175.10, committed as follows:

The defendant, in the County of New York and elsewhere, on or about August 1, 2017, with intent to defraud and intent to commit another crime and aid and conceal the commission thereof, made and caused a false entry in the business records of an enterprise, to wit, an entry in the Detail General Ledger for Donald J. Trump, bearing voucher number 863641, and kept and maintained by the Trump Organization.

TWENTY-SECOND COUNT

AND THE GRAND JURY AFORESAID, by this indictment, further accuses the defendant of the crime of **FALSIFYING BUSINESS**

RECORDS IN THE FIRST DEGREE, in violation of Penal Law § 175.10, committed as follows:

The defendant, in the County of New York and elsewhere, on or about August 1, 2017, with intent to defraud and intent to commit another crime and aid and conceal the commission thereof, made and caused a false entry in the business records of an enterprise, to wit, a Donald J. Trump account check and check stub dated August 1, 2017, bearing check number 002821, and kept and maintained by the Trump Organization.

TWENTY-THIRD COUNT

AND THE GRAND JURY AFORESAID, by this indictment, further accuses the defendant of the crime of **FALSIFYING BUSINESS RECORDS IN THE FIRST DEGREE,** in violation of Penal Law § 175.10, committed as follows:

The defendant, in the County of New York and elsewhere, on or about September 11, 2017, with intent to defraud and intent to commit another crime and aid and conceal the commission thereof, made and caused a false entry in the business records of an enterprise, to wit, an invoice from Michael Cohen dated September 11, 2017, marked as a record of Donald J. Trump, and kept and maintained by the Trump Organization.

TWENTY-FOURTH COUNT

AND THE GRAND JURY AFORESAID, by this indictment, further accuses the defendant of the crime of **FALSIFYING BUSINESS RECORDS IN THE FIRST DEGREE,** in violation of Penal Law § 175.10, committed as follows:

The defendant, in the County of New York and elsewhere, on or about September 11, 2017, with intent to defraud and intent to commit another crime and aid and conceal the commission thereof, made and caused a false entry in the business records of an enterprise, to wit, an entry in the Detail General Ledger for Donald J. Trump, bearing voucher number 868174, and kept and maintained by the Trump Organization.

TWENTY-FIFTH COUNT

AND THE GRAND JURY AFORESAID, by this indictment, further accuses the defendant of the crime of **FALSIFYING BUSINESS RECORDS IN THE FIRST DEGREE,** in violation of Penal Law § 175.10, committed as follows:

The defendant, in the County of New York and elsewhere, on or about September 12, 2017, with intent to defraud and intent to commit another crime and aid and conceal the commission thereof, made and caused a false entry in the business records of an enterprise, to wit, a Donald J. Trump account check and check stub dated September 12, 2017, bearing check number 002908, and kept and maintained by the Trump Organization.

TWENTY-SIXTH COUNT

AND THE GRAND JURY AFORESAID, by this indictment, further accuses the defendant of the crime of **FALSIFYING BUSINESS RECORDS IN THE FIRST DEGREE,** in violation of Penal Law § 175.10, committed as follows:

The defendant, in the County of New York and elsewhere, on or about October 18, 2017, with intent to defraud and intent to commit another crime and aid and conceal the commission thereof, made and caused a false entry in the business records of an enterprise, to wit, an invoice from Michael Cohen dated October 18, 2017, marked as a record of Donald J. Trump, and kept and maintained by the Trump Organization.

TWENTY-SEVENTH COUNT

AND THE GRAND JURY AFORESAID, by this indictment, further accuses the defendant of the crime of **FALSIFYING BUSINESS RECORDS IN THE FIRST DEGREE,** in violation of Penal Law § 175.10, committed as follows:

The defendant, in the County of New York and elsewhere, on or about October 18, 2017, with intent to defraud and intent to commit another crime and aid and conceal the commission thereof, made and caused a false entry in the business records of an enterprise, to wit, an entry in the Detail General Ledger for Donald J. Trump, bearing voucher number 872654, and kept and maintained by the Trump Organization.

TWENTY-EIGHTH COUNT

AND THE GRAND JURY AFORESAID, by this indictment, further accuses the defendant of the crime of **FALSIFYING BUSINESS RECORDS IN THE FIRST DEGREE**, in violation of Penal Law § 175.10, committed as follows:

The defendant, in the County of New York and elsewhere, on or about October 18, 2017, with intent to defraud and intent to commit another crime and aid and conceal the commission thereof, made and caused a false entry in the business records of an enterprise, to wit, a Donald J. Trump account check and check stub dated October 18, 2017, bearing check number 002944, and kept and maintained by the Trump Organization.

TWENTY-NINTH COUNT

AND THE GRAND JURY AFORESAID, by this indictment, further accuses the defendant of the crime of **FALSIFYING BUSINESS**

RECORDS IN THE FIRST DEGREE, in violation of Penal Law § 175.10, committed as follows:

The defendant, in the County of New York and elsewhere, on or about November 20, 2017, with intent to defraud and intent to commit another crime and aid and conceal the commission thereof, made and caused a false entry in the business records of an enterprise, to wit, an invoice from Michael Cohen dated November 20, 2017, marked as a record of Donald J. Trump, and kept and maintained by the Trump Organization.

THIRTIETH COUNT

AND THE GRAND JURY AFORESAID, by this indictment, further accuses the defendant of the crime of **FALSIFYING BUSINESS RECORDS IN THE FIRST DEGREE**, in violation of Penal Law § 175.10, committed as follows:

The defendant, in the County of New York and elsewhere, on or about November 20, 2017, with intent to defraud and intent to commit another crime and aid and conceal the commission thereof, made and caused a false entry in the business records of an enterprise, to wit, an entry in the Detail General Ledger for Donald J. Trump, bearing voucher number 876511, and kept and maintained by the Trump Organization.

THIRTY-FIRST COUNT

AND THE GRAND JURY AFORESAID, by this indictment, further accuses the defendant of the crime of **FALSIFYING BUSINESS RECORDS IN THE FIRST DEGREE**, in violation of Penal Law § 175.10, committed as follows:

The defendant, in the County of New York and elsewhere, on or about November 21, 2017, with intent to defraud and intent to commit another crime and aid and conceal the commission thereof, made and caused a false entry in the business records of an enterprise, to wit, a Donald J. Trump account check and check stub dated November 21, 2017, bearing check number 002980, and kept and maintained by the Trump Organization.

THIRTY-SECOND COUNT

AND THE GRAND JURY AFORESAID, by this indictment, further accuses the defendant of the crime of **FALSIFYING BUSINESS RECORDS IN THE FIRST DEGREE**, in violation of Penal Law § 175.10, committed as follows:

The defendant, in the County of New York and elsewhere, on or about December 1, 2017, with intent to defraud and intent to commit another crime and aid and conceal the commission thereof, made and caused a false entry in the business records of an enterprise, to wit, an invoice from Michael Cohen dated December 1, 2017, marked as a record of Donald J. Trump, and kept and maintained by the Trump Organization.

THIRTY-THIRD COUNT

AND THE GRAND JURY AFORESAID, by this indictment, further accuses the defendant of the crime of **FALSIFYING BUSINESS RECORDS IN THE FIRST DEGREE**, in violation of Penal Law § 175.10, committed as follows:

The defendant, in the County of New York and elsewhere, on or about December 1, 2017, with intent to defraud and intent to commit another crime and aid and conceal the commission thereof, made and caused a false entry in the business records of an enterprise, to wit, an entry in the Detail General Ledger for Donald J. Trump, bearing voucher number 877785, and kept and maintained by the Trump Organization.

THIRTY-FOURTH COUNT

AND THE GRAND JURY AFORESAID, by this indictment, further accuses the defendant of the crime of **FALSIFYING BUSINESS RECORDS IN THE FIRST DEGREE**, in violation of Penal Law § 175.10, committed as follows:

The defendant, in the County of New York and elsewhere, on or about December 5, 2017, with intent to defraud and intent to commit another crime and aid and conceal the commission thereof, made and caused a false entry in the business records of an enterprise, to wit, a Donald J. Trump account check and check stub dated December 5, 2017, bearing check number 003006, and kept and maintained by the Trump Organization.

ALVIN L. BRAGG, JR.
District Attorney

THE PEOPLE OF THE STATE OF NEW YORK

-against-

DONALD J. TRUMP,

Defendant.

INDICTMENT

FALSIFYING BUSINESS RECORDS IN THE FIRST DEGREE,
P.L. § 175.10, 34 Cts

ALVIN L. BRAGG JR., District Attorney

A True Bill

APPENDIX

Original Documents Case Indictment

UNITED STATES OF AMERICA v. DONALD J. TRUMP AND WALTINE NAUTA

UNITED STATES DISTRICT COURT
SOUTHERN DISTRICT OF FLORIDA
23-80101-CR-CANNON/REINHART

18 U.S.C. § 793(e)
18 U.S.C. § 1512(k)
18 U.S.C. § 1512(b)(2)(A)
18 U.S.C. § 1512(c)(1)
18 U.S.C. § 1519
18 U.S.C. § 1001(a)(1)
18 U.S.C. § 1001(a)(2)
18 U.S.C. § 2

UNITED STATES OF AMERICA

v.

DONALD J. TRUMP and

WALTINE NAUTA,

Defendants.

INDICTMENT

The Grand Jury charges that:

GENERAL ALLEGATIONS

At times material to this Indictment, on or about the dates and approximate times stated below:

Introduction

1. Defendant **DONALD J. TRUMP** was the forty-fifth President of the United States of America. He held office from January 20, 2017, until January 20, 2021. As president, **TRUMP** had lawful access to the most sensitive classified documents and national defense information gathered and owned by the United States government, including information from the agencies that comprise the United States Intelligence Community and the United States Department of Defense.

2. Over the course of his presidency, **TRUMP** gathered newspapers, press clippings, letters, notes, cards, photographs, official documents, and other materials in cardboard boxes that he kept in the White House. Among the materials **TRUMP** stored in his boxes were hundreds of classified documents.

3. The classified documents **TRUMP** stored in his boxes included information regarding defense and weapons capabilities of both the United States and foreign countries; United States nuclear programs; potential vulnerabilities of the United States and its allies to military attack; and plans for possible retaliation in response to a foreign attack. The unauthorized disclosure of these classified documents could put at risk the national security of the United States,

foreign relations, the safety of the United States military, and human sources and the continued viability of sensitive intelligence collection methods.

4. At 12:00 p.m. on January 20, 2021, **TRUMP** ceased to be president. As he departed the White House, **TRUMP** caused scores of boxes, many of which contained classified documents, to be transported to The Mar-a-Lago Club in Palm Beach, Florida, where he maintained his residence. **TRUMP** was not authorized to possess or retain those classified documents.

5. The Mar-a-Lago Club was an active social club, which, between January 2021 and August 2022, hosted events for tens of thousands of members and guests. After **TRUMP**'s presidency, The Mar-a-Lago Club was not an authorized location for the storage, possession, review, display, or discussion of classified documents. Nevertheless, **TRUMP** stored his boxes containing classified documents in various locations at The Mar-a-Lago Club—including in a ballroom, a bathroom and shower, an office space, his bedroom, and a storage room.

6. On two occasions in 2021, **TRUMP** showed classified documents to others, as follows:

a. In July 2021, at Trump National Golf Club in Bedminster, New Jersey ("The Bedminster Club"), during an audio-recorded meeting with a writer, a publisher, and two members of his staff, none of whom possessed a security clearance, **TRUMP** showed and described a "plan of attack" that **TRUMP** said was prepared for him by the Department of Defense and a senior military official. **TRUMP** told the individuals that the plan was "highly confidential" and "secret." **TRUMP** also said, "as president I could have declassified it," and, "Now I can't, you know, but this is still a secret."

b. In August or September 2021, at The Bedminster Club, **TRUMP** showed a representative of his political action committee who did not possess a security clearance a classified map related to a military operation and told the representative that he should not be showing it to the representative and that the representative should not get too close.

7. On March 30, 2022, the Federal Bureau of Investigation ("FBI") opened a criminal investigation into the unlawful retention of classified documents at The Mar-a-Lago Club. A federal grand jury investigation began the next month. The grand jury issued a subpoena requiring **TRUMP** to turn over all documents with classification markings. **TRUMP** endeavored to obstruct the FBI and grand jury investigations and conceal his continued retention of classified documents by, among other things:

a. suggesting that his attorney falsely represent to the FBI and grand jury that **TRUMP** did not have documents called for by the grand jury subpoena;

b. directing defendant **WALTINE NAUTA** to move boxes of documents to conceal them from **TRUMP**'s attorney, the FBI, and the grand jury;

c. suggesting that his attorney hide or destroy documents called for by the grand jury subpoena;

d. providing to the FBI and grand jury just some of the documents called for by the grand jury subpoena, while claiming that he was cooperating fully; and

e. causing a certification to be submitted to the FBI and grand jury falsely representing that all documents called for by the grand jury subpoena had been produced—while knowing that, in fact, not all such documents had been produced.

8. As a result of **TRUMP**'s retention of classified documents after his presidency and refusal to return them, hundreds of classified documents were not recovered by the United States government until 2022, as follows:

a. On January 17, nearly one year after **TRUMP** left office, and after months of demands by the National Archives and Records Administration for **TRUMP** to provide all missing presidential records, **TRUMP** provided only 15 boxes, which contained 197 documents with classification markings.

b. On June 3, in response to a grand jury subpoena demanding the production of all documents with classification markings, **TRUMP**'s attorney provided to the FBI 38 more documents with classification markings.

c. On August 8, pursuant to a court-authorized search warrant, the FBI recovered from **TRUMP**'s office and a storage room at The Mar-a-Lago Club 102 more documents with classification markings.

TRUMP's Co-Conspirator

9. Defendant **NAUTA** was a member of the United States Navy stationed as a valet in the White House during **TRUMP**'s presidency.

Beginning in August 2021, **NAUTA** became an executive assistant in The Office of Donald J. Trump and served as **TRUMP**'s personal aide or "body man." **NAUTA** reported to **TRUMP,** worked closely with **TRUMP,** and traveled with **TRUMP.**

The Mar-a-Lago Club

10. The Mar-a-Lago Club was located on South Ocean Boulevard in Palm Beach, Florida, and included **TRUMP**'s residence, more than 25 guest rooms, two ballrooms, a spa, a gift store, exercise facilities, office space, and an outdoor pool and patio. As of January 2021, The Mar-a-Lago Club had hundreds of members and was staffed by more than 150 full-time, part-time, and temporary employees.

11. Between January 2021 and August 2022, The Mar-a-Lago Club hosted more than 150 social events, including weddings, movie premieres, and fundraisers that together drew tens of thousands of guests.

12. The United States Secret Service (the "Secret Service") provided protection services to **TRUMP** and his family after he left office, including at The Mar-a-Lago Club, but it was not responsible for the protection of **TRUMP**'s boxes or their contents. **TRUMP** did not inform the Secret Service that he was storing boxes containing classified documents at The Mar-a-Lago Club.

Classified Information

13. National security information was information owned by, produced by, produced for, and under the control of the United States government. Pursuant to Executive Order 12958, signed on April 17, 1995, as amended by Executive Order 13292 on March 25, 2003, and Executive Order 13526 on December 29, 2009, national security information was classified as "TOP SECRET," "SECRET," or "CONFIDENTIAL," as follows:

a. Information was classified as TOP SECRET if the unauthorized disclosure of that information reasonably could be expected to cause exceptionally grave damage to the national security that the original classification authority was able to identify or describe.

b. Information was classified as SECRET if the unauthorized disclosure of that information reasonably could be expected to cause serious damage to the national security that the original classification authority was able to identify or describe.

c. Information was classified as CONFIDENTIAL if the unauthorized disclosure of that information reasonably could be expected to cause damage to the national security that the original classification authority was able to identify or describe.

14. The classification marking "NOFORN" stood for "Not Releasable to Foreign Nationals" and denoted that dissemination of that information was limited to United States persons.

15. Classified information related to intelligence sources, methods, and analytical processes was designated as Sensitive Compartmented Information ("SCI"). SCI was to be processed, stored, used, or discussed in an accredited Sensitive Compartmented Information Facility ("SCIF"), and only individuals with the appropriate security clearance and additional SCI permissions were authorized to have access to such national security information.

16. When the vulnerability of, or threat to, specific classified information was exceptional, and the normal criteria for determining eligibility for access to classified information were insufficient to protect the information from unauthorized disclosure, the United States could establish Special Access Programs ("SAPs") to further protect the classified

information. The number of these programs was to be kept to an absolute minimum and limited to programs in which the number of persons who ordinarily would have access would be reasonably small and commensurate with the objective of providing enhanced protection for the information involved. Only individuals with the appropriate security clearance and additional SAP permissions were authorized to have access to such national security information, which was subject to enhanced handling and storage requirements.

17. Pursuant to Executive Order 13526, information classified at any level could be lawfully accessed only by persons determined by an appropriate United States government official to be eligible for access to classified information and who had signed an approved non-disclosure agreement, who received a security clearance, and who had a "need-to-know" the classified information. After his presidency, **TRUMP** was not authorized to possess or retain classified documents.

18. Executive Order 13526 provided that a former president could obtain a waiver of the "need-to-know" requirement, if the agency head or senior agency official of the agency that originated the classified information: (1) determined in writing that access was consistent with the interest of national security and (2) took appropriate steps to protect classified information from unauthorized disclosure or compromise and ensured that the information was safeguarded in a manner consistent with the order. **TRUMP** did not obtain any such waiver after his presidency.

The Executive Branch Departments and Agencies Whose Classified Documents TRUMP Retained After His Presidency

19. As part of his official duties as president, **TRUMP** received intelligence briefings from high-level United States government officials,

including briefings from the Director of the Central Intelligence Agency, the Chairman of the Joint Chiefs of Staff, senior White House officials, and a designated briefer. He regularly received a collection of classified intelligence from the United States Intelligence Community ("USIC") known as the "President's Daily Brief."

20. The USIC's mission was to collect, analyze, and deliver foreign intelligence and counterintelligence information to America's leaders, including the president, policymakers, law enforcement, and the military, so they could make sound decisions to protect the United States. The USIC consisted of United States executive branch departments and agencies responsible for the conduct of foreign relations and the protection of national security.

21. After his presidency, **TRUMP** retained classified documents originated by, or implicating the equities of, multiple USIC members and other executive branch departments and agencies, including the following:

a. **The Central Intelligence Agency ("CIA").** CIA was responsible for providing intelligence on foreign countries and global issues to the president and other policymakers to help them make national security decisions.

b. **The Department of Defense ("DoD").** DoD was responsible for providing the military forces needed to deter war and ensure national security. Some of the executive branch agencies comprising the USIC were within DoD.

c. **The National Security Agency.** The National Security Agency was a combat support agency within DoD and a member of the USIC responsible for foreign signals intelligence and cybersecurity. This included collecting, processing, and disseminating to United States policymakers and military leaders foreign intelligence derived from communications and information systems; protecting national security systems; and enabling computer network operations.

d. **The National Geospatial Intelligence Agency.** The National Geospatial Intelligence Agency was a combat support agency within DoD responsible for the exploitation and analysis of imagery, imagery intelligence, and geospatial information in support of the national security objectives of the United States and the geospatial intelligence requirements of DoD, the Department of State, and other federal agencies.

e. **The National Reconnaissance Office.** The National Reconnaissance Office was an agency within DoD responsible for developing, acquiring, launching, and operating space-based surveillance and reconnaissance systems that collected and delivered intelligence to enhance national security.

f. **The Department of Energy.** The Department of Energy was responsible for maintaining a safe, secure, and effective nuclear deterrent to protect national security, including ensuring the effectiveness of the United States nuclear weapons stockpile without nuclear explosive testing.

g. **The Department of State and Bureau of Intelligence and Research.** The Department of State was responsible for protecting and promoting United States security, prosperity, and democratic values. Within the Department of State, the Bureau of Intelligence and Research was a member of the USIC and responsible for providing intelligence to inform diplomacy and support United States diplomats.

TRUMP's Public Statements on Classified Information

22. As a candidate for President of the United States, **TRUMP** made the following public statements, among others, about classified information:

a. On August 18, 2016, **TRUMP** stated, "In my administration I'm going to enforce all laws concerning the protection of classified information. No one will be above the law."

b. On September 6, 2016, **TRUMP** stated, "We also need to fight this battle by collecting intelligence and then protecting, protecting our classified secrets. . . . We can't have someone in the Oval Office who doesn't understand the meaning of the word confidential or classified."

c. On September 7, 2016, **TRUMP** stated, "[O]ne of the first things we must do is to enforce all classification rules and to enforce all laws relating to the handling of classified information."

d. On September 19, 2016, **TRUMP** stated, "We also need the best protection of classified information."

e. On November 3, 2016, **TRUMP** stated, "Service members here in North Carolina have risked their lives to acquire classified intelligence to protect our country."

23. As President of the United States, on July 26, 2018, **TRUMP** issued the following statement about classified information:

> As the head of the executive branch and Commander in Chief, I have a unique, Constitutional responsibility to protect the Nation's classified information, including by controlling access to it. . . . More broadly, the issue of [a former executive branch official's] security clearance raises larger questions about the practice of former officials maintaining access to our Nation's most sensitive secrets long after their time in Government has ended. Such access is particularly inappropriate when former officials have transitioned into highly partisan positions and seek to use real or perceived access to sensitive information to validate their political attacks. Any access granted to our Nation's secrets should be in furtherance of national, not personal, interests.

TRUMP's Retention of Classified Documents After His Presidency

24. In January 2021, as he was preparing to leave the White House, **TRUMP** and his White House staff, including **NAUTA,** packed items, including some of **TRUMP**'s boxes. **TRUMP** was personally involved in this process. **TRUMP** caused his boxes, containing hundreds of classified documents, to be transported from the White House to The Mar-a-Lago Club.

25. From January through March 15, 2021, some of **TRUMP**'s boxes were stored in The Mar-a-Lago Club's White and Gold Ballroom, in which events and gatherings took place. **TRUMP**'s boxes were for a time stacked on the ballroom's stage, as depicted in the photograph below (redacted to obscure an individual's identity).

26. In March 2021, **NAUTA** and others moved some of **TRUMP**'s boxes from the White and Gold Ballroom to the business center at The Mar-a-Lago Club.

27. On April 5, 2021, an employee of The Office of Donald J. Trump ("Trump Employee 1") texted another employee of that office ("Trump Employee 2") to ask whether **TRUMP**'s boxes could be moved out of the business center to make room for staff to use it as an office. Trump Employee 2 replied, "Woah!! Ok so potus specifically asked Walt for those boxes to be in the business center because they are his 'papers.'" Later that day, Trump Employee 1 and Trump Employee 2 exchanged the following text messages:

Trump Employee 2:

> We can definitely make it work if we move his papers into the lake room?

Trump Employee 1:

> There is still a little room in the shower where his other stuff

> is. Is it only his papers he cares about? Theres some other stuff in there that are not papers. Could that go to storage? Or does he want everything in there on property

Trump Employee 2:

> Yes—anything that's not the beautiful mind paper boxes can definitely go to storage. Want to take a look at the space and start moving tomorrow AM?

28. After the text exchange between Trump Employee 1 and Trump Employee 2, in April 2021, some of **TRUMP**'s boxes were moved from the business center to a bathroom and shower in The Mar-a-Lago Club's Lake Room, as depicted in the photograph below.

29. In May 2021, **TRUMP** directed that a storage room on the ground floor of The Mar-a-Lago Club (the "Storage Room") be cleaned out so that it could be used to store his boxes. The hallway leading to the Storage Room could be reached from multiple outside entrances, in-

cluding one accessible from The Mar-a-Lago Club pool patio through a doorway that was often kept open. The Storage Room was near the liquor supply closet, linen room, lock shop, and various other rooms.

30. On June 24, 2021, **TRUMP**'s boxes that were in the Lake Room were moved to the Storage Room. After the move, there were more than 80 boxes in the Storage Room, as depicted in the photographs below.

31. On December 7, 2021, **NAUTA** found several of **TRUMP**'s boxes fallen and their contents spilled onto the floor of the Storage Room, including a document marked "SECRET//REL TO USA, FVEY," which denoted that the information in the document was releasable only to the Five Eyes intelligence alliance consisting of Australia, Canada, New Zealand, the United Kingdom, and the United States. **NAUTA** texted Trump Employee 2, "I opened the door and found this . . ." **NAUTA** also attached two photographs he took of the spill. Trump Employee 2 replied, "Oh no oh no," and "I'm sorry potus had my phone." One of the photographs **NAUTA** texted to Trump Employee 2 is depicted below with the visible classified information redacted. **TRUMP**'s unlawful retention of this document is charged in Count 8 of this Indictment.

TRUMP's Disclosures of Classified Information in Private Meetings

32. In May 2021, **TRUMP** caused some of his boxes to be brought to his summer residence at The Bedminster Club. Like The Mar-a-Lago Club, after **TRUMP**'s presidency, The Bedminster Club was not an authorized location for the storage, possession, review, display, or discussion of classified documents.

33. On July 21, 2021, when he was no longer president, **TRUMP** gave an interview in his office at The Bedminster Club to a writer and a publisher in connection with a then-forthcoming book. Two members of **TRUMP**'s staff also attended the interview, which was recorded with **TRUMP**'s knowledge and consent. Before the interview, the media had published reports that, at the end of **TRUMP**'s term as president, a senior military official (the "Senior Military Official") purportedly feared that **TRUMP** might order an attack on Country A and that the Senior Military Official advised **TRUMP** against doing so.

34. Upon greeting the writer, publisher, and his two staff members, **TRUMP** stated, "Look what I found, this was [the Senior Military Official's] plan of attack, read it and just show . . . it's interesting." Later in the interview, **TRUMP** engaged in the following exchange:

TRUMP: Well, with [the Senior Military Official]—uh, let me see that, I'll show you an example. He said that I wanted to attack [Country A]. Isn't it amazing? I have a big pile of papers, this thing just came up. Look. This was him. They presented me this—this is off the record, but—they presented me this. This was him. This was the Defense Department and him.

WRITER: Wow.

TRUMP: We looked at some. This was him. This wasn't done by me, this was him. All sorts of stuff—pages long, look.

STAFFER: Mm.

TRUMP: Wait a minute, let's see here.

STAFFER: *[Laughter]* Yeah.

TRUMP: I just found, isn't that amazing? This totally wins my case, you know.

STAFFER: Mm-hm.

TRUMP: Except it is like, highly confidential.

STAFFER: Yeah. *[Laughter]*

TRUMP: Secret. This is secret information. Look, look at this. You attack, and—

* * *

TRUMP: By the way. Isn't that incredible?

STAFFER: Yeah.

TRUMP: I was just thinking, because we were talking about it. And you know, he said, "he wanted to attack [Country A], and what . . ."

STAFFER: You did.

TRUMP: This was done by the military and given to me. Uh, I think we can probably, right?

STAFFER: I don't know, we'll, we'll have to see. Yeah, we'll have to try to—

TRUMP: Declassify it.

STAFFER: —figure out a—yeah.

TRUMP: See as president I could have declassified it.

STAFFER: Yeah. *[Laughter]*

TRUMP: Now I can't, you know, but this is still a secret.

STAFFER: Yeah. *[Laughter]* Now we have a problem.

TRUMP: Isn't that interesting?

At the time of this exchange, the writer, the publisher, and **TRUMP**'s two staff members did not have security clearances or any need-to-know any classified information about a plan of attack on Country A.

35. In August or September 2021, when he was no longer president, **TRUMP** met in his office at The Bedminster Club with a representative of his political action committee (the "PAC Representative"). During the meeting, **TRUMP** commented that an ongoing military operation in Country B was not going well. **TRUMP** showed the PAC Representative a classified map of Country B and told the PAC Representative that he should not be showing the map to the PAC Representative and to not get too close. The PAC Representative did not have a security clearance or any need-to-know classified information about the military operation.

36. On February 16, 2017, four years before **TRUMP**'s disclosures of classified information set forth above, **TRUMP** said at a press conference:

> The first thing I thought of when I heard about it is, how does the press get this information that's classified? How do they do it? You know why? Because it's an illegal process, and the press should be ashamed of themselves. But more importantly, the people that gave out the information to the press should be ashamed of themselves. Really ashamed.

TRUMP's Production of 15 Cardboard Boxes to the National Archives and Records Administration

37. Beginning in May 2021, the National Archives and Records Administration ("NARA"), which was responsible for archiving presidential records, repeatedly demanded that **TRUMP** turn over presidential records that he had kept after his presidency. On multiple occasions, beginning in June, NARA warned **TRUMP** through his representatives that if he did not comply, it would refer the matter of the missing records to the Department of Justice.

38. Between November 2021 and January 2022, **NAUTA** and Trump Employee 2—at **TRUMP**'s direction—brought boxes from the Storage Room to **TRUMP**'s residence for **TRUMP** to review.

39. On November 12, 2021, Trump Employee 2 provided **TRUMP** a photograph of his boxes in the Storage Room by taping it to one of the boxes that Trump Employee 2 had placed in **TRUMP**'s residence. Trump Employee 2 provided **TRUMP** the photograph so that **TRUMP** could see how many of his boxes were stored in the Storage Room. The photograph, shown below, depicted a wall of the Storage Room against which dozens of **TRUMP**'s boxes were stacked.

40. On November 17, 2021, **NAUTA** texted Trump Employee 2 about the photograph Trump Employee 2 had provided to **TRUMP,** stating, "He mentioned about a picture of the 'boxes' he wants me to see it?" Trump Employee 2 replied, "Calling you shortly."

41. On November 25, 2021, Trump Employee 2 texted **NAUTA** about **TRUMP**'s review of the contents of his boxes, asking, "Has he mentioned boxes to you? I delivered some, but I think he may need more. Could you ask if he'd like more in pine hall?" Pine Hall was an entry room in **TRUMP**'s residence. **NAUTA** replied in three successive text messages:

> Nothing about boxes yet
>
> He has one he's working on in pine hall
>
> Knocked out 2 boxes yesterday

42. On November 29, 2021, Trump Employee 2 texted **NAUTA,** asking, "Next you are on property (no rush) could you help me bring 4 more boxes up?" **NAUTA** replied, "Yes!! Of course."

43. On December 29, 2021, Trump Employee 2 texted a **TRUMP** representative who was in contact with NARA ("Trump Representative 1"), "box answer will be wrenched out of him today, promise!" The next day, Trump Representative 1 replied in two successive text messages:

> Hey—Just checking on Boxes . . .
>
> would love to have a number to them today

Trump Employee 2 spoke to **TRUMP** and then responded a few hours later in two successive text messages:

> 12
>
> Is his number

44. On January 13, 2022, **NAUTA** texted Trump Employee 2 about **TRUMP**'s "tracking" of boxes, stating, "He's tracking the boxes, more to follow today on whether he wants to go through more today or tomorrow." Trump Employee 2 replied, "Thank you!"

45. On January 15, 2022, **NAUTA** sent Trump Employee 2 four successive text messages:

> One thing he asked
>
> Was for new covers for the boxes, for Monday m.
>
> Morning
>
> *can we get new box covers before giving these to them on Monday? They have too much writing on them..I marked too much

Trump Employee 2 replied, "Yes, I will get that!"

46. On January 17, 2022, Trump Employee 2 and **NAUTA** gathered 15 boxes from **TRUMP**'s residence, loaded the boxes in **NAUTA**'s car, and took them to a commercial truck for delivery to NARA.

47. When interviewed by the FBI in May 2022 regarding the location and movement of boxes before the production to NARA, **NAUTA** made false and misleading statements as set forth in Count 38 of this Indictment, including:

a. falsely stating that he was not aware of **TRUMP**'s boxes being brought to **TRUMP**'s residence for his review before **TRUMP** provided 15 boxes to NARA in January 2022;

b. falsely stating that he did not know how the boxes that he and Trump Employee 2 brought from **TRUMP**'s residence to the commercial truck for delivery to NARA on January 17, 2022, had gotten to the residence; and

c. when asked whether he knew where **TRUMP**'s boxes had been stored before they were in **TRUMP**'s residence and whether they had been in a secure or locked location, **NAUTA** falsely responded, "I wish, I wish I could tell you. I don't know. I don't—I honestly just don't know."

48. When the 15 boxes that **TRUMP** had provided reached NARA in January 2022, NARA reviewed the contents and determined that 14 of the boxes contained documents with classification markings. Specifically, as the FBI later determined, the boxes contained 197 documents with classification markings, of which 98 were marked "SECRET," 30 were marked "TOP SECRET," and the remainder were marked "CON-

FIDENTIAL." Some of those documents also contained SCI and SAP markings.

49. On February 9, 2022, NARA referred the discovery of classified documents in **TRUMP**'s boxes to the Department of Justice for investigation.

The FBI and Grand Jury Investigations

50. On March 30, 2022, the FBI opened a criminal investigation.

51. On April 26, 2022, a federal grand jury opened an investigation.

The Defendants' Concealment of Boxes

52. On May 11, 2022, the grand jury issued a subpoena (the "May 11 Subpoena") to The Office of Donald J. Trump requiring the production of all documents with classification markings in the possession, custody, or control of **TRUMP** or The Office of Donald J. Trump. Two attorneys representing **TRUMP** ("Trump Attorney 1" and "Trump Attorney 2") informed **TRUMP** of the May 11 Subpoena, and he authorized Trump Attorney 1 to accept service.

53. On May 22, 2022, **NAUTA** entered the Storage Room at 3:47 p.m. and left approximately 34 minutes later, carrying one of **TRUMP**'s boxes.

54. On May 23, 2022, **TRUMP** met with Trump Attorney 1 and Trump Attorney 2 at The Mar-a-Lago Club to discuss the response to the May 11 Subpoena. Trump Attorney 1 and Trump Attorney 2 told **TRUMP** that they needed to search for documents that would be responsive to the subpoena and provide a certification that there had been compliance with the subpoena. **TRUMP**, in sum and substance, made the following statements, among others, as memorialized by Trump Attorney 1:

a. I don't want anybody looking, I don't want anybody looking through my boxes, I really don't, I don't want you looking through my boxes.

b. Well what if we, what happens if we just don't respond at all or don't play ball with them?

c. Wouldn't it be better if we just told them we don't have anything here?

d. Well look isn't it better if there are no documents?

55. While meeting with Trump Attorney 1 and Trump Attorney 2 on May 23, **TRUMP**, in sum and substance, told the following story, as memorialized by Trump Attorney 1:

> [Attorney], he was great, he did a great job. You know what? He said, he said that it—that it was him. That he was the one who deleted all of her emails, the 30,000 emails, because they basically dealt with her scheduling and her going to the gym and her having beauty appointments. And he was great. And he, so she didn't get in any trouble because he said that he was the one who deleted them.

TRUMP related the story more than once that day.

56. On May 23, **TRUMP** also confirmed his understanding with Trump Attorney 1 that Trump Attorney 1 would return to The Mar-a-Lago Club on June 2 to search for any documents with classification markings to produce in response to the May 11 Subpoena. Trump Attorney 1 made it clear to **TRUMP** that Trump Attorney 1 would conduct the search for responsive documents by looking through **TRUMP**'s boxes

that had been transported from the White House and remained in storage at The Mar-a-Lago Club. **TRUMP** indicated that he wanted to be at The Mar-a-Lago Club when Trump Attorney 1 returned to review his boxes on June 2, and that **TRUMP** would change his summer travel plans to do so. **TRUMP** told Trump Attorney 2 that Trump Attorney 2 did not need to be present for the review of boxes.

57. After meeting with Trump Attorney 1 and Trump Attorney 2 on May 23, **TRUMP** delayed his departure from The Mar-a-Lago Club to The Bedminster Club for the summer so that he would be present at The Mar-a-Lago Club on June 2, when Trump Attorney 1 returned to review the boxes.

58. Between **TRUMP**'s May 23 meeting with Trump Attorney 1 and Trump Attorney 2 to discuss the May 11 Subpoena, and June 2, when Trump Attorney 1 returned to The Mar-a-Lago Club to review the boxes in the Storage Room, **NAUTA** removed—at **TRUMP**'s direction—a total of approximately 64 boxes from the Storage Room and brought them to **TRUMP**'s residence, as set forth below:

a. On May 24, 2022, between 5:30 p.m. and 5:38 p.m., **NAUTA** removed three boxes from the Storage Room.

b. On May 30, 2022, at 9:08 a.m., **TRUMP** and **NAUTA** spoke by phone for approximately 30 seconds. Between 10:02 a.m. and 11:51 a.m., **NAUTA** removed a total of approximately 50 boxes from the Storage Room.

c. On May 30, 2022, at 12:33 p.m., a Trump family member texted **NAUTA**:

> Good afternoon Walt,
>
> Happy Memorial Day!

I saw you put boxes to Potus room. Just FYI and I will tell him as well:

Not sure how many he wants to take on Friday on the plane. We will NOT have a room for them. Plane will be full with luggage.

Thank you!

NAUTA replied:

Good Afternoon Ma'am [Smiley Face Emoji]

Thank you so much.

I think he wanted to pick from them. I don't imagine him wanting to take the boxes.

He told me to put them in the room and that he was going to talk to you about them.

d. On June 1, 2022, beginning at 12:52 p.m., **NAUTA** removed approximately 11 boxes from the Storage Room.

59. On June 1, 2022, **TRUMP** spoke with Trump Attorney 1 by phone and asked whether Trump Attorney 1 was coming to The Mar-a-Lago Club the next day and for exactly what purpose. Trump Attorney 1 reminded **TRUMP** that Trump Attorney 1 was going to review the boxes that had been transported from the White House and remained in storage at The Mar-a-Lago Club so that Trump Attorney 1 could have a custodian of records certify that the May 11 subpoena had been complied with fully.

60. On June 2, 2022, the day that Trump Attorney 1 was scheduled to review **TRUMP**'s boxes in the Storage Room, **TRUMP** spoke with **NAUTA** on the phone at 9:29 a.m. for approximately 24 seconds.

61. Later that day, between 12:33 p.m. and 12:52 p.m., **NAUTA** and an employee of The Mar-a-Lago Club moved approximately 30 boxes from **TRUMP**'s residence to the Storage Room.

62. In sum, between May 23, 2022, and June 2, 2022, before Trump Attorney 1's review of **TRUMP**'s boxes in the Storage Room, **NAUTA**—at **TRUMP**'s direction—moved approximately 64 boxes from the Storage Room to **TRUMP**'s residence and brought to the Storage Room only approximately 30 boxes. Neither **TRUMP** nor **NAUTA** informed Trump Attorney 1 of this information.

The False Certification to the FBI and the Grand Jury

63. On the afternoon of June 2, 2022, as **TRUMP** had been informed, Trump Attorney 1 arrived at The Mar-a-Lago Club to review **TRUMP**'s boxes to look for documents with classification markings in response to the May 11 Subpoena. **TRUMP** met with Trump Attorney 1 before Trump Attorney 1 conducted the review. **NAUTA** escorted Trump Attorney 1 to the Storage Room.

64. Between 3:53 p.m. and 6:23 p.m., Trump Attorney 1 reviewed the contents of **TRUMP**'s boxes in the Storage Room. Trump Attorney 1 located 38 documents with classification markings inside the boxes, which Trump Attorney 1 removed and placed in a Redweld folder. Trump Attorney 1 contacted **NAUTA** and asked him to bring clear duct tape to the Storage Room, which **NAUTA** did. Trump Attorney 1 used the clear duct tape to seal the Redweld folder with the documents with classification markings inside.

65. After Trump Attorney 1 finished sealing the Redweld folder containing the documents with classification markings that he had found

inside **TRUMP**'s boxes, **NAUTA** took Trump Attorney 1 to a dining room in The Mar-a-Lago Club to meet with **TRUMP**. After Trump Attorney 1 confirmed that he was finished with his search of the Storage Room, **TRUMP** asked, "Did you find anything? . . . Is it bad? Good?"

66. **TRUMP** and Trump Attorney 1 then discussed what to do with the Redweld folder containing documents with classification markings and whether Trump Attorney 1 should bring them to his hotel room and put them in a safe there. During that conversation, **TRUMP** made a plucking motion, as memorialized by Trump Attorney 1:

> He made a funny motion as though—well okay why don't you take them with you to your hotel room and if there's anything really bad in there, like, you know, pluck it out. And that was the motion that he made. He didn't say that.

67. That evening, Trump Attorney 1 contacted the Department of Justice and requested that an FBI agent meet him at The Mar-a-Lago Club the next day, June 3, so that he could turn over the documents responsive to the May 11 Subpoena.

68. Also that evening, Trump Attorney 1 contacted another **TRUMP** attorney ("Trump Attorney 3") and asked her if she would come to The Mar-a-Lago Club the next morning to act as a custodian of records and sign a certification regarding the search for documents with classification markings in response to the May 11 Subpoena. Trump Attorney 3, who had no role in the review of **TRUMP**'s boxes in the Storage Room, agreed.

69. The next day, on June 3, 2022, at Trump Attorney 1's request, Trump Attorney 3 signed a certification as the custodian of records for The Office of Donald J. Trump and took it to The Mar-a-Lago Club to provide it to the Department of Justice and FBI. In the certification, Trump Attorney 3—who performed no search of **TRUMP**'s boxes, had

not reviewed the May 11 Subpoena, and had not reviewed the contents of the Redweld folder—stated, among other things, that "[b]ased upon the information that [had] been provided to" her:

a. "A diligent search was conducted of the boxes that were moved from the White House to Florida";

b. "This search was conducted after receipt of the subpoena, in order to locate any and all documents that are responsive to the subpoena"; and

c. "Any and all responsive documents accompany this certification."

70. These statements were false because, among other reasons, **TRUMP** had directed **NAUTA** to move boxes before Trump Attorney 1's June 2 review, so that many boxes were not searched and many documents responsive to the May 11 Subpoena could not be found—and in fact were not found—by Trump Attorney 1.

71. Shortly after Trump Attorney 3 executed the false certification, on June 3, 2022, Trump Attorney 1 and Trump Attorney 3 met at The Mar-a-Lago Club with personnel from the Department of Justice and FBI. Trump Attorney 1 and Trump Attorney 3 turned over the Redweld folder containing documents with classification markings, as well as the false certification signed by Trump Attorney 3 as custodian of records. **TRUMP,** who had delayed his departure from The Mar-a-Lago Club, joined Trump Attorney 1 and Trump Attorney 3 for some of the meeting. **TRUMP** claimed to the Department of Justice and FBI that he was "an open book."

72. Earlier that same day, **NAUTA** and others loaded several of **TRUMP**'s boxes along with other items on aircraft that flew **TRUMP** and his family north for the summer.

The Court-Authorized Search of The Mar-a-Lago Club

73. In July 2022, the FBI and grand jury obtained and reviewed surveillance video from The Mar-a-Lago Club showing the movement of boxes set forth above.

74. On August 8, 2022, the FBI executed a court-authorized search warrant at The Mar-a-Lago Club. The search warrant authorized the FBI to search for and seize, among other things, all documents with classification markings.

75. During the execution of the warrant at The Mar-a-Lago Club, the FBI seized 102 documents with classification markings in **TRUMP**'s office and the Storage Room, as follows:

Location	Number of Documents	Classification Markings
TRUMP's Office	27	Top Secret (6) Secret (18) Confidential (3)
Storage Room	75	Top Secret (11) Secret (36) Confidential (28)

COUNTS 1–31

Willful Retention of National Defense Information

(18 U.S.C. § 793(e))

76. The General Allegations of this Indictment are re-alleged and fully incorporated here by reference.

77. On or about the dates set forth in the table below, in Palm Beach County, in the Southern District of Florida, and elsewhere, the defendant,

DONALD J. TRUMP,

having unauthorized possession of, access to, and control over documents relating to the national defense, did willfully retain the documents and fail to deliver them to the officer and employee of the United States entitled to receive them; that is—**TRUMP**, without authorization, retained at The Mar-a-Lago Club documents relating to the national defense, including the following:

Count	Date of Offense / Classification Marking / Document Description
1	January 20, 2021 – August 8, 2022
	TOP SECRET//NOFORN//SPECIAL HANDLING
	Document dated May 3, 2018, concerning White House intelligence briefing related to various foreign countries
2	January 20, 2021 – August 8, 2022
	TOP SECRET//SI//NOFORN//SPECIAL HANDLING
	Document dated May 9, 2018, concerning White House intelligence briefing related to various foreign countries
3	January 20, 2021 – August 8, 2022
	TOP SECRET//SI//NOFORN//FISA
	Undated document concerning military capabilities of a foreign country and the United States, with handwritten annotation in black marker
4	January 20, 2021 – August 8, 2022
	TOP SECRET//SPECIAL HANDLING
	Document dated May 6, 2019, concerning White House intelligence briefing related to foreign countries, including military activities and planning of foreign countries
5	January 20, 2021 – August 8, 2022
	TOP SECRET//[redacted]/[redacted]//ORCON/NOFORN
	Document dated June 2020 concerning nuclear capabilities of a foreign country

<table>
<tr><td rowspan="3">6</td><td>January 20, 2021 – August 8, 2022</td></tr>
<tr><td>TOP SECRET//SPECIAL HANDLING</td></tr>
<tr><td>Document dated June 4, 2020, concerning White House intelligence briefing related to various foreign countries</td></tr>
<tr><td rowspan="3">7</td><td>January 20, 2021 – August 8, 2022</td></tr>
<tr><td>SECRET//NOFORN</td></tr>
<tr><td>Document dated October 21, 2018, concerning communications with a leader of a foreign country</td></tr>
<tr><td rowspan="3">8</td><td>January 20, 2021 – August 8, 2022</td></tr>
<tr><td>SECRET//REL TO USA, FVEY</td></tr>
<tr><td>Document dated October 4, 2019, concerning military capabilities of a foreign country</td></tr>
<tr><td rowspan="3">9</td><td>January 20, 2021 – August 8, 2022</td></tr>
<tr><td>TOP SECRET//[redacted]/[redacted]//ORCON/NOFORN/FISA</td></tr>
<tr><td>Undated document concerning military attacks by a foreign country</td></tr>
<tr><td rowspan="3">10</td><td>January 20, 2021 – August 8, 2022</td></tr>
<tr><td>TOP SECRET//TK//NOFORN</td></tr>
<tr><td>Document dated November 2017 concerning military capabilities of a foreign country</td></tr>
<tr><td rowspan="3">11</td><td>January 20, 2021 – August 8, 2022</td></tr>
<tr><td>No marking</td></tr>
<tr><td>Undated document concerning military contingency planning of the United States</td></tr>
<tr><td rowspan="3">12</td><td>January 20, 2021 – August 8, 2022</td></tr>
<tr><td>SECRET//REL TO USA, FVEY</td></tr>
<tr><td>Pages of undated document concerning projected regional military capabilities of a foreign country and the United States</td></tr>
</table>

13	January 20, 2021 – August 8, 2022
	TOP SECRET//SI/TK//NOFORN
	Undated document concerning military capabilities of a foreign country and the United States
14	January 20, 2021 – August 8, 2022
	SECRET//ORCON/NOFORN
	Document dated January 2020 concerning military options of a foreign country and potential effects on United States interests
15	January 20, 2021 – August 8, 2022
	SECRET//ORCON/NOFORN
	Document dated February 2020 concerning policies in a foreign country
16	January 20, 2021 – August 8, 2022
	SECRET//ORCON/NOFORN
	Document dated December 2019 concerning foreign country support of terrorist acts against United States interests
17	January 20, 2021 – August 8, 2022
	TOP SECRET//[redacted]/TK//ORCON/IMCON/NOFORN
	Document dated January 2020 concerning military capabilities of a foreign country
18	January 20, 2021 – August 8, 2022
	SECRET//NOFORN
	Document dated March 2020 concerning military operations against United States forces and others
19	January 20, 2021 – August 8, 2022
	SECRET//FORMERLY RESTRICTED DATA
	Undated document concerning nuclear weaponry of the United States
20	January 20, 2021 – August 8, 2022
	TOP SECRET//[redacted]//ORCON/NOFORN
	Undated document concerning timeline and details of attack in a foreign country

<table>
<tr><td rowspan="3">21</td><td>January 20, 2021 – August 8, 2022</td></tr>
<tr><td>SECRET//NOFORN</td></tr>
<tr><td>Undated document concerning military capabilities of foreign countries</td></tr>
<tr><td rowspan="3">22</td><td>January 20, 2021 – June 3, 2022</td></tr>
<tr><td>TOP SECRET//[redacted]//RSEN/ORCON/NOFORN</td></tr>
<tr><td>Document dated August 2019 concerning regional military activity of a foreign country</td></tr>
<tr><td rowspan="3">23</td><td>January 20, 2021 – June 3, 2022</td></tr>
<tr><td>TOP SECRET//SPECIAL HANDLING</td></tr>
<tr><td>Document dated August 30, 2019, concerning White House intelligence briefing related to various foreign countries, with handwritten annotation in black marker</td></tr>
<tr><td rowspan="3">24</td><td>January 20, 2021 – June 3, 2022</td></tr>
<tr><td>TOP SECRET//HCS-P/SI//ORCON-USGOV/NOFORN</td></tr>
<tr><td>Undated document concerning military activity of a foreign country</td></tr>
<tr><td rowspan="3">25</td><td>January 20, 2021 – June 3, 2022</td></tr>
<tr><td>TOP SECRET//HCS-P/SI//ORCON-USGOV/NOFORN</td></tr>
<tr><td>Document dated October 24, 2019, concerning military activity of foreign countries and the United States</td></tr>
<tr><td rowspan="3">26</td><td>January 20, 2021 – June 3, 2022</td></tr>
<tr><td>TOP SECRET//[redacted]//ORCON/NOFORN/FISA</td></tr>
<tr><td>Document dated November 7, 2019, concerning military activity of foreign countries and the United States</td></tr>
<tr><td rowspan="3">27</td><td>January 20, 2021 – June 3, 2022</td></tr>
<tr><td>TOP SECRET//SI/TK//NOFORN</td></tr>
<tr><td>Document dated November 2019 concerning military activity of foreign countries</td></tr>
</table>

28	January 20, 2021 – June 3, 2022
	TOP SECRET//SPECIAL HANDLING
	Document dated October 18, 2019, concerning White House intelligence briefing related to various foreign countries
29	January 20, 2021 – June 3, 2022
	TOP SECRET//[redacted]/SI/TK//ORCON/NOFORN
	Document dated October 18, 2019, concerning military capabilities of a foreign country
30	January 20, 2021 – June 3, 2022
	TOP SECRET//[redacted]//ORCON/NOFORN/FISA
	Document dated October 15, 2019, concerning military activity in a foreign country
31	January 20, 2021 – June 3, 2022
	TOP SECRET//SI/TK//NOFORN
	Document dated February 2017 concerning military activity of a foreign country

All in violation of Title 18, United States Code, Section 793(e).

COUNT 32

Conspiracy to Obstruct Justice
(18 U.S.C. § 1512(k))

78. The General Allegations of this Indictment are re-alleged and fully incorporated here by reference.

The Conspiracy and its Objects

79. From on or about May 11, 2022, through in or around August 2022, in Palm Beach County, in the Southern District of Florida, and elsewhere, the defendants,

DONALD J. TRUMP and
WALTINE NAUTA,

did knowingly combine, conspire, confederate, and agree with each other and with others known and unknown to the grand jury, to engage in misleading conduct toward another person and corruptly persuade another person to withhold a record, document, and other object from an official proceeding, in violation of 18 U.S.C. § 1512(b)(2)(A), and to corruptly conceal a record, document, and other object from an official proceeding, in violation of 18 U.S.C. § 1512(c)(1).

The Purpose of the Conspiracy

80. The purpose of the conspiracy was for **TRUMP** to keep classified documents he had taken with him from the White House and to hide and conceal them from a federal grand jury.

The Manner and Means of the Conspiracy

81. The manner and means by which the defendants sought to accomplish the objects and purpose of the conspiracy included, among other things, the following:

a. Suggesting that Trump Attorney 1 falsely represent to the FBI and grand jury that **TRUMP** did not have documents called for by the May 11 Subpoena;

b. moving boxes of documents to conceal them from Trump Attorney 1, the FBI, and the grand jury;

c. suggesting that Trump Attorney 1 hide or destroy documents called for by the May 11 Subpoena;

d. providing to the FBI and grand jury just some of the documents called for by the May 11 Subpoena, while **TRUMP** claimed he was cooperating fully;

e. causing a false certification to be submitted to the FBI and grand jury representing that all documents with classification markings had been produced, when in fact they had not; and

f. making false and misleading statements to the FBI.

All in violation of Title 18, United States Code, Sections 1512(k).

COUNT 33

Withholding a Document or Record

(18 U.S.C. §§ 1512(b)(2)(A), 2)

82. The General Allegations of this Indictment are re-alleged and fully incorporated here by reference.

83. From on or about May 11, 2022, through in or around August 2022, in Palm Beach County, in the Southern District of Florida, and elsewhere, the defendants,

DONALD J. TRUMP and

WALTINE NAUTA,

did knowingly engage in misleading conduct toward another person, and knowingly corruptly persuade and attempt to persuade another person, with intent to cause and induce any person to withhold a record, document, and other object from an official proceeding; that is—(1) **TRUMP** attempted to persuade Trump Attorney 1 to hide and conceal documents from a federal grand jury; and (2) **TRUMP** and **NAUTA** misled Trump Attorney 1 by moving boxes that contained documents with classification markings so that Trump Attorney 1 would not find the documents and produce them to a federal grand jury.

All in violation of Title 18, United States Code, Sections 1512(b)(2)(A) and 2.

COUNT 34

Corruptly Concealing a Document or Record (18 U.S.C. §§ 1512(c)(1), 2)

84. The General Allegations of this Indictment are re-alleged and fully incorporated here by reference.

85. From on or about May 11, 2022, through in or around August 2022, in Palm Beach County, in the Southern District of Florida, and elsewhere, the defendants,

DONALD J. TRUMP and
WALTINE NAUTA,

did corruptly conceal a record, document, and other object, and attempted to do so, with the intent to impair the object's integrity and availability for use in an official proceeding; that is—**TRUMP** and **NAUTA** hid and concealed boxes that contained documents with classification markings from Trump Attorney 1 so that Trump Attorney 1 would not find the documents and produce them to a federal grand jury.

All in violation of Title 18, United States Code, Sections 1512(c)(1) and 2.

COUNT 35

Concealing a Document in a Federal Investigation (18 U.S.C. §§ 1519, 2)

86. The General Allegations of this Indictment are re-alleged and fully incorporated here by reference.

87. From on or about May 11, 2022, through in or around August 2022, in Palm Beach County, in the Southern District of Florida, and elsewhere, the defendants,

DONALD J. TRUMP and
WALTINE NAUTA,

did knowingly conceal, cover up, falsify, and make a false entry in any record, document, and tangible object with the intent to impede, obstruct, and influence the investigation and proper administration of any matter within the jurisdiction of a department and agency of the United States, and in relation to and contemplation of any such matter; that is—during a federal criminal investigation being conducted by the FBI, (1) **TRUMP** and **NAUTA** hid, concealed, and covered up from the FBI **TRUMP**'s continued possession of documents with classification markings at The Mar-a-Lago Club; and (2) **TRUMP** caused a false certification to be submitted to the FBI.

All in violation of Title 18, United States Code, Sections 1519 and 2.

COUNT 36

Scheme to Conceal

(18 U.S.C. §§ 1001(a)(1), 2)

88. The General Allegations of this Indictment are re-alleged and fully incorporated here by reference.

89. From on or about May 11, 2022, through in or around August 2022, in Palm Beach County, in the Southern District of Florida, and elsewhere, the defendants,

DONALD J. TRUMP and
WALTINE NAUTA,

in a matter within the jurisdiction of the judicial branch and executive branch of the United States government, did knowingly and willfully falsify, conceal, and cover up by any trick, scheme, and device a material fact; that is—during a federal grand jury investigation and a federal criminal investigation being conducted by the FBI, **TRUMP** and **NAUTA** hid and concealed from the grand jury and the FBI **TRUMP**'s continued possession of documents with classification markings.

All in violation of Title 18, United States Code, Sections 1001(a)(1) and 2.

COUNT 37

False Statements and Representations

(18 U.S.C. §§ 1001(a)(2), 2)

90. The General Allegations of this Indictment are re-alleged and fully incorporated here by reference.

91. On or about June 3, 2022, in Palm Beach County, in the Southern District of Florida, and elsewhere, the defendant,

DONALD J. TRUMP,

in a matter within the jurisdiction of the judicial branch and executive branch of the United States government, did knowingly and willfully make and cause to be made a materially false, fictitious, and fraudulent statement and representation; that is—during a federal grand jury investigation and a federal criminal investigation being conducted by the FBI, **TRUMP** caused the following false statements and representations to be made to the grand jury and the FBI in a sworn certification executed by Trump Attorney 3:

a. "A diligent search was conducted of the boxes that were moved from the White House to Florida";

b. "This search was conducted after receipt of the subpoena, in order to locate any and all documents that are responsive to the subpoena"; and

c. "Any and all responsive documents accompany this certification."

92. The statements and representations set forth above were false, as **TRUMP** knew, because **TRUMP** had directed that boxes be removed from the Storage Room before Trump Attorney 1 conducted the June 2, 2022 search for documents with classification markings, so that Trump Attorney 1's search would not and did not include all of **TRUMP**'s boxes that were removed from the White House; Trump Attorney 1's search would not and did not locate all documents responsive to the May 11 Subpoena; and all responsive documents were not provided to the FBI and the grand jury with the certification. In fact, after June 3, 2022, more than 100 documents with classification markings remained at The Mar-a-Lago Club until the FBI search on August 8, 2022.

All in violation of Title 18, United States Code, Sections 1001(a)(2) and 2.

COUNT 38

False Statements and Representations

(18 U.S.C. § 1001(a)(2))

93. The General Allegations of this Indictment are re-alleged and fully incorporated here by reference.

94. On May 26, 2022, **NAUTA** participated in a voluntary interview with the FBI. During the interview, the FBI explained to **NAUTA** that the FBI was investigating how classified documents had been kept at The Mar-a-Lago Club, and the FBI asked **NAUTA** questions about the location and movement of **TRUMP**'s boxes before **TRUMP** provided 15

boxes to NARA on January 17, 2022. **NAUTA** was represented by counsel, and the FBI advised **NAUTA** that the interview was voluntary and that he could leave at any time. The FBI also advised **NAUTA** that it was a criminal offense to lie to the FBI. The interview was recorded.

95. On or about May 26, 2022, in Palm Beach County, in the Southern District of Florida, and elsewhere, the defendant,

WALTINE NAUTA,

in a matter within the jurisdiction of the executive branch of the United States government, did knowingly and willfully make a materially false, fictitious, and fraudulent statement and representation; that is—in a voluntary interview during a federal criminal investigation being conducted by the FBI, **NAUTA** was asked the following questions and gave the following false answers:

Question: Does any—are you aware of any boxes being brought to his home—his suite?

Answer: **No.**

* * *

Question: All right. So, so to the best of your knowledge, you're saying that those boxes that you brought onto the truck, first time you ever laid eyes on them was just the day of when [Trump Employee 2] needed you to—

Answer: **Correct.**

Question: —to take them. Okay.

* * *

Question: In knowing that we're trying to track the life of

these boxes and where they could have been kept and stored and all that kind of stuff—

Answer: Mm-hm.

Question: —do you have any information that could—that would—that could help us understand, like, where they were kept, how they were kept, were they secured, were they locked? Something that makes the intelligence community feel better about these things, you know?

Answer: **I wish, I wish I could tell you. I don't know. I don't—I honestly just don't know.**

* * *

Question: And what—so, so you only saw the 15 boxes, 15, 17 boxes—

Answer: Mm-hm.

Question: —the day of the move? Even—they just showed up that day?

Answer: They were in Pine Hall. [Trump Employee 2] just asked me, hey, can we move some boxes?

Question: Okay.

Answer: And I was like, okay.

Question: So, you didn't know—had no idea how they got there before?

Answer: **No.**

96. The underscored statements and representations above were false, as **NAUTA** knew, because (1) **NAUTA** did in fact know that the boxes in Pine Hall had come from the Storage Room, as **NAUTA** himself, with the assistance of Trump Employee 2, had moved the boxes from the Storage Room to Pine Hall; and (2) **NAUTA** had observed the boxes in and moved them to various locations at The Mar-a-Lago Club.

All in violation of Title 18, United States Code, Section 1001(a)(2).

JACK SMITH
SPECIAL COUNSEL
UNITED STATES
DEPARTMENT OF JUSTICE

UNITED STATES DISTRICT COURT
SOUTHERN DISTRICT OF FLORIDA

PENALTY SHEET

Defendant's Name: Donald J. Trump

Counts #: 1–31

Willful Retention of National Defense Information, 18 U.S.C. § 793(e)

* **Max. Term of Imprisonment: 10 years**
* **Mandatory Min. Term of Imprisonment (if applicable): N/A**
* **Max. Supervised Release: 3 years**
* **Max. Fine: $250,000**

Count #: 32

Conspiracy to Obstruct Justice, 18 U.S.C. § 1512(k)

* **Max. Term of Imprisonment: 20 years**
* **Mandatory Min. Term of Imprisonment (if applicable): N/A**
* **Max. Supervised Release: 3 years**
* **Max. Fine: $250,000**

Count #: 33

Withholding a Document or Record, 18 U.S.C. § 1512(b)(2)(A)

* **Max. Term of Imprisonment: 20 years**
* **Mandatory Min. Term of Imprisonment (if applicable): N/A**
* **Max. Supervised Release: 3 years**
* **Max. Fine: $250,000**

Count #: 34

Corruptly Concealing a Document or Record, 18 U.S.C. § 1512(c)(1)

* **Max. Term of Imprisonment: 20 years**
* **Mandatory Min. Term of Imprisonment (if applicable): N/A**
* **Max. Supervised Release: 3 years**
* **Max. Fine: $250,000**

***Refers only to possible term of incarceration, supervised release and fines. It does not include restitution, special assessments, parole terms, or forfeitures that may be applicable.**

Count #: 35

Concealing a Document in a Federal Investigation, 18 U.S.C. §§ 1519, 2

* **Max. Term of Imprisonment: 20 years**
* **Mandatory Min. Term of Imprisonment (if applicable): N/A**
* **Max. Supervised Release: 3 years**
* **Max. Fine: $250,000**

Count #: 36

Scheme to Conceal, 18 U.S.C. §§ 1001(a)(1), 2

* **Max. Term of Imprisonment: 5 years**
* **Mandatory Min. Term of Imprisonment (if applicable): N/A**
* **Max. Supervised Release: 3 years**
* **Max. Fine: $250,000**

Count #: 37

False Statements and Representations, 18 U.S.C. §§ 1001(a)(2), 2

* **Max. Term of Imprisonment: 5 years**
* **Mandatory Min. Term of Imprisonment (if applicable): N/A**
* **Max. Supervised Release: 3 years**
* **Max. Fine: $250,000**

***Refers only to possible term of incarceration, supervised release and fines. It does not include restitution, special assessments, parole terms, or forfeitures that may be applicable.**

UNITED STATES DISTRICT COURT
SOUTHERN DISTRICT OF FLORIDA

PENALTY SHEET

Defendant's Name: Waltine Nauta

Count #: 32

Conspiracy to Obstruct Justice, 18 U.S.C. § 1512(k)

* **Max. Term of Imprisonment: 20 years**
* **Mandatory Min. Term of Imprisonment (if applicable): N/A**
* **Max. Supervised Release: 3 years**
* **Max. Fine: $250,000**

Count #: 33

Withholding a Document or Record, 18 U.S.C. § 1512(b)(2)(A)

* **Max. Term of Imprisonment: 20 years**
* **Mandatory Min. Term of Imprisonment (if applicable): N/A**
* **Max. Supervised Release: 3 years**
* **Max. Fine: $250,000**

Count #: 34

Corruptly Concealing a Document or Record, 18 U.S.C. § 1512(c)(1)

* **Max. Term of Imprisonment: 20 years**
* **Mandatory Min. Term of Imprisonment (if applicable): N/A**
* **Max. Supervised Release: 3 years**
* **Max. Fine: $250,000**

Count #: 35

Concealing a Document in a Federal Investigation, 18 U.S.C. §§ 1519, 2

* **Max. Term of Imprisonment: 20 years**
* **Mandatory Min. Term of Imprisonment (if applicable): N/A**
* **Max. Supervised Release: 3 years**
* **Max. Fine: $250,000**

***Refers only to possible term of incarceration, supervised release and fines. It does not include restitution, special assessments, parole terms, or forfeitures that may be applicable.**

Count #: 36

Scheme to Conceal, 18 U.S.C. §§ 1001(a)(1), 2

- **Max. Term of Imprisonment: 5 years**
- **Mandatory Min. Term of Imprisonment (if applicable): N/A**
- **Max. Supervised Release: 3 years**
- **Max. Fine: $250,000**

Count #: 38

False Statements and Representations, 18 U.S.C. § 1001(a)(2)

- **Max. Term of Imprisonment: 5 years**
- **Mandatory Min. Term of Imprisonment (if applicable): N/A**
- **Max. Supervised Release: 3 years**
- **Max. Fine: $250,000**

***Refers only to possible term of incarceration, supervised release and fines. It does not include restitution, special assessments, parole terms, or forfeitures that may be applicable.**

ABOUT

MARINER BOOKS

MARINER BOOKS traces its beginnings to 1832 when William Ticknor cofounded the Old Corner Bookstore in Boston, from which he would run the legendary firm Ticknor and Fields, publisher of Ralph Waldo Emerson, Harriet Beecher Stowe, Nathaniel Hawthorne, and Henry David Thoreau. Following Ticknor's death, Henry Oscar Houghton acquired Ticknor and Fields and, in 1880, formed Houghton Mifflin, which later merged with venerable Harcourt Publishing to form Houghton Mifflin Harcourt. HarperCollins purchased HMH's trade publishing business in 2021 and reestablished their storied lists and editorial team under the name Mariner Books.

Uniting the legacies of Houghton Mifflin, Harcourt Brace, and Ticknor and Fields, Mariner Books continues one of the great traditions in American bookselling. Our imprints have introduced an incomparable roster of enduring classics, including Hawthorne's *The Scarlet Letter,* Thoreau's *Walden,* Willa Cather's *O Pioneers!,* Virginia Woolf's *To the Lighthouse,* W.E.B. Du Bois's *Black Reconstruction,* J.R.R. Tolkien's *The Lord of the Rings,* Carson McCullers's *The Heart Is a Lonely Hunter,* Ann Petry's *The Narrows,* George Orwell's *Animal Farm* and *Nineteen Eighty-Four,* Rachel Carson's *Silent Spring,* Margaret Walker's *Jubilee,* Italo Calvino's *Invisible Cities,* Alice Walker's *The Color Purple,* Margaret Atwood's *The Handmaid's Tale,* Tim O'Brien's *The Things They Carried,* Philip Roth's *The Plot Against America,* Jhumpa Lahiri's *Interpreter of Maladies,* and many others. Today Mariner Books remains proudly committed to the craft of fine publishing established nearly two centuries ago at the Old Corner Bookstore.